C000264825

Henry VIII's Divorce:
Literature and
the Politics of the Printing Press

Henry VIII's Divorce:
Literature and
the Politics of the Printing Press

J. Christopher Warner

THE BOYDELL PRESS

© J. Christopher Warner 1998

All Rights Reserved. Except as permitted under current legislation
no part of this work may be photocopied, stored in a retrieval system,
published, performed in public, adapted, broadcast,
transmitted, recorded or reproduced in any form or by any means,
without the prior permission of the copyright owner

First published 1998
The Boydell Press, Woodbridge

ISBN 0 85115 642 8

The Boydell Press is an imprint of Boydell & Brewer Ltd
PO Box 9, Woodbridge, Suffolk IP12 3DF, UK
and of Boydell & Brewer Inc.
PO Box 41026, Rochester, NY 14604–4126, USA

A catalogue record for this book is available
from the British Library

Library of Congress Catalog Card Number: 98–35600

This publication is printed on acid-free paper

Printed in Great Britain by
St Edmundsbury Press Ltd, Bury St Edmunds, Suffolk

Contents

Acknowledgments

During the course of this book's preparation I have benefited greatly from the advice and encouragement of friends, teachers, and colleagues, especially John Webster, Alan Fisher, Joanne Altieri, Malcolm Griffith, William Streitberger, Ron Corthell, and Barrett Beer. I am also much indebted to Stephen Gunn, whose insightful recommendations helped me to make substantial improvements to the final manuscript. A grant from Kent State University's Office of Research and Graduate Studies enabled me to complete the primary research for this study at the Cambridge University Library, the Bodleian Library, and the British Library. I am grateful to the staffs of these institutions, and of the Houghton Library at Harvard and the Center for Research Libraries in Chicago, for their expert assistance. I have relied, too, on the library services of my own campus, and I thank Susan Weaver and Denise Fitzpatrick for their help at crucial stages of this project.

Opportunities to present some of my work on Thomas Elyot and John Rastell were given me by the organizers of a joint meeting of the Central and South Central Renaissance Conferences, and by Albert Geritz, organizer of the sessions on Thomas More and His Circle at the International Congress on Medieval Studies at Kalamazoo. For permission to reprint material published in earlier form beforehand, I thank François Paré and the Canadian Society for Renaissance Studies, for my essay "Sir Thomas More, *Utopia*, and the Representation of Henry VIII," *Renaissance and Reformation / Renaissance et Réforme* 20 (1996): 59–72; Clare Murphy and Amici Thomae Mori, for "John Rastell's *A New Book of Purgatory* and the Obligations of a Christian Prince," *Moreana* 33 (1996): 29–40; and Frank Cass and Co. Ltd., for "No Humanist Fiction This: Henry VIII's Prose Dialogue *A Glass of the Truth*," *Prose Studies: History, Theory, Criticism* 18 (1995): 123–34.

Finally, thanks are due to my wife Ding Xiang, who is busy enough with her work in medieval Chinese literature, but graciously read my manuscript and advised me on several points.

Abbreviations

Full publication details are given in the Bibliography.

CW	*The Complete Works of St. Thomas More.*
Documents	Gerald Bray, ed. *Documents of the English Reformation.*
Hall	Edward Hall. *Hall's Chronicle.*
LP	J. S. Brewer, James Gairdner, et al., eds. *Letters and Papers, Foreign and Domestic, of the Reign of Henry VIII.*
SP	*State Papers . . . of King Henry VIII.*
SP, Spanish	Pascual de Gayangos, ed. *Calendar of Letters, Despatches, and State Papers, relating to the Negotiations between England and Spain.*
SP, Venetian	Rawdon Brown, ed. *Calendar of State Papers, and Manuscripts, relating to English Affairs, existing in the Archives and Collections of Venice, and in Other Libraries of Northern Italy.*
Statutes	*The Statutes of the Realm.*
STC	A. W. Pollard and G. R. Redgrave. *A Short-Title Catalogue of Books Printed in England, Scotland, and Ireland and of English Books Printed Abroad, 1475–1640* (2nd edition, revised and enlarged by W. A. Jackson, F. S. Ferguson, and Katherine Pantzer).
TRP	Paul L. Hughes and James F. Larkin, eds. *Tudor Royal Proclamations.*

A Note on Texts

For the sake of uniformity and convenience I have modernized the spelling and capitalization of quotations from sixteenth-century editions of English books and from modern editions of these books that retain the original spelling. I have also modernized when appropriate the spelling of translations out of other languages. Citations of the Roman classics are from the Loeb series, but the translations have ordinarily been adjusted. When citing obscure texts, or differentiating between editions, I have provided their numbers from the *Short-Title Catalogue*.

Introduction

Representing Henry VIII:
The Rhetoric of "Reticent Delicacy"

The period from 1529 to 1535 saw Henry replace his first queen, Catherine of Aragon, with his second, Anne Boleyn, and sever his nation's ties to Rome by arranging for Parliament to declare him supreme head of church and state in England. It saw too the fall of Cardinal Thomas Wolsey, the rise of Thomas Cromwell, and the rise and fall and execution of Sir Thomas More. Yet as interesting as this period is, its texts have inspired little enthusiasm in students of English literature.[1] As Alistair Fox explains it, there was at the time a "retreat from fictive literature": men of letters were not writing poetry and plays but religious polemics, government propaganda, and political philosophy.[2] These are the sorts of works consulted by historians, whose accounts of Henry's reign and the progress of the English Reformation rely on the era's flood of pamphlets for testimony of its political and religious controversies and for indications of shifting government policy. Accordingly, scholars have treated Henrician tracts under a variety of topics in the fields of political, religious, and intellectual history, such as the impact of Reformation theology on government, the rise of the

---

[1] The poems by Thomas Wyatt are the exception, but though many were written in the 1530s we are not very certain which ones. The dating of his corpus is so problematic that we can only speak of the Henrician court as a context for Wyatt's poetry by conceiving of it in its span from 1524 to 1542, the years of Wyatt's royal service.

[2] Fox surveys the late 1520s and 1530s in the chapter titled "Propaganda and Polemic: The Retreat from Fictive Literature after 1525," in *Politics and Literature in the Reigns of Henry VII and Henry VIII* (London: Basil Blackwell, 1989), pp. 209–31. A few scholars have found the period's texts of some literary or rhetorical interest: John King, for example, discusses them briefly in the context of the development of Protestant literary themes in *English Reformation Literature: The Tudor Origins of the Protestant Tradition* (Princeton: Princeton University Press, 1982); Rainer Pineas studies their argumentative techniques in *Thomas More and Tudor Polemics* (Bloomington: Indiana University Press, 1968); and David Birch points out that the polemics, propaganda, and legal texts of the 1520s and 1530s mark the inception of the printing of original English prose compositions, in *Early Reformation English Polemics*, Salzburg Studies in English Literature (Salzburg: Institut für Anglistik und Amerikanistik, 1983).

humanist movement in England, the development of modern political theory, and the machinery of an early police state.[3]

Because I am interested in the uses of language, I have a different story to tell. This book examines the fictions that Henry had published to discourage resistance to his divorce, and it illustrates how these fictions in turn elicited and shaped other works of fiction printed by those who opposed the king's policies. I call these texts "fictions," in part, because so many are prose dialogues, which (Fox's assessment notwithstanding) do present fictional scenes and characters and do warrant, as I shall show, our attention to their literary forms as much as to their engagement in political and religious controversies. Less obviously, but just as crucial to understanding the rhetorical designs of the period's literature, these works contribute towards and are governed by a deliberately

---

[3] For example, on Reformation theology and government see Joan Lockwood O'Donovan, *Theology of Law and Authority in the English Reformation*, Emory University Studies in Law and Religion, no. 1 (Atlanta: Scholars Press, 1991); Edward R. Riegler, "Printing, Protestantism, and Politics: Thomas Cromwell and Religious Reform" (Ph.D. dissertation, UCLA, 1978); Leo F. Solt, *Church and State in Early Modern England, 1509–1640* (Oxford: Oxford University Press, 1990). On early modern political theory in England see Franklin le van Baumer, *The Early Tudor Theory of Kingship* (New Haven: Yale University Press, 1940); Quentin Skinner, *The Foundations of Modern Political Thought*, 2 vols. (Cambridge: Cambridge University Press, 1978); W. Gordon Zeeveld, *Foundations of Tudor Policy* (Cambridge, Mass.: Harvard University Press, 1948). The classic studies of English humanism are F. Caspari, *Humanism and the Social Order in Tudor England* (Chicago: University of Chicago Press, 1954); Arthur B. Ferguson, *The Articulate Citizen and the English Renaissance* (Durham, North Carolina: Duke University Press, 1965); James Kelsey McConica, *English Humanists and Reformation Politics under Henry VIII and Edward VI* (Oxford: Oxford University Press, 1965). A study of Henry VIII's propaganda in the context of his government's broader efforts to keep control of society during this period of radical reform is in G. R. Elton, *Policy and Police: The Enforcement of the Reformation in the Age of Thomas Cromwell* (Cambridge: Cambridge University Press, 1972).

The standard histories of the Reformation in England include A. G. Dickens, *The English Reformation*, 2nd ed. (University Park, Pennsylvania: Pennsylvania State University Press, 1989), and the same author's *Thomas Cromwell and the English Reformation* (London: English Universities Press, 1959); G. R. Elton, *Reform and Reformation: England, 1509–1558*, New History of England, vol. 2 (Cambridge, Mass.: Harvard University Press, 1977); John Guy, *Tudor England* (Oxford: Oxford University Press, 1988); and Philip Hughes, *The Reformation in England*, 3 vols. (London: Hollis & Carter, 1950–54); while the standard biography of Henry VIII is still J. J. Scarisbrick's *Henry VIII* (Berkeley: University of California Press, 1968). On the king's divorce from Catherine of Aragon see Geoffrey de C. Parmiter, *The King's Great Matter: A Study of Anglo-Papal Relations, 1527–1534* (New York: Barnes and Noble, 1967); and Henry Ansgar Kelly, *The Matrimonial Trials of Henry VIII* (Stanford: Stanford University Press, 1976). Stanford E. Lehmberg chronicles the political and legislative maneuvers within Parliament and the court in *The Reformation Parliament, 1529–1536* (Cambridge: Cambridge University Press, 1970).

crafted image of the king.[4] Books published by the royal printer, Thomas Berthelet, represent Henry VIII as a humanistic scholar- or philosopher-king, a learned and temperate ruler who solicits the counsel of wise men assembled at his court, in the universities, and in the two houses of Parliament. This image was designed to assure the realm that such a king, guided by such good counsel, was directing the government's actions in what everyone recognized were dangerous times. Henry was determined to have his way despite the dangers, but he was also anxious to minimize them by encouraging his subjects not to think him a tyrant. The philosopher-king image lent itself to this public relations campaign because it appeared to allow space for dissent, portraying Henry as a disinterested seeker after truth who, for the good of the realm, welcomed open debate and truthful counsel. At the same time this image allowed Henry to retain almost total control over the published expression of that dissent. According to the logic of the image not just anyone was qualified to participate. Only court counselors and others with legitimate connections to the government were in a position to offer advice or to represent the king and his interests. Also, as we shall see, the nature of Henry's philosopher-king image stipulated that only one particular form of conventional humanist discourse was acceptable for public debate: that of a philosophical inquiry into a general question, a form that diluted criticism of the king's specific actions.

Whatever his claims to the contrary, therefore, Henry left little room for an opposition to print counter-propaganda within England. Those who had connections to the government and who were in a position to attempt it still had to abide by the discursive rules imposed by the king's fiction in striving to achieve their very real suasive aims.[5] This is what we

---

[4] In the last two decades historians have argued that Henry's propaganda campaign was initiated earlier, and directed by the king to a greater degree, than has traditionally been supposed. See John Guy, *Christopher St. German on Chancery and Statute*, Selden Society Supplementary Series, vol. 6 (London: Selden Society, 1985), pp. 19–55; Guy, "Thomas More and Christopher St. German: The Battle of the Books," in Alistair Fox and John Guy, *Reassessing the Henrician Age: Humanism, Politics and Reform, 1500–1550* (Oxford: Basil Blackwell, 1986), pp. 95–120; Steven Haas, "The *Disputatio inter clericum et militem*: Was Berthelet's 1531 Edition the First Henrician Polemic of Thomas Cromwell?" in *Moreana* 14 (1977): pp. 65–72. My study continues this trend, treating several works that have until now not been considered relevant to this campaign.

[5] Here I allude to Michel Foucault's theory of the formation of "discursive practices" or "strategies." In such formations, the more and less authoritative speakers and writers within a discursive community – Foucault's examples are drawn mainly from the fields of science in the nineteenth century – establish and honor implicitly codified rules of discourse, which in effect function as constraints for those who aspire to enter into and remain within those communities (see *The Archaeology of Knowledge*, trans. A. M. Sheridan Smith [New York: Pantheon,

see in the publications of John Rastell (before his religious conversion in 1531) and of his son William Rastell, who were kinsmen to the lord chancellor, Sir Thomas More, and the printers of all More's polemical works. By virtue of this connection and their own occasional court service, the Rastells were in a legitimate position to address the king and to represent his interests, and for a time they did so in an effort to sway Henry's actions, if not into strict conformity with those of his image, at least toward some middle ground between it and tyranny.

I am describing, then, not only Henry VIII's literary self-representation to his subjects but also a rhetorical contest, waged with literature, between and among the king and those who represented him. This was the first time in England's short printing history that the ideals of humanism were put to such extended test, when men used the equipment of the new learning in systematic, public attempts to steer the ship of state. The king and the More circle were trying, in other words, to exert literary pressures on actual behavior, employing a set of conventions from the traditions of imaginative and speculative writing, from fiction and philosophy, which they hoped would have power in the real world. For everyone would have understood that the philosopher-king image carried with it both a pledge and a bidding. It advanced the proposition that Henry, the members of his court, and all the subjects of his realm would act according to a prescribed range of conventional and logical

1972], pp. 31–9 and 64–76; originally published as *L'Archéologie du Savoir* [Paris: Gallimard, 1969]). Or, as Foucault states elsewhere: "None may enter into discourse on a specific subject unless he has satisfied certain conditions or if he is not, from the outset, qualified to do so" ("The Discourse on Knowledge," appendix to *The Archaeology of Knowledge*, trans. Rupert Swyer, pp. 224–5; originally published as *L'ordre du discours* [Paris: Gallimard, 1971], translation first published in *Social Science Information* 10.2 [April, 1971], pp. 7–30).

An explication of discursive formations in later Renaissance literary history is in Annabel Patterson's *Censorship and Interpretation: The Conditions of Writing and Reading in Early Modern England* (Madison: University of Wisconsin Press, 1984), which describes the ways that Sidney, Jonson, and other Elizabethan and Stuart authors exploited the "functional ambiguity" of government censorship. Patterson sees "the prevailing codes of communication, the implicit social contract between authors and authorities, intelligible to all parties at the time, as being a fully deliberate and conscious arrangement" (p. 17), which articulates well what this study details in the period of Henry's divorce crisis. Richard Helgerson, in his *Forms of Nationhood: The Elizabethan Writing of England* (Chicago: Chicago University Press, 1992), also adopts Foucault's terminology in his analysis of the discursive practices shared by the various professional, religious, and literary communities striving toward the formation of an English national identity (see especially pp. 12–16). And with a similar interest to mine in the public and courtly image of the monarch, Susan Frye invokes Foucault's thesis on power and discourse in her study of the contested representation of Queen Elizabeth, in *Elizabeth I: The Competition for Representation* (Oxford: Oxford University Press, 1993), p. 17.

guidelines. But it was also clear that there was room to maneuver within those guidelines. By strategically reformulating in their texts the idealized image of the king, his court, and his country, Henry VIII and the More circle could attempt to restrict and define actions according to their own political, religious, and personal commitments, thereby making the image work – as each would insist – in the best interests of the realm.[6]

II

If it seems unlikely that Henry would have gone to the trouble to initiate and sustain such an elaborate press campaign, we need to keep in mind how high were the stakes. The general, roundabout nature of Henry's propaganda allowed him to tread lightly at a time when he and the country perceived real disasters to be imminent. As Henry moved closer toward open defiance of Rome over the matter of the divorce, he increasingly risked excommunication and a bull from Pope Clement VII declaring holy war against England. Rumor had it that the queen's nephew, Charles V of Spain, was prepared to lead an invasion personally if Henry dared remarry.[7] Public sympathy, too, was with Catherine. Edward Hall records that among the people there was much "grumbling and murmuring" against the king, and open expressions of support when the queen appeared in public (pp. 781–2).[8] Once, these "grumbling" subjects even ventured an attempt on Anne Boleyn's life, if we can believe

[6] In the context of this study's focus on the 1530s, "the More circle" refers to More and those of his allies who, it is likely, coordinated their activities with More's own in trying to protect the Church in England. Compare my argument in this section to Greg Walker's point that Henry's "affable" image gave More and other counselors "certain freedoms" to give advice and debate policy, in *Persuasive Fictions: Faction, Faith and Political Culture in the Reign of Henry VIII* (Aldershot: Scolar Press, 1996), pp. 110–14.

[7] This threat was taken so seriously that the Duke of Norfolk, head of Henry's council, asked Spain's ambassador in England outright whether or not Charles would attack if the English Church granted Henry his divorce (*SP, Spanish*, vol. 4, pt. 1, no. 290). As has become clear, I follow general practice in using the term "divorce" in this study, even though technically Henry neither sought nor, with Bishop Cranmer's eventual solution to the crisis, secured a divorce (which is the dissolution of a valid marriage) but an annulment (a decision that his marriage had been void from the beginning). This annulment was declared on the grounds that the pope could not dispense against the prohibitions in Leviticus 18:16 and 20:21 against a man marrying the wife of his brother (as Pope Julius II had done for Henry, so that he could marry Catherine after the death of Prince Arthur). In 1527 Henry began to insist that the Old Testament law applied to his case, and that his lack of a male heir was his punishment from God for breaking it.

[8] Also see *SP, Spanish*, vol. 3, pt. 2, no. 586.

a 1531 report to the French ambassador in Venice that "a mob of from seven to eight thousand women of London went out of the town to seize Boleyn's daughter, the sweetheart of the king of England, who was supping at a villa on a river, the king not being with her; and having received notice of this, she escaped by crossing the river in a boat. The women had intended to kill her; and amongst the mob were many men, disguised as women."[9] The royal propaganda campaign was designed to prevent uprisings such as this. Henry fed the perception that he was surrounded by wise and admiring counselors at court and in Parliament because this image, he hoped, would help to allay fears at home, and discourage enemies' hopes both at home and abroad, that the ship of state was being piloted by a lone and unpopular tyrant ripe for deposing by revolt or foreign invasion.[10]

Henry had delivered similar messages before. In fact, the Tudor court was from the beginning adept at devising propaganda to bolster its claims to legitimacy and encourage loyalty in the king's subjects. In Sydney Anglo's seminal study of the political purposes of court spectacle, for example, one is impressed by the propagandistic coherence of such events as the coronations of Henry VII and VIII, the various Tudor progresses through the English countryside, the London pageants for the receptions of Catherine of Aragon in 1501 and Charles V in 1522, and especially the "Field of Cloth of Gold" that celebrated the momentous, if short-lived, "Universal Peace" among Europe's rulers.[11] To similar purpose, in the 1510s and 1520s Henry's acting company, the King's Players, and the Gentleman and Children of the Chapel Royal were engaged to perform in disguisings and other entertainments that were intended to reinforce the court's position at times of negotiations with French and Imperial diplomats. An example is the play performed before Charles V and his entourage in 1522, in which a proud horse representing Louis XII was tamed and bridled by characters named Prudence and Policy (representing Henry and Charles). As Greg Walker explains, the play was not just "partisan self-congratulation," but a means to "dispel suggestions of English diplomatic ambivalence or duplicity" at a time when the emperor was receiving reports from his ambassadors that

---

[9] *SP, Venetian*, vol. 4, no. 701.

[10] This was the characterization of Henry that Catherine's English allies were presenting the Imperial ambassador in England, Eustache Chapuys, and that Chapuys was sending on to Charles. See, for example, *LP*, vol. 7, no. 1206.

[11] *Spectacle, Pageantry, and Early Tudor Policy* (Oxford: Clarendon Press, 1969). On Henry VIII's coronation see too Jennifer Loach, "The Function of Ceremonial in the Reign of Henry VIII," *Past and Present* 143 (1994): pp. 43–68, in which Loach demonstrates that "royal ceremonial at this period did not merely seek to convince intellectually and visually: it offered tangible evidence that loyalty would be well rewarded" (p. 68).

"England's commitment to the enterprise against France was at best lukewarm."[12] In this way the simple story of the proud horse exemplifies Walker's definition of plays that are *political* "not merely because they touched upon political acts, but because they were themselves political acts."[13]

Additionally, Henry VIII used the printing press for self-promotion several times before the 1530s, commissioning Richard Pynson, royal printer before Thomas Berthelet, to publish besides the statutes and proclamations tracts that would generate support for the government's policies and actions.[14] The first major press campaign coincided with England's alliance with Spain, Venice, and Pope Julius II in the Holy League against Louis XII of France. As Henry dispatched troops to the Continent in 1512, and then prepared to lead them himself the following year, several tracts were issued by Pynson's press that rallied England for war: James Whytstons' *De Iusticia et sanctitate belli* (*STC* 25585) describes the schism in the church caused by Louis and defends the pope's call for France's invasion; the *Gardener's Pastance touching the Outrage of France* (*STC* 11562.5) achieves the same end by way of an allegorical tale (the central characters being a rose and a lily). Pynson also printed in 1512 an *inspeximus* of the papal bull absolving the subjects of France from their allegiance to Louis (*STC* 25947.7).[15]

Henry's failure in 1513 to depose the French king meant he was not granted the title that Julius II had dangled before him as a prize: "Most Christian King."[16] But in 1521, Pope Leo X granted Henry the title

---

[12] *Plays of Persuasion: Drama and Politics at the Court of Henry VIII* (Cambridge: Cambridge University Press, 1991), p. 17. For Walker's discussion of other political plays at court in the years before the divorce crisis see pp. 15–19. Another analysis of the play (which is reported in Hall, p. 641 and *SP, Spanish*, vol. 2, no. 437) is in Anglo, *Spectacle, Pageantry and Early Tudor Policy*, pp. 203–4; and Anglo, "William Cornish in a Play, Pageants, Prison and Politics," *Review of English Studies*, New Series, 10 (1959): pp. 357–60.

[13] Walker, *Plays of Persuasion*, p. 2.

[14] Two studies chronicle Richard Pynson's activity as royal printer: Pamela Ayers Neville, "Richard Pynson, King's Printer (1506–1529): Printing and Propaganda in Early Tudor England" (Ph.D. dissertation, University of London, Warburg Institute, 1990); and Stanley Howard Johnston, Jr., "A Study of the Career and Literary Publications of Richard Pynson" (Ph.D. dissertation, University of Western Ontario, 1977).

[15] On these tracts see Neville, "Richard Pynson, King's Printer," pp. 107–8; Johnston, "A Study of Richard Pynson," pp. 87–9. Neville is probably right also to include in this press campaign the *History, Siege and Destruction of Troy* (*STC* 5579), which Pynson states was "imprinted at the commandment of our sovereign Lord the king Henry VIII" and which John Lydgate had originally translated for presentation to Henry V, Henry VIII's model for winning victory in France (cf. Scarisbrick, *Henry VIII*, p. 23 n. 3).

[16] Scarisbrick, *Henry VIII*, pp. 33–4.

defensor fidei for having written a book, the *Assertio Septem Sacramen-torum adversus M. Lutherum.*[17] The press campaign against Luther during the 1520s was the government's most concerted propaganda effort before 1530, and the one most relevant to this study because it is marked by the obvious cultivation of Henry's image as a philosopher-king. The title-page's wood-cut by Holbein and the text in roman type distinguished the *Assertio* as a self-consciously humanist production,[18] and though it hardly set back the advance of the Reformation it publicized the self-image and inspired the kind of praise for which Henry was eager. Shortly after the *Assertio*'s publication, for instance, the renowned humanist at the University of Rome, Pierius Valernius, said about Henry and his treatise in a public lecture that, "The most pious writings of this king are in the hands of all – so learned, so devout, so ardent – by which he has most successfully demolished the most vile enterprises of the Lutheran faction (or should I say, pestilence?) which had begun to overthrow the laws, religion, and all secular things; so that you may understand from this one man what hope exists for the future if, as Plato argued, citizens will be of the same quality as their kings."[19]

Henry's divorce crisis was not the first occasion in which the printing press was used to publicize a ruler's image as a philosopher-king to justify his supremacy. Quentin Skinner reminds us that humanist tracts arguing for the concentration of power in the hands of a single "prudent and philosophical ruler" began to appear in Florence in the 1470s and 1480s, when Lorenzo de Medici was intent on discouraging a growing popular nostalgia for the city's republican past.[20] When Henry VIII

---

[17] First edition *STC* 13078. See Neville, "Richard Pynson, King's Printer," pp. 124–5; Johnston, "A Study of Richard Pynson," pp. 144–5. As Neville explains, a good number of men are given credit for contributing to the *Assertio* besides (or instead of) Henry; on this question see also Hughes, *The Reformation in England*, vol. 1, pp. 146–8; Scarisbrick, *Henry VIII*, pp. 112–15.

[18] Neville stresses this point in "Richard Pynson, King's Printer," p. 124.

[19] *Praelectiones in Catullum* (Vat. Lat. 5215), fols. 162ᵛ–163ʳ, quoted and translated in Julia Haig Gaisser, *Catullus and his Renaissance Readers* (Oxford: Clarendon Press, 1993), pp. 132–3, 348 n. 102. Thomas More's *Responsio ad Lutherum* (first edition 1523; *STC* 18088.5) also contributed to the court's campaign. Then in 1526 Henry countered Luther's rebuttal of the *Assertio* with the tract *Literarum, quibus inuictissimus princeps, Henricus octauus, respondit, ad quandam epistolam M. Lutheri* (first edition *STC* 13084; English translation *STC* 13086). See Neville, "Richard Pynson, King's Printer," pp. 172–3; Johnston, "A Study of Richard Pynson," p. 149. The print war against Luther is discussed in its broader religious context by David V. N. Bagchi in *Luther's Earliest Opponents: Catholic Controversialists, 1518–1525* (Minneapolis: Fortress Press, 1991).

[20] See "Political Philosophy," *The Cambridge History of Renaissance Philosophy*, ed. Charles B. Schmitt and Quentin Skinner (Cambridge: Cambridge University Press, 1988), pp. 426–30. The examples Skinner cites of works extolling monarchy as

began to plot his divorce from Catherine of Aragon, therefore, the cultivation of a philosopher-king image was a strategy based on historical precedent and personal, past success. It naturally became a chief tactic in pursuing his "great matter."[21]

Even before the inception of the press campaign, Henry invoked the philosopher-king image for the legatine trial that opened in 1529 to investigate the validity of his marriage.[22] This trial was convened after Cardinal Thomas Wolsey, Henry's lord chancellor prior to More, requested authorization from Rome to decide the king's case, and Pope Clement VII reluctantly agreed. Clement then appointed two papal legates to preside as joint inquisitors for the trial: Cardinal Wolsey and Cardinal Lorenzo Campeggio, a former bishop of Salisbury whom Wolsey hoped would go along with the verdict that he knew his king expected. When the trial opened Henry declared how painful this whole business was for him. Really, he insisted, he loved Catherine as much as ever.[23] But the serious doubts that troubled his conscience had to be settled, he continued with a show of bravery, and that was why he had consented to this trial – because the discovery of truth takes precedence over personal feelings. Such professions did more than mask real motives. They established ground rules for the proceedings, making it clear that Henry expected Catherine's counsel to present its case in accordance with an official fiction of his personal disinterest and the trial's integrity.

Not everyone was willing to play along. John Fisher, the Bishop of Rochester who, with More, would be executed in 1535 for refusing to acknowledge the king's supremacy, at one point during the trial personally vouched for the validity of Henry's marriage, offering, prophetically, to lay down his life in its defense.[24] Henry instructed his secretary, Stephen Gardiner, to prepare his response to Fisher, and this was shortly afterwards delivered before the judges as an oration, either by the king himself or one of his counsel.[25] Because Henry's image and the discursive

---

"the best state of a commonwealth" are the *Disputationes Camaldulenses* by Cristoforo Landino and *De legibus et iudiciis* by Bartolomeo Scala, Lorenzo's chancellor.

[21] This was how ambassadors and others regularly referred to Henry's divorce crisis in their correspondence, as can be seen in the contents of *LP*, vols. 4–7.

[22] The records of this trial are summarized and given extensive analysis in Kelly, *The Matrimonial Trials of Henry VIII*, pp. 75–131.

[23] Ibid., p. 81.

[24] Ibid., p. 92.

[25] The Latin text of Henry's response to Fisher, which survives in MS, is edited with facing-page translation (slightly modified in the excerpt below) by Pierre Janelle in Gardiner, *Obedience in Church and State: Three Political Tracts by Stephen Gardiner* (Cambridge: Cambridge University Press, 1930), pp. 2–9.

rules it stipulated had been challenged and needed explicit reassertion, his answer to Fisher illustrates the nature of the image and its rules especially well. For this reason it is worth quoting a substantial excerpt.

Since in this matrimonial cause now to be investigated, or in the controversy now to be determined, we have attempted or designed nothing, on our own authority, which were unsuited to the office of a true Christian prince; but on the contrary have always had regard before everything to equity, justice and truth, and have everywhere held that the judgment of the Church was to be deferred to with great respect; relying upon our consciousness of this our innocence, we hoped, Judges, that we should have all the best men as supporters of our honor, our efforts and our purposes, and hardly thought that there might come forth any one, to disparage such a dutiful mind of ours, show enmity to our virtue, and jealousy of our fame. If this was to be (and we are not ignorant how many things have deceived the very wisest, even in regard to their own concerns, and to public affairs), yet we never supposed, Judges, that the bishop of Rochester would take up before your tribunal that accusation against ourselves, which would rather befit the hatred, or better still the fury, of bad citizens, and a multitude seditiously roused, than his own virtue and dignity. Of a certainty, Judges, we did unfold to this Rochester, and this already some months ago, and more than once, how far we had been from purposely seeking out or rashly devising those reasons, which long before had engendered in us scruples of conscience, in regard to this illegitimate and incestuous marriage. Which reasons this very Rochester thus far then approved, and deemed so weighty and powerful, that unless we applied to the oracle of our most serene Lord [the pope] (which he then thought it necessary to consult upon those matters) he did not believe that our former peace of mind could be restored to us.[26] Now when this same our most holy Lord (yet not without the advice and opinion of some of the most reverend cardinals of the apostolic see, and of other members of the Roman court, most eminent for their worthiness and erudition) has judged that these same reasons made the cause of our marriage so intricate and ambiguous, that only through the ruling of the best chosen and wisest judges could it be treated and set forth according to its dignity and magnitude; and when he has,

---

[26] This claim that Fisher had once conceded the intricacy of the king's matter, warranting an appeal to "the wisest judges," probably refers to the result of Wolsey's interview with him in 1527 concerning Henry's plans, when Fisher was assured that "the king's intentions were altogether honorable" (Gardiner, *Obedience in Church and State*, p. 2 n. 3). In a letter to Wolsey, Fisher maintained that "it belongs to the pope to clear ambiguous passages of scripture, after hearing the opinions of the best divines," though he insisted that this matter had already been settled by the fact that Julius had issued Henry a dispensation before his marriage to Catherine: "this alone should determine the question," said Fisher (*LP*, vol. 4, pt. 2, no. 3148).

most in accordance with your deserts, entrusted it to you, Judges, and to your scrupulousness, to be wholly determined; and has sent thee here, most reverend Campeggio, for no other reason, to the great charges indeed of his Holiness, and to thy great peril and travail through the dangers of so many things and ways;[27] what shall we believe, Judges, to have come into the mind of this Rochester, or by what spirit shall we think he has been led, to come forward here so impudently and so much out of season, in order to declare his own personal view of the matter, now at length after so many months, and even here before such a great and illustrious assembly as that of your court. It had been of constancy on his part, not to ascribe now at last in public those scruples of conscience, which he had once thought we were right in harboring, to mere commonplaces (as he calls them), to subtleties only probable in appearance, and other gilded persuasions of rhetoricians. (pp. 3–5)

A number of the references in this speech to Fisher's objections reveal that he had not only challenged the reasons supplied for judging Henry's marriage invalid, but also attacked the hypocrisy of both the king's professed motives and his counsel's language. This is clear from Fisher's reported scorn for the "mere commonplaces," the "subtleties only probable in appearance," and the "gilded persuasions of rhetoricians" that he claims are being marshaled to argue the king's case. Of course Fisher is invoking Socrates' objections to sophistry here,[28] implying that the king's counsel is making use of tools more suited to academic exercises – and deception – than to an inquiry into the truth. Also, every participant in the trial would have recognized Fisher's outright assertion of the validity of the royal marriage for what it was: a denial that the court was an assembly of impartial judges who could be trusted to discover and affirm truth. Henry accuses the bishop, consequently, of having insulted the sacred authority of these proceedings. The pope himself, he says, sanctioned this trial upon the advice of "the most reverend cardinals of the apostolic see, and of other members of the Roman court," and these are the "wisest of judges" now gathered to hear

[27] Gardiner/Henry is referring to Campeggio's long journey from Rome at a time when he suffered severely from the gout (see Parmiter, *The King's Great Matter*, p. 63).

[28] As in *Phaedrus*, 272d–e: "There is . . . absolutely no need for the budding orator to concern himself with the truth about what is just or good conduct . . . In the law courts nobody cares a rap for the truth about these matters, but only what is plausible. And that is the same as what is probable, and is what must occupy the attention of the would-be master of the art of speech." References in this study to Plato are to the translations in *Plato: The Collected Dialogues*, ed. Edith Hamilton and Huntington Cairns, Bollingen Series 71 (Princeton: Princeton University Press, 1961); citations from this and other classical texts are to the marginal sigla.

the case. The king asserts, too, that Fisher himself had once admitted how "intricate and ambiguous" this question is, and therefore, says Henry, it is a marvel to him that the bishop of Rochester should now assert a "personal view of the matter," before the judges have heard all the evidence and handed down their sentence.

Despite being "intricate and ambiguous," however, this matter *is* the king's, and the king, being pressed, departs just briefly from the form of general, disinterested inquiry that he demands of Fisher and the rest of the defense team to remind everyone that his marriage is plainly "illegitimate and incestuous." Henry's intention in making this flat pronouncement was not to stop the spectacle of debate, to be sure. In a trial, opposition is required, and he was determined that this one would provide a legitimate and decisive solution to his problem. His aim was rather to dilute the opposition, to restrict debate to a form that allowed the contending sides in the trial to carry on contending without actually threatening the outcome. In the end, Fisher only succeeded in voicing what everyone could see already, that Henry's image and its discursive rules were hypocritical. The king was put on the defensive rhetorically, but by reasserting the image and its rules – mingled with threats – he made it clear that he would not back down merely because the fiction of his image was obvious. This was a power struggle, and "the quint-essential sign" of power, in Stephen Greenblatt's formulation, "is the ability to impose one's fictions upon the world."[29]

Unhappily for Henry at the time, the reach of his authority did not extend beyond Wolsey to the other papal legate, Cardinal Campeggio, and his hopes for the trial were eventually thwarted. After two months of testimony on the validity of the 1503 papal dispensation that had allowed Henry to marry his brother's widow, Campeggio took the action that Clement VII may even have instructed him to take prior to the trial: he announced that the case was too important to be decided without consulting the pope, and he adjourned the court.[30] Shortly afterwards, Clement declared the removal of the cause to Rome. For Henry this was far worse than a serious setback, in part because of other events at home and in Europe. Cardinal Wolsey, who had been striving to keep the

---

[29] *Renaissance Self-Fashioning: From More to Shakespeare* (Chicago: University of Chicago Press, 1980), p. 13.

[30] The traditional view of Campeggio's abrupt end to the legatine trial is that it was met by Wolsey and Henry as an unexpected shattering of their hoped-for success (Scarisbrick, *Henry VIII*, p. 227; Parmiter, *The King's Great Matter*, pp. 104–5; Kelly, *The Matrimonial Trials of Henry VIII*, pp. 128–9). In contrast, Peter Gwyn argues that it came rather as "a relief" to Wolsey, and was accepted by him and Henry as a "compromise" solution to a trial that did not promise to conclude in the king's favor (*The King's Cardinal: The Rise and Fall of Thomas Wolsey* [London: Barrie and Jenkins, 1990], pp. 525–30).

papacy from the control of Charles V, had encouraged Henry to strike an alliance with France in 1526, and in January 1528 to declare war against Charles; but after the French were routed at the Battle of Landriano in June France sued for peace, and without even informing England, France and Spain signed the treaty of Cambrai, leaving Charles virtually in control of Italy and completely in control of the pope. With the avocation of the king's cause to Rome, the queen's nephew had Henry's great matter in his hands as well.

With the failure of the trial Wolsey lost Henry's confidence and protection against his political enemies. In October Wolsey was accused of *praemunire* (that is, obeying a foreign authority over the statutes of the realm, which, ironically, he had done on the king's behalf by assuming the papal legateship), and he confessed to this and other crimes.[31] The king stripped Wolsey of his property and all his titles but archbishop of York, just after instructing him to call for the convening of Parliament. This request appeared to signal Henry's new strategy for pursuing his divorce, but during its first few sessions Henry did not make it clear what he expected from Parliament.[32] He continued his efforts, instead, to convince the pope to return his case to England for a domestic trial. Ambassadors' reports give the impression that Clement was hearing petitions on this subject almost daily. In the meantime, to prepare against the day when Henry might actually have to defy Rome, the court initiated a propaganda campaign to represent to the public the justice of the king's position, and the injustice of a pope exercising temporal powers within England.

Historians are intrigued by Henry's careful behavior during this period, observing that he only fitfully and uncertainly asserted his regal authority in the first years of the Reformation Parliament. The king's apparent indecisiveness led G. R. Elton, for example, to call 1529–1532 "the years without a policy."[33] The hesitant character of Henry's

[31] Wolsey's confession and the indictment brought against him are calendared in *LP*, vol. 4, pt. 3, nos. 6017 and 6035. The circumstances behind Wolsey's fall have been much contested recently. For arguments that Wolsey was a victim of political faction see E. W. Ives, "The Fall of Wolsey," in *Cardinal Wolsey: Church, State and Art*, ed. S. J. Gunn and P. G. Lindley (Cambridge: Cambridge University Press, 1991), pp. 286–315; and Joseph S. Block, *Factional Politics and the English Reformation, 1520–1540* (London/Royal Historical Society, 1993), pp. 1–25. For the view that a greater emphasis should be placed on the king's dissatisfaction with Wolsey see Gwyn, *The King's Cardinal*, pp. 583–98; and G. W. Bernard, "The Fall of Wolsey Reconsidered," *Journal of British Studies* 35 (1996): pp. 277–310.

[32] Members of Parliament knew from the start that Henry had plans for their participation in resolving his divorce crisis, so they were puzzled, even if relieved, that in the first sessions they were not pressed to take any explicit action on the matter. On this point see Lehmberg, *The Reformation Parliament*, pp. 105–7 and 128–30.

[33] *England under the Tudors*, 3rd edition (London: Routledge, 1991), p. 122. Or

rule could be attributed to his naturally impulsive disposition, a trait he exhibited all his life, or to the understandable uncertainty and trepidation he must have felt as he ventured into ever more dangerous waters. It has also been noted that Henry was between right-hand men during this period: Wolsey was gone, Cromwell was rising but not yet firmly in power, and the new chancellor, Sir Thomas More, would not have anything to do with the matter that most occupied his prince. But the promulgation of an image of hesitancy can itself be effective policy, and in Henry's case, I will maintain, this image was consciously cultivated as part of a strategy to avoid the appearance of tyranny, of the king ruling outside the law, at a time when the law was being rewritten to suit the king's will. A philosopher-king, as everyone knows, does not act rashly. For the good of his realm, he waits until he has weighed all arguments, all options, before taking action. This was precisely the mode of behavior Henry had on display during the early 1530s, both in print and in his personal presentation at court and in Parliament.

We can, of course, find instances from this period of Henry wielding his power with a heavy hand. One of the most famous occurred during Parliament's third session, when a bill threatening the Church's powers of taxation and also preparing the way for Henry to resolve his matter at home was meeting with strong resistance in the House of Commons. This bill was the Act in Conditional Restraint of Annates, which not only limited the payment of the year's revenues or "first fruits" to the See of Rome, but also, as J. R. Tanner points out, "set up the provisional machinery for the consecration of archbishops and bishops without the necessary bulls from Rome, and defied interdict and excommunication in advance."[34] To overcome the resistance Henry made the unprecedented step of entering the House at the time of the vote and requesting those "who would stand for his success and the welfare of the realm" to one side, and those who would not to the other, with the effect that several members belonging one moment before to the opposition had a sudden change of heart and the measure was passed.[35]

We must keep in mind, though, that the published result of this episode accorded perfectly well with Henry's official image. It was not

alternatively, in Joseph Block's words, "these were not years without policy; they were years bereft of political will. Henry would not yield to conservative pleas that he submit to Roman jurisdiction, but neither did he commit himself beyond theoretical agreement to the radical policy of schism and reform" (*Factional Politics*, p. 33).

[34] J. R. Tanner, ed., *Tudor Constitutional Documents, A.D. 1485–1603, with an Historical Commentary* (Cambridge: Cambridge University Press, 1922), p. 25. For the Act in Conditional Restraint of Annates see *Statutes*, 23 Henry VIII, c. 20 (reprinted in *Documents*, no. 8).

[35] Lehmberg, *The Reformation Parliament*, pp. 137–8; Imperial ambassador Chapuys's report of this incident is calendared in *LP*, vol. 5, no. 898.

a royal proclamation, but an act of Parliament. From the perspective of the public, therefore, this bill was not made law because Henry VIII intimidated its opponents into submission, but – as the text of the statute puts it – by the request of "the noblemen . . . and wise, sage, politic commons" of "the whole body of this realm."

And in general, Henry seems to have maintained a careful court behavior that was more consistent with his public image as a temperate, reasonable king. Edward Hall reports that later in the same session House Speaker Sir Thomas Audley and several of his fellow members presented to Henry the Commons' Supplication against the Ordinaries beseeching the king to redress "the extreme and uncharitable behavior and dealings" of many clerics. While Henry could have acted on this personally, he instead passed it on to Convocation, the assembly of bishops that met concurrently with Parliament, and invited its response. As he told Audley,

> It is not the office of a king which is a judge to be too light of credence, nor I have not, nor will not use the same: for I will hear the party that is accused speak ere I give any sentence. (p. 784)

When Convocation had prepared its Answer of the Ordinaries defending the clergy's conduct and traditional privileges, Henry sent it directly to Audley and his party, with the observation,

> We think their answer will smally please you, for it seemeth to us very slender. You be a great sort of wise men; I doubt not but you will look circumspectly on the matter, and we will be indifferent between you. (p. 788)[36]

This was the king's "sentence," then: a profession of indifference and a promise not to interfere in the deliberations. But of course, any real sentence or direct action on Henry's part was unnecessary. His observations on the slenderness of the answer and the wisdom of those in the Lower House were enough to embolden Commons to pass before their Easter recess four more acts restricting the rights of clerics.[37]

---

[36] The Supplication and Convocation's Answer are printed in *Documents*, nos. 4 and 5. There is speculation that Cromwell was behind the original drafting of the Supplication, which would make Henry's "indifference" all the more ironic: see G. R. Elton, "The Commons' Supplication of 1532: Parliamentary Manoevres in the Reign of Henry VIII," *English Historical Review* 66 (1951): pp. 507–34 (reprinted in Elton, *Studies in Tudor and Stuart Politics and Government*, 4 vols. [Cambridge: Cambridge University Press, 1974–1992], vol. 2, pp. 107–36); J. P. Cooper, "The Supplication against the Ordinaries Reconsidered," *English Historical Review* 72 (1957): pp. 616–41; Lehmberg, *The Reformation Parliament*, p. 139.

[37] 23 Henry VIII, cc. 1 (preventing the release of clerics who are guilty of crimes), 9 (prohibiting bishops from citing laymen out of their own dioceses), 10 (prohibiting

III

The official propaganda of this time indicates a similar unwillingness on Henry's part to pass judgment too hastily, by portraying him as a prudent ruler who would hear the opinions of all his wise counselors and of biblical scholars throughout Christendom before speaking or taking action. Henry's most pressing reason for this self-representation, as I have said, was to convince his subjects of the justice of his cause and thereby to avoid rebellion when Anne replaced Catherine as his queen. But Henry had another strong motive for publicizing his philosopher-king image, which was a consequence of the popular conviction that Cardinal Wolsey first questioned the validity of the royal marriage and had pursued its nullification because of his own political ambitions. Catherine herself made this accusation against Wolsey, prompting him to open the legatine trial with a denial that he had any personal design in the king's great matter. He appealed to Henry to confirm his words, and gave his assurances to the court that his sentence would be bound by the demands of justice.[38] Wolsey had been making this protest for two years, but apparently he was unconvincing. Even after his death, as we shall see, Henry was impelled to combat the perception that he was acting on the bad advice of his disgraced, former chancellor.

Yet that effort only led Henry into another difficult position. As he distanced himself from Wolsey, he risked giving his subjects the impression that he was embracing the opinions of William Tyndale and the other religious reformers who were the most outspoken of Wolsey's enemies. Naturally the reformers were quite eager to encourage that impression, and toward the end of the 1520s they began to do so in satires forecasting the lord chancellor's looming fall. It is well known that attacks on Wolsey had long been circulating in manuscript – most familiar are John Skelton's *Why Come Ye Not to Court?* and *Colin Clout.* Now, in Wolsey's last years, the reformers apparently found a model in Skelton's daring accusation that the king had been hoodwinked out of his rule of the realm. For example, in one place Skelton declares that

> [Wolsey] diggeth so in the trench
> Of the court royal
> That he ruleth them all.

the permanent settlement of lands on parish churches and chapels), and 11 (making it a felony for clerics to break prison), in *Statutes.*

[38] Wolsey's declaration is summarized in Kelly, *Matrimonial Trials of Henry VIII,* p. 81.

So he doth undermind,
And such sleights doth find,
That the king's mind
By him is subverted.[39]

In the same vein, a passage from a popular ballad of the late 1520s depicts Wolsey as a usurper of Henry VIII's power:

thou hast ascended as high as may be;
thou canst no higher, but one degree; –
    Men muse much whither thou wilt; –
on the which degree thine one foot doth stand,
and most of his power thou hast in thy hand,
    and all is cost, lost and spilt.[40]

The anonymous satirist's stance toward the king in this rhyme is subtly more insistent than Skelton's, however. By referring to what men "wonder," he challenges Henry to reclaim his rightful sovereignty over England:

. . . every man on other doth stare,
    wondering what they may do,
looking ever when their sovereign lord
will set all thing in due accord,
    as him belongeth unto.   (p. 358)

By synecdoche Wolsey stood for the yoke of papal laws, and in numerous pamphlets, most printed in the relative safety of Antwerp, the reformers made the image of Henry's compromised sovereignty one of their favorite polemical tropes. Simon Fish uses it in his *Supplication for the Beggars* (1529), where he adopts the voice of an English commoner beggared by avaricious clergymen. Fish condemns the usual list of clerical enormities – drinking, whoring, selling indulgences, and threatening with accusations of heresy anyone who objects to clerical privileges – but he also laments that his king has been fettered and bankrupted by the priests. Even Parliament, he says, is in their control:

What a number of bishops, abbots, and priors are lords of your Parliament? Are not all the learned men in your realm in fee with them

---

[39] *Why Come Ye Not to Court?* lines 434–40, in *John Skelton: The Complete English Poems*, ed. John Scattergood (New Haven: Yale University Press, 1983). Greg Walker stresses the bold criticism of these and similar lines in the poem in *John Skelton and the Politics of the 1520s* (Cambridge: Cambridge University Press, 1988), pp. 170–2.

[40] "An Impeachment of Wolsey," in Frederick J. Furnivall, ed., *Ballads from Manuscripts*, 2 vols. (London and Hertford: Ballad Society, 1868–73), vol. 1, p. 359.

to speak in your Parliament House for them against your crown, dignity, and common wealth of your realm, a few of your own learned council only excepted?[41]

William Roy and Jerome Barlow, two former associates of William Tyndale, bait Henry in the same way in their verse dialogue *Read Me and Be Not Wroth, for I Say No Thing but Truth* (1528). This tract includes on its title page a mock coat of arms for Wolsey, with a cardinal's hat and (as described in the preface) a "mastiff cur bred in Ipswich town / Gnawing with his teeth a king's crown."[42] The image prepares us for the strategy of the text. Like Fish's *Supplication, Read Me and Be Not Wroth* feeds popular resentment of the clergy, but also tries to provoke Henry into breaking with Rome by portraying him as an impotent king:

> . . . the religious sects,
> Unto no laws are subjects,
> Obeying neither God nor king.
> If the king will their service use,
> Forthwith they lay for an excuse,
> That they must do God's business.
> And if in it they be found negligent,
> They say the king is impediment,
> Because they must do him service.
> And if the king shall them compel,
> Then obstinately they do rebel,
> Fleeing to the pope's maintenance.
> Of whom they obtain exemptions,
> From all the jurisdictions,
> Of temporal governance.   (lines 2488–502)

Tyndale expressed distaste at what he called these "railing rhymes" by his former colleagues.[43] But in *The Obedience of a Christian Man* (1528)

---

[41] Fish, *Supplication*, in *CW*, vol. 7, p. 417.

[42] Jerome Barlowe and William Roye, *Rede Me and Be Nott Wrothe*, ed. Douglas Parker (Toronto: University of Toronto Press, 1992), pp. 50–2. The facsimile of the coat of arms in this edition is not as clear as the reproduction in Edward Arber, ed., *English Reprints* (Westminster: A. Constable, 1895), pp. 19–20.

[43] See Tyndale's preface to *The Parable of the Wicked Mammon*, in *Doctrinal Treatises and Introductions to Different Portions of the Holy Scriptures by William Tyndale*, ed. Rev. Henry Walter, The Parker Society (Cambridge: Cambridge University Press, 1848), p. 41. On the topic of Tyndale's soured relations with Roy and Barlow see David Daniell, *William Tyndale: A Biography* (New Haven: Yale University Press, 1994), pp. 157–8; William A. Clebsch, *England's Earliest Protestants, 1520–1535*, Yale Publications in Religion, ed. David Horne, vol. 11 (New Haven: Yale University Press, 1964), pp. 229–40; and J. F. Mozley, *William Tyndale* (New York: MacMillan, 1937), pp. 56–60 and 130–4.

he employed the same rhetorical strategy, enticing Henry with the theme of a king's divine right to supremacy within his realm. "The king is, in this world, without law," Tyndale writes, "and may at his lust do right or wrong, and shall give accounts but to God only." It is a sin to resist either the king or his officers who execute the king's commandments, he continues, because both tyrants and their henchmen are "reserved unto the judgment, wrath, and vengeance of God."[44] Finally, he contrasts this image of kingship with the lamentable state of the present monarchies: kings today are "but shadows, vain names and things idle, having nothing to do in the world, but when our holy father needeth their help" (p. 186). Tyndale never had any delusion that Henry would convert to the beliefs of the reformers, but like Roy and Barlow he recognized that one way to rid England of the papacy was to convince the king it was in his best interests. Religious conviction did not have to be his motive. So while Tyndale does speak in *The Obedience* on familiar Protestant themes – justification by faith alone, the denunciation of confession, and the abolition of profane images, to name a few – he relies also on the persuasive power of provoking the king and his subjects to feel shame and indignation, by portraying Henry as one of the clergy's puppets:

> There seest thou the cause why it is impossible for kings to come to the knowledge of the truth. For the sprites [priests] lay await for them, and serve their appetites at all points; and through confession buy and sell and betray both them and all their true friends, and lay baits for them, and never leave them, till they have blinded them with their sophistry, and have brought them into their nets. And then, when the king is captive, they compel all the rest with violence of his sword.
>
> (pp. 341–2)

Not only early reformers but many historians have given *The Obedience* and other Protestant books credit for shaping Henry's conception of kingship. Invariably cited is the story that Henry "delighted in [Tyndale's *Obedience*] . . . 'For,' saith he, 'this book is for me and all kings to read,'"[45] as well as John Foxe's statement that Henry kept Fish's *Supplication for the Beggars* "in his bosom three or four days, as is credibly reported."[46] In recent years the thesis that the

---

[44] *Doctrinal Treatises by William Tyndale*, p. 177.

[45] Recorded in John Strype, *Ecclesiastical Memorials, relating chiefly to Religion . . . under King Henry VIII, King Edward VI, and Queen Mary I*, 3 vols. (Oxford: Clarendon Press, 1822), vol. 1, pt. 1, p. 172.

[46] *The Acts and Monuments of John Foxe*, ed. Rev. Stephen Reed Cattley, 8 vols. (London: R. B. Seeley and W. Burnside, 1837–41), vol. 4, p. 657; reprinted in *CW*, vol. 7, p. 420.

reformers supplied Henry with the idea of royal supremacy has been considered at least overstated, but it does reflect accurately the rhetorical aims of the reformers' treatises: to encourage the king to assert his power against Rome, and to place such an assertion of power in the context of a Protestant reformation.

Henry himself was determined not to accept this interpretation of his conflict with Rome. That would have guaranteed his excommunication and increased the possibility of an uprising or even a holy war. It is true that Cromwell, for a brief period in the early 1530s, attempted to hire Tyndale, Fish, Barlow, and other reformers who were living in exile on the Continent, but Henry made their disavowal of past heresies a condition of their "guaranteed passage" back to England.[47] He offered them safety and government employment in order to stop their inflammatory literature and to exploit their polemical skills in his own cause.

No doubt Henry also conceived of his efforts to lure the heretics home again as part of his strategy to put pressure on the pope. Early in his negotiations with Rome, he instructed his ambassadors at the papal court to hint discretely that Clement's indecision made some of the reformers' ideas increasingly attractive to their king. In an exchange that Cardinal Campeggio recounts between himself and Henry VIII just before the opening of the legatine trial, we learn that Henry even took part in this gambit personally. Like the oration that was delivered at that trial against Bishop Fisher, this exchange between the king and the pope's representative is especially instructive about the nature of the public image Henry would shortly afterwards be promulgating through his press, and it merits quoting at length:

> During these holy days (Easter week) certain Lutheran books, in English, of an evil sort, have been circulated in the king's court. As yet I have been unable to obtain one, but I will endeavor to do so. I understand that by this book the Lutherans promise to abrogate all the heresies affecting the articles of the faith, and to believe according to the divine law, provided that this king, with the Most Christian King [Francis I], will undertake to reduce the ecclesiastical state to the condition of the primitive Church, taking from it all its temporalities. I told the king that this was the devil dressed in angels' clothing, in order that he might the more easily deceive, and that their object was to seize the property of the Church; nor could any one promise the abrogation of so much heresy as now largely pervades the people. I represented

---

[47] Mozley, *William Tyndale*, pp. 187–8; Daniell, *William Tyndale*, pp. 208–17. The exchange of letters between Cromwell and Stephen Vaughan, the agent sent to Antwerp to approach Tyndale and Frith, is calendared in *LP*, vol. 5, nos. 65, 153, 201, 246, 248. One who took up the king's offer was Simon Fish (see Clebsch, *England's Earliest Protestants*, p. 244).

that by councils and theologians it had been determined that the Church justly held her temporal goods. His majesty remarked that these [Lutherans] say that those decisions were arrived at by ecclesiastics, insinuating that now it is necessary for the laity to interpose. In reply I adduced various reasons, partly theological and partly temporal, telling him that this would be directly against his interests, for, as matters now stood, he obtained large sums of money; but if the laity had the goods of the Church this would no longer be the case, and they would probably grow rich and rebellious. The king also remarked that these men allege that the ecclesiastics, and especially the court of Rome, live very wickedly, and that we have erred in many things from the divine law. I replied that I would allow there were sins in Rome and in the court, because we are but men, but the Holy See had not deviated a jot from the true faith. Finally, his majesty assured me of his good will, and that he had been and always would remain a good Christian, but that he had desired to communicate to me what had been told him by others; and if I wished to write to Rome, he was content, provided I did not state that I heard it from his own mouth.[48]

This incident reflects the nature of Henry's tactics for several years after the legatine trial. He does not argue with the Church's "councils and theologians," he merely cites what "others" have told him. In this way he could convey thinly disguised threats, encourage anti-clerical legislation, and tie his cooperation in diplomatic maneuvers and international treaties to the pope's acquiescence. But he was careful not to question Church theology. In fact, in 1530 he publicly confirmed his orthodoxy by publishing two proclamations forbidding the sale and possession of heretical books, including those by Tyndale and Fish.[49] These proclamations maintained Henry's official stance as defender of the faith, even while other government tracts were advertising his professed intellectual independence – from the Church every bit as much as from other "interested" parties – by representing him as the judicious philosopher-king, the neutral quester after truth who hears and weighs arguments on each side of the question.

Through those proclamations Henry was also sending a message to Clement that so long as a defender of the faith was ruler of England, the Church had a responsibility to accommodate him in his reasonable requests. Otherwise, the pope left the door open for "others" to influence

---

[48] *LP*, vol. 4, pt. 3, no. 5416.

[49] These are A Proclamation Enforcing Statutes against Heresy and Prohibiting Unlicensed Preaching, Heretical Books (21 Henry VIII) and A Proclamation Prohibiting Erroneous Books and Bible Translations (22 Henry VIII), in *TRP*, vol. 1, nos. 122 (incorrectly dated 20 Henry VIII; see Elton, *Policy and Police*, p. 218 n. 5) and 129.

Henry. To underscore both these messages, propaganda from the royal press attacked the Church, but took the form of *others'* opinions. Evidence and arguments used in the legatine trial supplied much of the material for this propaganda, but more was needed. In the first half of the 1530s, Henry and his agents requested and often purchased supporting opinions on the divorce question from the most esteemed university faculties in England and Europe. In addition Henry sent scholars to cull relevant historical precedents from chronicles found in university and private libraries, alley book shops, and even (under the pretense of researching other matters) the Vatican.[50] These were shown to the public in the 1531 treatise *Gravissimae, atque exactissimae illustrissimarum totius Italiae, et Galliae Academiarum censurae*, printed soon afterwards in translation as *The Determinations of the Most Famous and Most Excellent Universities of Italy and France, that it is So Unlawful for a Man to Marry his Brother's Wife, that the Pope hath No Power to Dispense Therewith.*[51]

Elton observes that while this treatise proves how early "Henry VIII and Cromwell discovered the use of printing as an instrument for convincing the people of their claims," it nevertheless maintains a curious "reticent delicacy." "The most remarkable thing about it," says Elton, "is the fact that it never once mentions King or Queen or the particular marriage dispute. A stranger coming upon it would have to

---

[50] See Kelly, *Matrimonial Trials of Henry VIII*, pp. 173–89; Parmiter, *The King's Great Matter*, pp. 120–43. The progress of this search for authoritative opinions and historical precedents is seen in most detail in the entertaining letters from Richard Croke calendared in *LP*, vol. 4, pt. 3.

[51] The *Censurae* (*STC* 14286) and *Determinations* (*STC* 14287) are reprinted in Edward Surtz, S. J. and Virginia Murphy, eds., *The Divorce Tracts of Henry VIII* (Angers: *Moreana*, 1988). The *Censurae* is dated 1530 in *STC*, but Murphy puts its publication in spring, 1531 (p. iv). A royal proclamation citing (in English) at least some of these university determinations apparently was issued in 1530, but is lost (ibid.). A precise study of the compilation and interrelation between manuscript and printed treatises on the divorce question is Murphy, "The Debate over Henry VIII's First Divorce" (Ph.D. dissertation, Cambridge University, 1984), its main arguments given summary in Murphy, "The Literature and Propaganda of Henry VIII's First Divorce," in Diarmaid MacCulloch, ed., *The Reign of Henry VIII: Politics, Policy, and Piety* (London: MacMillan, 1995), pp. 135–58. See, also, the collected studies of the university determinations and the opinions of individual doctors of theology in Guy Bedouelle and Patrick Le Gal, eds., *Le "Divorce" du Roi Henry VIII: Etudes et documents*, Travaux d'Humanisme et Renaissance No. 221 (Geneva: Librairie Droz S.A., 1987). For a useful discussion of the strain that politics put on scholars' biblical interpretations pertaining to the validity of Henry's marriage, see Guy Bedouelle, "The Consultations of the Universities and Scholars Concerning the 'Great Matter' of King Henry VIII," trans. John L. Farthing, in *The Bible in the Sixteenth Century*, ed. David C. Steinmetz (Durham: Duke University Press, 1990), pp. 21–36.

regard it as a peculiar academic exercise."[52] It is peculiar in this way because the document presents itself as the collected conclusions reached by independent-minded academics and theologians throughout Christendom to a deliberative argument on a general question – an argument made merely on its own account. In the terminology of the rhetoric handbook, the *Determinations* is the product of debates "consisting in the discussion of policy" rather than of particular persons or courses of action. These are "causes in which the subject of itself engenders the deliberation," in which any "extraneous motives" are not considered, and "the entire discourse is devoted to the subject itself."[53] In other words, this is an exercise in "philosopher talk" – the kind of dialogues about truth and virtue that humanists engage in when they meet in their gardens and villas, and, so it was implied, at Henry's court.

Practically speaking, the treatise unmistakably delivers the king's answer to his own question. Nobody who was not a stranger, Elton concedes, would have mistaken it for anything but official propaganda. The significance of its academic form, therefore, lies in the assertion of its own discursive rules for discussing the king's great matter. In progressing toward the specific conclusion that divine law declares the king's marriage invalid, neither the views of the king nor specific references to the king's case are relevant, because this is ostensibly an inquiry into a general, not a specific question. In the event of future public deliberations the same rules would apply to others. No specific references to the king's case, no personal views, no "extraneous motives," would be permitted.

IV

One advantage that everyone gained from such an arrangement was the privilege of deniability. Henry opposed Rome, and More and the Rastells opposed Henry, but both sides could always say, "That was not *me* speaking." After releasing the *Determinations*, Henry remained in this manner one step removed from his propaganda. Rather than being expressions or justifications of his will alone, the king's tracts are exhortations from members of his learned council, letters from leading scholars, and, the greatest number, prose dialogues. By virtue of their genre readers could be expected to associate these dialogues with others in the humanist tradition, from Cicero's *De oratore* and *De officiis* to Erasmus's colloquies and More's *Utopia.* Such associations would have contributed to Henry's campaign because of the way that humanist

---

[52] Elton, *Policy and Police*, p. 175.
[53] *Rhetorica ad Herennium*, 1.2.2 and 3.2.2.

dialogues, in Joel Altman's terms, are in the "explorative mode": they raise dilemmas, argue *in utramque partem*, and "cultivate ambivalence" as part of a moral program to train the intellect to discover fuller, deeper truths than are reached by syllogism or maxim.[54] Through disputation, so the theory goes, wise men become wiser, and that, Henry wanted it to be known, was what was going on at his court.

While Henry was eager to represent himself as an enlightened king who encouraged intellectual exploration, his dialogues directly concerning the divorce and royal supremacy do not, as we shall see, explore. And as time passed Henry increasingly limited the spectacle of debate even as he claimed to welcome it. I tell this part of the story in chapter 1, by showing how such works as the later *Doctor and Student* dialogues by Christopher St. German and *A Glass of the Truth* – rumored to be by the king himself – maintained Henry's public stance of reticent delicacy while increasingly emphasizing his authority to judge and to speak for the whole body of the realm. In chapters 2 and 3 I examine the place and writings of prominent humanists in Henry's service. Sir Thomas More was appointed lord chancellor just before the opening of Parliament in 1529, a promotion that was supposed to contribute to the king's image as a philosopher-king. But More refused to involve himself in court business relating to the king's matter, and instead wrote religious polemics designed to feed expectations that a true defender of the faith would prove more an ally of the Church than Henry possibly could remain and still achieve the verdict he wanted. The royal press countered More's challenge by printing a wide range of humanist works, and I examine Thomas Starkey's *Dialogue between Pole and Lupset* as a work that was intended for this campaign. The court patronized another prominent humanist, however, Thomas Elyot, whose books were better suited to the king's divorce propaganda. *The Governor, Pasquil the Plain*, and *Of the Knowledge which Maketh a Wise Man* are *speculi principes* well known for holding rulers to high moral standards and even conveying Elyot's thinly-veiled criticism of Henry's actions, but the fact

---

[54] See *The Tudor Play of Mind: Rhetorical Inquiry and the Development of Elizabethan Drama* (Berkeley: University of California Press, 1978), pp. 13–30, for Altman's distinction between "explorative" and "demonstrative" fiction. The latter term describes the morality play, which reinforces for its audience the verity of known truths; see pp. 53–65 and 79–87 for analyses of *The Praise of Folly* and *Utopia* as examples of explorative fiction. On the subject of the idealization of dialogue and disputation in the Renaissance see too C. J. R. Armstrong, "The Dialectical Road to Truth," in *French Renaissance Studies, 1540–70: Humanism and the Encyclopedia*, ed. Peter Sharratt (Edinburgh: Edinburgh University Press, 1976), pp. 36–51 (but cf. J. F. Tinkler, "Humanism and Dialogue," *Parergon*, New Series, 6 [1988]: pp. 197–214, in which a parallel is drawn between the ambivalent form of the humanist dialogue and the ambivalent direction of the authors' careers).

that they abide by the discursive rules established by Henry's philosopher-king image, and were published by the royal press, meant that Elyot's specific criticism was obscured and that his general warnings against tyranny attested to the king's eagerness for good counsel. Chapter 4 serves as a short transition to my analyses of books from the Rastells' two presses, by assessing the status of the king's printer during this time. As it turns out his position was not a secure one, for though he unambiguously represented the king's interests he did not have a monopoly on government business, and this left room for others to offer what the public might perceive to be official views, or officially sanctioned debate and "wise counsel." This was the nature of the Rastells' competition with the king's press, as I argue in chapters 5 and 6. On the strength of their connection to Thomas More and their relationship with the government as quasi-official printers, they too attempted to influence the king, printing besides More's polemics John Rastell's *A New Book of Purgatory*, William Barlow's *A Dialogue on the Lutheran Factions*, John Skelton's *Magnificence*, and John Heywood's *Play of the Weather*. Only the first two in this list were unquestionably new compositions in the 1530s, but as I propose to show the Rastells saw very well how the two plays, both written by court entertainers who were orthodox Catholics, could put public pressure on the king to strive toward the ideal of his own public image.

My story ends with an account of what we might call the "discursive reformation" that occurred in 1534 with the passage of the supremacy legislation in Parliament. Henry abruptly abandoned the philosopher-king image for that of supreme head of church and state in England, and that, of course, meant a whole new set of rules.

1

"Where the word of a king is":
Dialogues Printed by Thomas Berthelet,
1530–1532

Where the word of a king is, there is power:
and who may say unto him, What doest thou?

(Ecclesiastes 8:4)

Robert Wakefield, England's foremost Hebrew scholar in the reign of Henry VIII, explicates the biblical passages pertaining to the divorce question in the treatise *Kotser Codicis R. Wakfeldi*, published by Thomas Berthelet in 1533.[1] A letter from Richard Pace to Henry VIII that is appended to the *Kotser Codicis* explains how this study came to be written. Pace, a Greek scholar and champion of humanistic education, reminds Henry of a pamphlet against the royal marriage that he had recently written with some assistance from Wakefield, and had presented to Henry for evaluation. At that time, Pace recalls, "it pleased your grace to show unto me, that some of your learned counsel had written that the book of the old law named Deuteronomy, doth take away and annul the other book named Leviticus" (sig. P3ʳ). Though Pace gave his assurance that "such opinions can in no wise be true," the king was not easily convinced. Shortly afterwards, Wakefield heard of Henry's continued doubts and asked Pace if he thought the king would appreciate a deeper examination of the scriptural evidence in its original language, to discover, says Pace to Henry, "whether it were against you or for you." Pace then repeats the answer he gave to Wakefield: "that your grace intended nothing, but that was convenient to the person of a noble and a virtuous prince, and that he should do unto your grace right acceptable service, if he would study for to show unto you the said truth of the matter" (sig. P3ᵛ).

We observe that in the process of telling his story, Pace represents the king – dutifully, I would say – acting with even more "reticent delicacy"

---

[1] *STC* 24943. On Wakefield's role in the advance of Hebrew studies during the early sixteenth century see G. Lloyd Jones, *The Discovery of Hebrew in Tudor England: A Third Language* (Manchester: Manchester University Press, 1983).

than characterizes the *Determinations of the Most Famous Universities.*
According to this official portrait, Henry so values truth that he
prudently hesitates to embrace the opinions Pace and Wakefield offer
in favor of his cause. Henry's own "learned counsel" has compiled
counter-arguments against the Levitical law that scholars and theologians are citing to deny the validity of his marriage, and the king himself
forwards these on to others who might too rashly judge in his favor. This
does not mean that the king will forever be a bystander in this debate.
Pace also says in his letter that he is sending Henry a Hebrew alphabet,
and he speaks of Henry having "within the space of one month . . .
sufficient knowledge of the Hebrew tongue, for to judge thereby the
Latin translation" of the relevant passages himself (sigs. P3^v–4^r). But for
now the king is withholding his judgment, waiting to hear from all sides
in this disputation among experts.

With like purpose, several prose dialogues printed by Berthelet during
this period allow Henry to remain strategically vague about "where the
word of the king is," even as they impart the wisdom Henry means for
his subjects to acquire. The dialogue form lends itself to this aim because
it gives the impression of wise discourse, whether it is a master-student
type of exchange, where one speaker teaches the other, or a disputation
that leads to a profounder understanding than either speaker first
possessed.[2] Wise discourse is also implied through association. The
long history of literary dialogues, stretching from Plato to Cicero to
Augustine and from the Italian humanists to Erasmus and More,
elevated the status of the dialogue in the eyes of English authors and
readers. The ancients and their Renaissance imitators wrote dialogues
designed to model the discovery of deeper truths, and such a discovery
could be invoked simply by adopting the form in which they wrote. This
explains the dialogue's fitness for Henry VIII's campaign to represent
himself as a philosopher-king. Like the "great sort of wise men" then
assembled in Parliament, and the learned theologians debating Henry's
case in the universities, his dialogues' speakers carry out their search for
truth and justice while he, ostensibly, remains indifferent between them.

Another advantage to the dialogue is the opportunity it provides to
speak for whole groups of people. As in the morality play, characters are
often types rather than individuals, and their discourse purports to
convey general opinions and universal truths rather than the idiosyncratic ideas of, say, a Raphael Hythlodaeus. A staged debate between a
lawyer and a priest, or between a knight and a cleric, ostensibly offers the
representative thoughts and character traits, virtues and vices, of the

---

[2] The distinction between these types is made by Roger Deakins in "The Tudor
Prose Dialogue: Genre and Anti-Genre," *Studies in English Literature, 1500–1800* 20
(1980): pp. 5–23.

social groups portrayed. In the case of dialogues from the official press, this feature allows us, I suggest, to trace Henry's developing conception of the king's relationship to his realm. Furthermore, in the interactions between the speakers of these dialogues we may be reading not only Henry's desired self-representation, but the representation of relations between different social groups in the realm that Henry envisioned himself ruling. That this vision was "developing" is indicated by the changes that occurred from dialogue to dialogue in the representation of those relations. In the first place, Henry found a way, without quite having to sacrifice his rhetoric of reticent delicacy and officially neutral stance, to heighten his readers' awareness of his own presence between the lines of the anonymous dialogues printed by Thomas Berthelet. Secondly, each of these dialogues includes a priest as one of the speakers, and this priest's status and authority steadily change in relation to the other speaker's. With each new dialogue from the king's press, a vision of the clergy's reconceived place in Henry's commonwealth comes more clearly into focus.

II

Both the magnification of Henry's presence and changes in the clergy's representation occurred within Christopher St. German's *Doctor and Student* dialogues, which appeared in various versions and sequels from 1528 to 1531. St. German was a prominent London lawyer who had been associated with John Rastell at the Middle Temple since the beginning of the century, and his first book (published anonymously, as were his later works), was the *Dialogus de fundamentis legum Anglie et de conscientia*, a dialogue between a doctor of divinity and a student of the law printed by John Rastell in 1528.[3] Theirs is a genuinely neutral interaction, in that the speakers are not disputants voicing opposing views over a controversial issue. Instead, they contribute equally to an exposition of the various grounds of English law (the laws of God, of nature, and of reason, and the traditional maxims and customs of England), and the two take turns illustrating how these grounds help to untangle difficult, particular cases. The *Dialogus* is a primer, a master-student dialogue in which the speakers team-teach. They learn from one another, and the reader learns from

---

[3] *STC* 21559. For a synopsis of St. German's career see Pearl Hogrefe, "The Life of Christopher St. German," *Review of English Studies* 13 (1937): pp. 398–404. On the basis of an entry in Ames' *Typographical Antiquities* (1749), scholars sometimes refer to a first but no longer extant 1523 edition of the *Dialogus*, but it is likely Ames was in error.

both, happily finding now accessible the kind of material that until then had existed only in Law French.[4]

In 1530, St. German's English translation of the *Dialogus* was printed, followed by a slightly expanded version in 1531.[5] The preface to this edition of *Doctor and Student*, as it is now usually called, advertises that its contents are different from the Latin original: "it can not be taken as a translation out of that dialogue in Latin," we are warned, "for there be divers things put in to this dialogue in English that be not in the said Latin dialogue: and in like wise there be some things in the Latin dialogue that be omitted in this, as to the reader will appear" (p. 3 n. 1). But upon first examination, the differences between the Latin and English editions seem only to be minor abridgments and simplifications of the text. The fourth or fifth example of the application of a law cited in the Latin text is discarded in the English version, or a more straightforward case is substituted for an intricate one. Changes like these are consistent with the decision to translate *Doctor and Student* into English and thus make it more accessible to the young law student or the literate layman, but they only slightly alter the character of the dialogue.

There are, however, two brief additions within the text, and an addition at the end, that do qualify its pretensions to being just a student primer. The first of these, in the midst of the chapter entitled "The Law of God," is an expansion of the sentence, "Yet nevertheless all the laws canon be not the laws of God, for many of them be made only for the political rule and conversation of the people, and should be reckoned as human law rather than divine."[6] The addition elaborates on this point, not only distinguishing between the Church's jurisdiction over spiritual

---

[4] The standard law texts of the time were the *Natura Brevium*, Littleton's *Tenures*, and Fitzherbert's *Diversite de courtz*.

[5] *STC* 21561 and 21562. These were published not by Rastell but by Robert Wyer, one of London's many "popular printers," as E. Gordon Duff calls him in *The Printers, Stationers, and Bookbinders of Westminster and London from 1476 to 1535* (Cambridge: Cambridge University Press, 1906), p. 156, although as the decade progressed Wyer emerged as a major publisher of Protestant literature. The theory that a hired translator was responsible for the English version rather than St. German (argued by S. E. Thorne, "St. German's 'Doctor and Student,'" *The Library*, Fourth Series, 10 [1930]: pp. 421–6) is convincingly refuted by J. L. Barton in his introduction to *St. German's Doctor and Student*, ed. T. F. T. Plucknett and J. L. Barton, Selden Society, vol. 91 (London: Selden Society, 1974), pp. xvi–xix. Subsequent references to the Latin and English texts of *Doctor and Student*, as well as to *The Second Dialogue between a Doctor and a Student* and *The New Additions to the Second Dialogue between a Doctor and a Student*, are to this edition.

[6] Translating "Sed tamen non omnes leges canonice sunt de iure divino, nam plures earum ad politicam solum populi conversationem sunt accommodate, que potius inter leges humanas quam divinas numerande sunt" in the original (p. 22).

matters and the state's jurisdiction over temporal goods, but also introducing for the first time into *Doctor and Student* criticism of those who fail to keep this distinction straight. Priests who call the goods of the Church spiritual, or the decrees of the pope laws of God, say so "but unproperly," and are "deceived, and also deceive other the which judge though things to be spiritual, the which all men know be things material and carnal" (pp. 23–5). Then in the other insertion into the Latin text, the Student remarks that "it is somewhat to marvel that spiritual men have not endeavored them self in time past to have more knowledge of the king's laws than they have done, or that they yet do, for by the ignorance thereof they be oft times ignorant of that, that should order them according to right and justice; as well concerning them self as other that come to them for counsel" (p. 131).

By making these two revisions Christopher St. German entered into the debate that preoccupied Parliament and Convocation during its first session, in 1529, on the question of Church jurisdiction over temporal property within the realm. The Commons had opened the session complaining of the taxes raised by the clergy in the form of tithes, mortuaries, probate fees, and other means by which they perceived that priests and the See of Rome were profiting off English parishioners.[7] St. German clearly decided that his textbook, with a few revisions, could help the Commons' cause, and with this intent he made one other addition to *Doctor and Student*, at the end, that raises the stakes in the conflict by representing the king as an interested participant in this controversy. Here St. German expands his criticism of the clergy and, after the manner of the Protestant polemics, makes an appeal to temporal authority to amend clerical abuses. According to the Doctor of Divinity, "when any thing is used to the displeasure of God, it hurteth not only the body but also the soul. And temporal rulers have not only cure of the bodies, but also of the souls, and shall answer for them if they perish in their default" (p. 172). The Student agrees, and follows with the observation that "many spiritual rulers be in great offense against God," because "they have in open sermons and in divers other open communications and counsels caused it to be openly notified and known that they should be all accursed that put priests to answer, or that maintain the said statute, or any other like to it" (p. 173). England's temporal rulers, the Student concludes, need to take legislative action to put the erring spiritual men in their place:

---

[7] See Lehmburg, *The Reformation Parliament*, pp. 81–3, 92. By the end of the session three bills were passed limiting the clergy's powers to raise money: These are 21 Henry VIII c. 5 (regulating probate fees), c. 6 (regulating mortuaries), and c. 13 (restricting non-residence and pluralities), in *Statutes*.

And I beseech all mighty God that some good man may so call upon all these matters that we have now communed of, so they that be in authority might somewhat ponder them, and to order them in such manner that offense of conscience grow not so lightly thereby hereafter as hath done in time past. And verily he that on the cross knew the price of man's soul will hereafter ask a right straight account of rulers, for every soul that is under them and that shall perish through their default. (p. 174)

There is a difference, we should note, between this call for action and that of the religious reformers who were asking when the king would rise up to reclaim his sovereignty by ejecting the Roman Church from the realm. St. German asks when England's *rulers* will put the realm in order by paying better heed to the existing laws that distinguish church and state. St. German uses the plural because he means the king *with his Parliament*, which includes the right-minded spiritual men such as the Doctor of Divinity taking part in this dialogue.[8] Unsurprisingly, St. German the professional lawyer would like to see the power of law elevated within England, but he is not proposing to cast out the Church. As depicted in this dialogue priests are in general reasonable men, and necessary not only for the spiritual well-being of the realm but also for understanding many of the most important grounds of its laws. A number of these priests have overreached their station lately, he admits, but they need only to be reminded, by king and Parliament, of their properly modest role in governing the realm.

In St. German's next installment, *The Second Dialogue in English between a Doctor and a Student* (1530; *STC* 21565), the thesis is repeated with more urgency. The preface states that "it is right necessary to all men in this realm both spiritual and temporal for the good ordering of their conscience to know many things of the law of England that they be ignorant in" (p. 176), and again the "men spiritual" have the most studying to do. About a third of *The Second Dialogue* attacks the ambition of priests and presents legal arguments against their claim to jurisdiction over things temporal, particularly denouncing the clergy's recent defense of its "spiritual right" to take tenths in the collection of tithes. What is innovative in these arguments is the Student of the Law's citations of scripture against the Doctor of Divinity. In the first dialogue

---

[8] Useful contexts for St. German's argument are provided in G. R. Elton's essays describing the sixteenth century transition from the idea of "the medieval 'king and Parliament'" to that of the "modern 'king-in-Parliament'" in *"The Body of the Whole Realm": Parliament and Representation in Medieval and Tudor England* (Charlottesville: University Press of Virginia, 1969), and in James McVey Hunter, "Christopher St. German's 'Doctor and Student': The Scholastic Heritage of a Tudor Dialogue" (Ph.D. dissertation, University of Colorado at Boulder, 1984).

the Doctor supplied all the scriptural grounds of laws, and the Student cited statutes and court cases. Even though the Student readily concedes that the Church "cannot err in matters of faith" (p. 309), his practice in this second dialogue illustrates that St. German believes lawyers have first rights to the interpretation of biblical passages that pertain to property.[9] Even within the province of scriptural exegesis, then, temporal topics are the business of temporal men.

Probably it was Thomas Cromwell, now increasingly more active in the court's legal and parliamentary maneuvers in 1531, who recognized that the *Doctor and Student* dialogues could do service for the king. They lent themselves to Henry's strategy of reticent delicacy because they supported the government's authority to override Church law without representing the king as the sole and therefore potentially tyrannical executor of that authority. And like the Commons' demands for the restriction of Church privileges, St. German's dialogues were part of an anti-clerical movement that was essentially independent of Henry's great matter, but they nonetheless offered themselves for his exploitation because they challenged the Church's jurisdiction over property, the very thing that enabled the clergy to maintain a state of mutual dependency with the king. Henry wanted to encourage restrictions on Rome's ability to exact taxes in order to put pressure on the pope to return his case to England, and to fan the popular anti-papal sentiments that Henry would need to rely on if one day he should be forced to defy Rome. But he did not want to appear personally responsible for his government's attacks on the Church. The *Doctor and Student* dialogues suit these aims by representing the king working in conjunction with his Parliament, limiting the power of the Church not according to royal whim but by the hallowed authority of English law. Indeed, some passages in *Doctor and Student* seem to suggest that even the king is bound by this law,[10] and though Henry did not easily accept that

[9] For examples in *The Second Dialogue* of the Student's citation of scripture, see especially pp. 300–2. The Student's concession that the Church "cannot err in matters of faith" indicates that St. German wanted to avoid being accused of heresy, as those who were attacking clerical privileges in the Commons sometimes were. E.g., Hall reports that Fisher said in the House of Lords one day, "now with the Commons is nothing but done with the Church, and all this me seemeth is for lack of faith only." The Commons took this remark "grievously," says Hall, "for they imagined that the bishop esteemed them as heretics" (p. 766).

[10] E.g., "And over this I would somewhat move further in this matter thus. That though the action were untrue, and the defendant not guilty, that yet the goods be forfeited to the king for his not appearance in the law and also in conscience, and for this cause, the king as sovereign and head of the law is bounden of justice to grant such writs and such processes as be appointed in the law to every person that will complain" (p. 182).

constraint in practice, on paper this representation of limits on his power he could live with for a time.

Henry's purposes were also served by *The Second Dialogue* because it is religiously orthodox and retains the educational aim of imparting knowledge of English law. Two thirds of it do not concern the division between temporal and spiritual realms at all, but instead treat a variety of other important legal topics, from horse theft to inheritance laws. In the midst of a string of chapters defining the proper jurisdiction of the Church, for example, chapter 38 interrupts to address the question, "If a house by chance falls upon a horse that is borrowed, who shall bear the loss?" To some degree, therefore, this is the sort of legal text ordinarily published by the king's printer. Who could say for sure, when Thomas Berthelet published St. German's third installment of *Doctor and Student* in 1531, that it signified an "official" challenge to the Church?

Three printings of this third version were issued, by the title *A Little Treatise called the New Additions (to be added to the Second Dialogue)* (*STC* 21563, 21563.5, 21564). The Doctor and Student characters once more discuss the day's controversial topics, including the state's right to arrest priests, Parliament's duty to decide for the realm in case of a schism in the papacy, and the right of England's courts to punish the abusers of pilgrimages and miracles. In each case, St. German claims the government has sole power over the property and person of anyone residing within England. This was already the central thesis of the earlier versions, as we saw, but now it carried the weight of Henry's implicit approval. For the first time, a *Doctor and Student* dialogue had "Thomas Bertheletus regius impressor excudebat . . . Cum privilegio a rege indulto" printed at the end (p. 340).[11]

Coupled with this switch of printers is an utter change in the roles of the dialogue's two speakers, ominously modeling a changed real-life relationship between the two groups they represent. In the very opening lines, the Student tells the Doctor that there are limits to what he may think and say:

> *Doctor:* I pray thee let me know thy mind in this question, whether lay men (as thee thinketh) have power to make any laws of mortuaries?
> *Student:* There was a law made of mortuaries in the Parliament

---

[11] G. R. Elton, overlooking Berthelet's editions of St. German's dialogues, excluded him from his study of state propaganda in *Policy and Police*, because, though "this vigorous septuagenarian lawyer, coming more and more into the open in defence of the royal supremacy, was certainly to be a most useful ally for the King's propagandists . . . there is no sign at all that he was in any way connected with the government" (p. 173). John Guy corrects this judgment, though partly on the basis of evidence unknown to Elton, in *Christopher St. German on Chancery and Statute*, pp. 19–55.

holden in the twenty-first year of our sovereign lord king Henry the VIII by the assent of the king, and of all the lords spiritual and temporal of the realm, and of all the commons: and I hold it not best to reason or to make arguments, whether they had authority to do that they did or not. For I suppose, that no man would think, that they would do any thing, that they had not power to do. (p. 317)[12]

When the Student in this passage takes the word *power*, by which the Doctor means "legal authority," and uses it to say that the king and Parliament by necessity have the authority to do whatever they can show they have already accomplished, it is not at all clear that St. German is still arguing for the supremacy of English law rather than voicing the doctrine that "might makes right." Neither can the Student's happy picture of perfect accord between Henry and every member of Parliament obscure the unsettling implications of his position, especially when shortly afterwards he adopts the tone of a royal proclamation by stating that this dialogue's intent is "for the good order of conscience of many persons, and the appeasing of many and great diversities of opinions in this realm" (p. 319). As the spokesman for that opinion, the Student now monopolizes the dialogue. In fact he does all the teaching, while the Doctor of Divinity's role has contracted to that of ignorant pupil, or rather, of a rebellious objector whose opinion must be corrected.

This change in the speakers' relationship produces a contradiction between the Student's portrait of harmony among "all the lords spiritual and temporal of the realm, and of all the commons," on the one hand, and the state of discord staged in this version of *Doctor and Student*, on the other. And this contradiction, situated as it is in a piece of state propaganda, puts into serious question any future role the clergy may hope to claim in the "reformed" government towards which court policy was tending. St. German may still grant that the "lords spiritual" are important members of Parliament, because their consensus with the "lords temporal" contributes to the authority of the statutes of the realm, but the figure who now represents the clergy in *Doctor and Student* needs silencing and instruction to stop up his treasonous objections against the legislation favored by the temporal authorities. There is in this picture a simple message for the Church. The king in his Parliament will continue to pass laws limiting clerical privileges, and though the clergy's consent to these laws would be a sign of their loyalty to the king, ultimately it is not necessary. This very treatise demonstrates, after all,

---

[12] The act regulating mortuary fees under discussion here is 21 Henry VIII c. 6 in *Statutes*, one of the three "anti-clerical" laws passed during the first session of Parliament in 1529.

that consent can always be declared in retrospect through the king's press.

Another prose dialogue, printed the same year as St. German's *New Additions*, conveys a similar vision of the clergy's reduced power: Thomas Berthelet's 1531 edition of the anonymous *Disputatio inter clericum et militem*, which Steven Haas has argued is the first example of Cromwell's involvement in Henry's developing propaganda campaign.[13] The *Disputatio* was originally written under the sponsorship of France's King Philip I in the late 1290s, to protest the clerical taxes that were going to Rome rather than toward Philip's war effort against England. In Haas's words, it "attacks clerical privilege – monetary and legal – and it strives to enhance royal prerogative at the expense of ecclesiastical dominion."[14] Pope Boniface VIII condemned it as heretical, ensuring its fame, and it was recycled several times afterwards: John of Trevisa produced an English translation in the fourteenth century that was "a popular Wycliffite piece into the early fifteenth century," and "by 1500 at least six Latin editions served the purposes of princes in Germany and the Low Countries."[15] When Cromwell dispatched Stephen Vaughan to Antwerp to seek out Tyndale in 1530, he also asked him to look for a copy of the *Disputatio*. Vaughan found one and sent it to Cromwell in January, 1531.[16] By October Berthelet's edition was printed, and in 1533 a new English translation appeared.[17]

Haas points out that Berthelet used the same page ornamentation for the Latin edition of the *Disputatio* that he had used for *The Determinations of the Most Famous Universities*, which was printed the next month (November, 1531).[18] Perhaps this was a coincidence; perhaps it suggests an intention, in these earliest examples of the king's propa-

[13] *STC* 12510. The history that follows relies on Haas, "The *Disputatio*." A more extensive study of the thirteenth-century *Disputatio*'s history, including an edition and translation of the text, is Norma Nadine Erickson's *"A Dispute between a Priest and a Knight"* (Ph.D. dissertation, University of Washington, 1966).

[14] "The *Disputatio*," p. 65.

[15] Ibid., p. 66, where Haas also observes that, "for some reason, the Tudor era labeled it a work of William of Ockham," which is how Stephen Vaughan refers to it in the following reference.

[16] *LP*, vol. 5, no. 65.

[17] *STC* 12511. References are to the 1533 English edition, *A Dialogue between a Knight and a Clerk concerning the Power Spiritual and Temporal*, printed as a parallel text with Trevisa's Middle English version in *Trevisa's Dialogus inter Militem et Clericum*, ed. Aaron Jenkins Perry, Early English Text Society, Original Series, no. 167 (London: EETS, 1925 for 1924), followed by citation of the corresponding passage in the 1531 Latin text.

[18] Haas, "The *Disputatio*," p. 70. This is plate 21 in R. B. McKerrow and F. S. Ferguson, *Title-Page Borders used in England and Scotland, 1485–1640* (London: Bibliographical Society, 1932).

ganda, to provide a visual indicator that the two books have something in common and are worth careful reading. Certainly the *Disputatio* had plenty of contemporary application, and it suited Henry's requirements precisely. It does not, to begin with, challenge Church theology and ritual, as we see when the Knight (*Miles*) exclaims, "he that would deny" that "the holy Church shall correct men for sins" shall "deny penance and confession" (p. 11/ sig. A5^r), two practices the sixteenth-century reformers were indeed denouncing. The government's position in respect to religion, so the king's press indicated, was orthodox, for at the time Henry wanted no part of doctrinal controversies. His problems lay in power relations, and the *Disputatio* offers a vision of these comparable to St. German's in that the Church is denied any jurisdiction over temporal goods or authority to pass laws outside of Rome:

> *Clericus:* I have seen in my time that kings, princes and all other nobles have had the Church in right great worship; and now I see the contrary, the Church is made a prey to you all, and many things are challenged of us, and nothing is given us. If we give not our goods, they be taken from us by strong hand, our good and cattle is destroyed, our laws and freedom be not holden, but despised and withsaid.
> *Miles:* I can not lightly believe, that the king (of whose council they of the clergy be) will deal unjustly with you nother destroy your law.
> *Clericus:* Yea truly against all law, we suffer innumerable wrongs.
> *Miles:* I would fain know what ye call law.
> *Clericus:* I call law the statutes and ordinances of bishops of Rome, and decrees of holy fathers.
> *Miles:* Whatever they ordain, or other have ordained in time past of temporality, may well be law to you, but not to us. For no man hath power to ordain statutes of things, over the which he hath no lordship. As the king of France may ordain no statutes upon the empire, nother the emperor upon the king of England. And likewise as princes of the world may ordain no statutes of your spirituality, over the which they have no power; no more ye may ordain no statutes of their temporalities, over the which ye have nother power nor authority.
> (pp. 1–3/ sig. A2^{r-v})

Though the Knight is inclined to strip the clergy of its accustomed powers, we see from his parenthetical aside that he includes the clergy among the "king's council." Like the *Doctor and Student* dialogues, then, the *Disputatio* does not plainly evict priests from their position in the government. The difference is this dialogue's more explicit threats than *Doctor and Student's* that priests risk punishment for their resistance. The Knight tells the Clerk, "so much as ye usurp and take upon that, that belongeth unto other, it is right meet, that ye suffer as ye do" (p. 15/ sig. A6^v), and warns him, "For as much as ye can not be content, and patiently (to your profit) suffer the princes, I fear me, that after due and just barking, ye shall feel biting" (p. 19/ sig. A8ʳ). "Refrain your tongue," concludes the Knight, "and acknowledge the king by his royal power to be above your laws, customs, privileges, and liberties; and that he may by the advice of his nobles add or diminish what so ever he think according with equity and reason: and therefore what so ever he changeth in those days for the wealth of the realm, take it well in worth and patiently suffer it" (pp. 36–7/ sig. B6ʳ). In sum, at the very moment Henry's propaganda was representing him as a philosopher-king working harmoniously with all the "lords temporal and spiritual" in Parliament for the betterment of the realm, that same propaganda was also warning many of Parliament's members – the priests – to stifle their protests, to expect just penalties for their past presumptions, and to accept what laws the king himself might pass.

III

Tyndale's *The Practice of Prelates: Whether the King's Grace may be Separated from his Queen because she was his Brother's Wife* (Antwerp, 1530), was one of countless texts that opposed Henry's divorce from the Continent, but no doubt because it was in English and by Tyndale himself the king perceived it as a major blow to his cause.[19] The tract begins with Tyndale's promise that "in the glass following" the reader will see the source of all the present wickedness, insurrection, and fall of princes (p. 246), which, he says, is in general the Catholic Church, and in England Cardinal Wolsey. He accuses "Wolfsee" of first "bewitching" Henry with magic in order to win his trust and steal his powers,[20] and

---

[19] Printed in *Expositions and Notes on Sundry Portions of the Holy Scriptures, together with The Practice of Prelates, by William Tyndale, Martyr, 1536*, ed. Rev. Henry Walter, The Parker Society (Cambridge: Cambridge University Press, 1849), pp. 237–344.

[20] Perhaps Tyndale was inspired for this accusation by Skelton's lines in *Why Come Ye Not to Court?*:

> It is a wonders case:
> That the King's grace
> Is toward him so minded,
> And so far blinded,
> That he can not perceive
> How he doth him deceive.
> I doubt, lest by sorcery
> Or such other loselry
> As witchcraft or charming.   (lines 657–65)

For a discussion of Skelton's apparent aims in this passage, see Walker, *John Skelton and the Politics of the 1520s*, pp. 171–2.

then of "inspir[ing] the king that the queen was not his wife" (p. 319). Tyndale claims the plot against Catherine was only the first step in Wolsey's larger plan to sacrifice the commonweal in order to obtain the papacy, and he warns his readers, "the mischief that [Wolsey] hath wrought for divorcement of the marriage . . . shall cost the whole realm of England" (p. 322).

These accusations, which comprise most of the first half of *The Practice of Prelates*, were not designed to topple Henry's right-hand man. Wolsey was already dead and Tyndale knew it.[21] The point of it all was to strengthen the association in the public's mind between Henry's aims and the ambitions of his unpopular and disgraced former chancellor. With this accomplished, Tyndale finally turns to analyze Leviticus 18:16 and 20:21, the scriptural passages relevant to Henry's case, and he quickly concludes that their prohibition, "Thou shalt not unhele [i.e., uncover] the secrets of thy brother's wife, for they are thy brother's secrets" (p. 323), means only "that Moses forbiddeth a man to take his brother's wife as long as his brother liveth" (p. 328). Because Henry married Catherine after Prince Arthur left her a widow, no scruples of conscience were justified.

Henry had every reason to feel this pronouncement – from the man who had given his subjects the word of God in their own tongue, no less – seriously damaged his case in the eyes of the public.[22] All the worse, Tyndale attacked the hypocrisy of Henry's professed neutrality even more explicitly than Bishop Fisher had done in the legatine trial. *The Practice of Prelates* was published while the king's agents were gathering university opinions on the royal marriage, and Tyndale took the occasion to challenge Henry to discard the reticent delicacy and philosopher-king image that he had adopted in the trial and was preparing for print:

> If the king's most noble grace will needs have another wife, then let him search the laws of God, whether it be lawful or not; forasmuch as he himself is baptized to keep the laws of God, and hath proposed them and hath sworn them. If the law of God suffer it, then let his grace put forth a little treatise in print, and even in the English tongue, that all men may see it, for his excuse and the defense of his deed, and say, "Lo, by the authority of God's word do I this." And then let not

---

[21] "And finally, concerning the cardinal's putting down, I consider many things: first, that I never heard or read that any man, being so great a traitor, was so easily put to death" (*Practice of Prelates*, p. 334). Wolsey was not actually executed. A year after his demotion he was arrested, and on the journey from York to the Tower of London he fell ill and died at Leicester Abbey.

[22] Tyndale's translation of the New Testament was widely available in England by the fall of 1526, and by the fall of 1530 so was his translation of the Pentateuch.

his grace be afraid either of the emperor, or of his lords, or of his commons and subjects: for God hath promised to keep them that keep his laws. (p. 323)

In making this request for Henry to abandon his neutral pose and announce in his own voice "I do this," Tyndale puts his finger on the very reason Henry so far has been unwilling to make such a declaration. The king *does* fear the emperor, and the very existence and nature of his propaganda campaign indicates that he is not confident of his subjects' support, either.

Henry soon answered Tyndale's challenge, but he found a way to do it without having to abandon his stance of reticent delicacy. He did in fact "put forth a little treatise in print, and even in the English tongue," but anonymously: the prose dialogue *A Glass of the Truth* (Berthelet, 1531).[23] Henry's agents then spread the word that the king had written the work himself, allowing him thereby to say in effect, but not on record, "I do this." Various authors, from Cranmer to St. German, have been credited for writing *A Glass of the Truth*, but as Pocock remarks, "the work has as much right to be considered the king's as the *Assertio Septem Sacramentorum* which bears his name,"[24] by which he means it doesn't, but we need not worry the point because authorship is not the issue.[25] The

---

[23] *STC* 11919. *A Glass of the Truth* has been dated anywhere from 1530 to 1535, but Steven Haas seems to have settled the question in "Henry VIII's 'Glasse of Truthe,'" *History* 64 (1979): pp. 353–62. Examining the condition of the borderfaces and minor changes in content, Haas argues that *STC* 11919 is the first edition, and that *STC* 11918 is a second edition (1532; both are dated 1532? in *STC*). Berthelet also published a French translation in 1532 (*Le myrouer de verite*; *STC* 11919.5). Nicholas Hawkins, Archdeacon of Ely, was given the job of translating *A Glass* into Latin (and in a letter to Henry reporting his progress he calls it "your dialogue" [*SP*, vol. 7, p. 389]). Hawkins soon afterwards announced his completion of the work (ibid., p. 404), though no record exists of it ever having been printed, perhaps because of his question to the king, "One thing therein I would most humbly desire Your prudent Highness to consider, whether it be best that those complaints on Your Highness's people, and to them made of their unkindness and unnaturalness, and such other, be turned into any other language than ours, or no" (ibid., p. 389). Hawkins' letters are calendared in *LP*, vol. 5, nos. 1564 and 1660. References to *A Glass of the Truth* are to the second edition, reprinted in Nicholas Pocock, ed., *Records of the Reformation: The Divorce, 1527–1533*, 2 vols. (Oxford: Clarendon Press, 1870), vol. 2, pp. 385–421.

[24] *Records of the Reformation*, vol. 1, p. xxiii.

[25] After all, as Graham Nicholson explains, *A Glass of the Truth* was compiled from material in the "Collectanea satis copiosa," the massive collection of manuscripts concerning the divorce question that survives in the Public Record Office and British Library. Nicholson identifies BL Cleopatra E 6, fos. 98–1096 as the main source ("The Acts of Appeals and the English Reformation," in *Law and Government under the Tudors*, ed. Claire Cross, David Loades, and J. J. Scarisbrick [Cambridge: Cambridge University Press, 1988], pp. 20–1).

salient fact is that readers understood these tracts were to be taken as the king's. In Richard Croke's report to Cromwell that he had "bestowed every copy of *A Glass of the Truth*," he admits that "many besides [John] Roper [Doctor of Divinity at Christ Church] cannot believe it is the king's writing, and, though they admit his wit, think that he lacketh leisure to search and bolt out so difficult a matter,"[26] but we can bet that Roper and the "many besides" read *A Glass* with as much attention as they read royal proclamations. That reading experience would have been overdetermined by the felt presence of the dialogue's reputed author: you would not have assumed that it represented the opinions of different groups in society, but instead modeled the opinions that the king wanted you to hold. And as the dialogue makes clear, to improvise in a discussion on this topic, meaning to hold a different opinion of the king's marriage or of the king's interpretation of the relevant biblical passages, would be treason and heresy.

The preface to *A Glass of the Truth* is addressed "To the gentle readers and sincere lovers of truth" (p. 385), and it promises readers that the following dialogue is a "clear glass within which ye shall see and behold (if ye look well and leisurely in it) the plain truth of our most noble and loving prince's cause, which by unmeet handling, hath hitherto had so overlong a stay" (p. 386). In other words, this tract offers a clearer glass than Tyndale's. Before readers are invited to gaze into it and see the evidence laid out against the validity of the royal marriage, however, the preface first spells out the dangers that await England if the king is not able to produce a male heir to the throne:

> [The prince's] lack of heirs male is a displeasure to him but for his lifetime, as lacking that which naturally is desired of all men to have children. But our lack shall be permanent so long as the world lasteth, except that God provide; for though we have a female heir [in Mary], which is both endued with much virtue and grace in many dotes [i.e., endowments] and gifts, yet if a male might be attained, it were much more sure, if we well perpend and ponder many urgent and weighty causes: amongst which this one is deeply to be foreseen, that if the female heir shall chance to rule, she cannot continue long without an husband, which, by God's law, must then be her governor and head, and so finally shall direct this realm. (p. 386)

It is, of course, a foreign husband that is the peril: Englishmen would naturally find the prospect of foreign domination intolerable, and the memory of the court's several attempts to arrange a political marriage for Princess Mary over the years – most recently to the Duke of Orleans,

[26] *LP*, vol. 5, no. 1338. For the identification of Roper see ibid., no. 1181 and p. 894.

Francis I's second son – would have given readers a foundation for the fears this passage exploits.[27] If the biblical evidence does not convince readers that Henry's marriage to Catherine is void, then this summary of political circumstances can be counted on to instill in them a desire to have a new, more fertile queen.

The preface ends with an admonition to "imprint well in your hearts this mere and sincere truth, and so to follow it that you may do a thing acceptable to the pleasure of Almighty God, and contentation of our sovereign and prince" (p. 388). But once more the messages that readers should "imprint" in their hearts go well beyond the king's matter. They are conveyed in *A Glass*'s representation of the relationship between the king and his subjects, and between the two groups of subjects personified by the dialogue's speakers. Like St. German's original *Doctor and Student*, this dialogue is between a priest and a lawyer discoursing on equal terms. They agree completely with one another, and provide mutually supporting arguments in favor of the king's cause. The result is an "us against them" positioning, but not of temporal versus spiritual men. It is rather between English patriots and hostile foreign powers such as the See of Rome. The priest in this dialogue is an Englishman first, a religious man second, or rather, he is the more religious because he is the king's loyal subject.

This harmony between the two speakers reflects the consensus that Henry will, in a few years, openly demand. There is in truth no room for open debate on the question of the king's marriage, and for that matter the Lawyer makes it clear that there has already been too much discussion of it. "The great, weighty cause of Christendom, concerning the king's separation from the queen," he laments, "is tossed and turned over the high mountains, labored and vexed at Rome, from judge to judge, without certain end or effect, being very perilous for his highness, and much more dangerous (if God help not) for us his poor and loving subjects" (p. 389). Henry had held completely the opposite position in the 1529 legatine trial, when he confessed that the validity of his marriage is an intricate matter needing the study of the wisest minds. But that does not mean he has given up the idea of another trial, because *A Glass* insists that his case should be returned to England, to be "ordained in the right and due course" in a trial "within the realm . . . as law and reason would it should have been." Only, this dialogue now takes over for the wisest minds, scripting their judgment by declaring the one allowable reading of the evidence. As the Lawyer asserts, any trial's outcome should be a foregone conclusion: "I marvel," he says, "why many thus call this matter disputable, seeing that there is but one truth therein; and why that

---

[27] On the various plans to wed Mary to foreign royalty see Scarisbrick, *Henry VIII*, pp. 71–3, 126, 137–8, 145.

truth is not embraced and openly showed by all learned men" (p. 390). Or as he says soon after, "It may evidently appear now that this matter is not disputable, but already judged and concluded, since it is determined that he shall be taken for a very heretic that holdeth or upholding disputeth to the contrary" (p. 396).

Conceivably, such threats would reduce the risk of rebellion once Henry decided more openly to say "I do this," but there was still the possibility that he would have to rely on his subject's willingness to go to war in his defense. The proceeding section of the dialogue is therefore aimed, like the preface, at rallying readers round their sovereign, and tellingly it is the priest who declares, "I doubt not (God assisting us) but that this his realm will rather stick with him in this his manifest right, according to their duty, than put their necks under the yoke of the pope" (p. 410). Henry's subjects, by definition, must ultimately accept *A Glass*'s "plain truth" on the basis of their duty to their king:

> *The Lawyer:* Alas, is it not great pity, the prince having so manifest and plain grounds for him, he being also so loving to us as he is, so glad and so hearty to take pains for this his commonwealth, that we, which that be his subjects, should be to him so unnatural, that either for other consideration worldly, or for reports of sinister persons, should let to do our very duty to him; yea, and leaving the plain truth, rather to believe maligners against his cause, which soweth more division than obedience, and not according to our very duties to stick fastly and surely unto him which is in the very right? Though, peradventure, he say little, yet may it fortune that he marketh all: wherefore both duty and reverence with fear, is to be had to him which is so loving and hearty to us, to the intent that these being joined both on his part and ours, we may withstand the malignity of all backbiters and slanderers, and utterly in our hearts conceive that it is far from our duty of allegiance to believe untrue reports and false malignations against our sovereign. (p. 398)

There is something of the quality of an in-joke, I think, in the remark about this loving prince who "says little." On the one hand it reminds readers of *A Glass of the Truth*'s official anonymity, and of Henry's public image as a temperate and wise ruler, which he has been cultivating and will continue to cultivate in such publications as the 1533 *Kotser Codicis*. On the other hand, it is ironically reflexive. As the reputed author of this dialogue the king is saying a lot, and in the reference to his "keeping mark" of all his subjects good reason is given for that "reverence with fear" that is "to be had to him." There is as well another sense to this statement that the king "marks all." By means of this dialogue he is writing his subjects' opinions, and apparently with success. As Richard Croke reports to Cromwell, "It is confessed that [*A Glass of the Truth*] has done more for the king's cause than all that ever has been written, and many have altered their stubborn minds to the contrary . . . No man can do more than the king has done, and all arguments to the contrary seem very heavy as compared with it."[28]

After *A Glass of the Truth* Henry continued to utilize its ventriloquial technique while maintaining his official stance of neutrality. In 1533, for example, Berthelet printed the *Articles Devised by the Whole Consent of the King's Most Honorable Council, his Grace's License obtained thereto, not only to Exhort, but also to Inform his Loving Subjects of the Truth.*[29] This consists of nine brief statements of policy, for instance that "no living creature [including the pope] hath power to dispense with God's laws," and that it is the pope's duty to respect a king's supremacy within his own realm. Although the *Articles* does not mandate obedience to any particular royal wish, it represents a consensus of opinion designed to close down the space for debate. Just as occurs in *A Glass of the Truth*, a "whole consent" is ascribed to the members of Henry's council, who then request it of everyone else:

> The king's most honorable council to the residue of his loving subjects. Since it is the part of all honorable and elect persons chosen by the prince, when they do declare and utter matters of weight, to observe an equity and truth in uttering of them, and to show benevolence to the people, which be under their prince, in admonishing them of things which are necessary for them to know; we therefore, the king our sovereign's most faithful counselors and subjects, with whole assent and by his license, have thought most convenient and necessary to intimate unto you (the rest of his subjects) these articles following for your better condition and knowledge, and to open unto you truly the manifold injuries done unto our king and sovereign, which (we being his true and faithful subjects) may in no wise sustain or suffer: but study and endeavor ourselves by all ways to us possible, to redouble [i.e., redress] and requite the same, and to take the injuries and wrongs done to his person (in whom is all our wealth and joy) more earnestly than if it were done to us alone. (p. 524)

Similarly, a number of statutes prepared by Cromwell, passed by Parliament, and then printed by Berthelet during 1532–1534 give the impression that England's lawmakers had arrived at their studied judgment of a matter and were now offering their counsel to Henry. In terms of rhetorical stance this was quite different from the norm. Typically the language of the statutes represented king and Parliament acting together to establish new laws. "Be it enacted by the King our

[28] *LP*, vol. 5, no. 1338.
[29] Reprinted in Pocock, *Records of the Reformation*, vol. 2, pp. 523–31.

Sovereign Lord and the Lords spiritual and temporal and the Commons in this present Parliament assembled and by the authority of the same" is a standard lead-in to new legislation. In contrast, such acts as that for the Exoneration from Exactions Paid to the See of Rome and for the Establishment of the King's Succession (25 Henry VIII cc. 21 and 22), like four other acts passed during Parliament's fifth session in early 1534, directly address the king, as if all the members of the Upper and Lower Houses are jointly urging Henry to take the wise actions they propose.[30] In this way, readers of Berthelet's publication of c. 22 (known as the First Act of Succession), for example, encountered a greeting "unto your Majesty" from "your most humble and obedient subjects the Lords spiritual and temporal and the Commons in this present Parliament assembled," followed by the statement that, "since it is the natural inclination of every man gladly and willingly to provide for the surety of both his title and succession . . . therefore most rightful and dreadful Sovereign Lord [we] reckon ourselves much more bounden to beseech and instant your Highness, although we doubt not of your princely heart and wisdom mixed with a natural affection to the same, to forsee and provide for the perfect surety of both you and of your most lawful succession and heirs, upon which dependeth all our joy and wealth." In a sense such language puts readers in the same position as an interceptor of correspondence between two other parties. But of course, the Lords and Commons are charged to speak *for* the English people as well as *to* their king. By giving the impression of unanimity among all the members of Parliament, therefore, the text assumes the same unanimity from Henry's loyal subjects.

Royal proclamations published by Berthelet during the early 1530s likewise emphasize that Henry is acting on the advice and authority of Parliament. R. W. Heinze has remarked that Cromwell "introduced a new concept" of "the relationship between statutes and proclamations," in that he sought "statutory authority" for the royal proclamations that were issued.[31] The result is that in this most autocratic mode of legislation the image of a king ruling by decree is mitigated. Even the Proclamation Depriving Catherine of Royal Style and Warning of Praemunire,[32] which explicitly warns that "every person henceforth take good heed and respect, at their perils," that "the King's majesty

---

[30] 25 Henry VIII cc. 21 and 22, in *Statutes*. Excerpts are printed in *The Tudor Constitution: Documents and Commentary*, 2nd ed., ed. G. R. Elton (Cambridge: Cambridge University Press, 1982), pp. 6–12 and 360–4. See, too, 23 Henry VIII c. 31; 24 Henry VIII cc. 3 and 11; and 25 Henry VIII cc. 3, 8, 14, and 32, in *Statutes*.

[31] *The Proclamations of the Tudor Kings* (Cambridge: Cambridge University Press, 1976), p. 109.

[32] *TRP*, no. 140 (dated 5 July 1533, 25 Henry VIII).

hath lawfully married" Anne Boleyn, "now Queen of England," and that "Lady Catherine should not henceforth have or use the name, style, title or dignity of Queen of this realm," is equally explicit that this proclamation is only reinforcing a statute already passed "by the common assent of the lords spiritual and temporal, and the commons of this realm, by authority of Parliament, as also by the assent and determinations of the whole clergy in their several convocations." Again, the assurance of unanimity contributes to Henry's public image as a prudent philosopher-king, an image that the court worked to maintain right up until the passage of the supremacy legislation in the sixth session of Parliament. Practically speaking, we may believe, there was from the beginning of the royal propaganda campaign little to distinguish between the king's rhetoric of reticent delicacy and the mandate of the loyalty oath. But until that oath was actually required, Henry appeared to govern according to the freely-wrought consensus of England's wisest men.

2

Thomas More, The King's Orator

In 1534 Thomas More wrote to Thomas Cromwell defending himself against the charge of opposition to the king's second marriage. More states that when Henry VIII offered him the lord chancellorship, in 1529, he made it clear he could not support Henry's efforts to obtain a divorce, but at the same time he agreed not to hinder them. The king in reply, according to More, declared that he would never "put any man in ruffle or trouble of his conscience."[1] On the strength of this letter historians were once unanimous in the opinion that "More took office only on condition that he would not be involved in the divorce to which he was immovably opposed," as G. R. Elton once put it.[2] But this version of events has since been complicated, by Elton as much as by others, with attention to evidence that Henry pressured More from the first year the divorce became an issue, in 1527, until More's resignation in 1532, urging him to accept the view that the royal marriage was invalid and to assist in the court's negotiations with Rome to have the cause returned to England for another trial.[3]

William Roper's *Life of Sir Thomas More* contains some of this evidence, in the form of testimony to the king's determination to sway his new chancellor at the time of More's appointment:

Now upon the coming home of the bishop of Durham and Sir Thomas More from Cambrai [in 1529], the king was as earnest in persuading Sir Thomas More to agree unto the matter of his marriage as before,

[1] *The Correspondence of Sir Thomas More*, ed. E. F. Rogers (Princeton: Princeton University Press, 1947), no. 199.

[2] Elton, *England under the Tudors*, p. 122; R. W. Chambers claimed that More only accepted the chancellorship after obtaining Henry's "promise" that he would not have to assist in the king's great matter, in *Thomas More* (New York: Harcourt Brace, 1935), p. 236.

[3] See Elton, "Sir Thomas More and the Opposition to Henry VIII," in *Bulletin of the Institute of Historical Research* 41 (1968): pp. 19–21; reprinted in Elton, *Studies in Tudor and Stuart Politics*, vol. 1, pp. 155–7; John Guy, *The Public Career of Sir Thomas More* (Brighton, Sussex: Harvester Press, and New Haven: Yale University Press, 1980), pp. 99–103; and Richard Marius, *Thomas More* (New York: Knopf, 1984), pp. 361–2.

by many and divers ways provoking him thereunto. For the which cause, as it was thought, he the rather [i.e., all the more quickly] soon after made him lord chancellor.[4]

If the king and his advisors could not convince More that the royal marriage was incestuous and void, then perhaps a promotion to the highest office in the government would bring him round. Such was the king's strategy, "as it was thought," and such is John Guy's explanation of Henry's choice for the great seal: On the one hand More "was the man of the moment, because a layman was required as chancellor, because he knew best the judicial work of Council and Chancery, and because he was not Wolsey's protégé," but on the other hand "his appointment as lord chancellor seems plainly to have rested partly on the miscalculation that [Henry] could win More round sooner or later to supporting the divorce."[5] By promoting him to lord chancellor, in other words, Henry would have put Thomas More under a greater obligation to serve according to his king's conscience, or rather, to come to the realization that his own conscience and his king's ought properly to be in accord. Henry could reasonably have hoped, therefore, that More's change of heart would shortly follow his promotion.

More's change of heart did not come at all, it turns out, and Henry grew increasingly impatient with his chancellor's stubborn refusal to get involved in the court's most important business. Within a year after More took office, in fact, Imperial ambassador Chapuys wrote to Charles V that "the chancellor is still in danger of being dismissed, and this solely because he hesitated to sign with the others the king's letters to the pope."[6] More never was dismissed, we know, and if this seems odd – that Henry would keep in a position of power one who so openly refused to agree with him on this of all issues – Guy also explains that, as a layman, More's actual political power was negligible compared to that of the pre-eminent peers at the time, the Dukes of Suffolk and Norfolk, especially. "The divorce crisis marked Henry VIII's first prolonged attention to public affairs, the result being a major shift of political gravity away from Star Chamber towards the court," Guy explains, so while More was engaged in judicial duties at Chancery and Star Chamber, policy was being made by the king and an "inner ring" led by Norfolk within the Court Council. Right from the beginning, then, More's position was one of "relative isolation."[7] He

---

[4] Roper, *Life of Sir Thomas More*, in *Two Early Tudor Lives*, ed. Richard S. Sylvester and Davis P. Harding (New Haven: Yale University Press, 1962), p. 217.
[5] Guy, *The Public Career of Sir Thomas More*, pp. 97, 101.
[6] *SP, Spanish*, vol. 4, pt. 1, no. 460.
[7] Guy, *The Public Career of Sir Thomas More*, pp. 97–9, 128.

could withhold his support of the king's divorce, but he had no power to prevent it.

That seems to return us to More's expertise in common law as an explanation of his value to Henry. But the divorce was by far Henry's chief concern at the time he appointed More, so one would think he would have wanted a chancellor who did not require isolating – someone who would help him in his cause. In an important sense More did help, simply by holding the office of lord chancellor. This is because one facet of Henry's "cause" was the building of his philosopher-king image, and in the context of that campaign More's appointment was something like a shrewd public relations move. As Elton has observed, "More was Henry's pledge of Renaissance excellence, his intellectual courtier,"[8] albeit I am citing these words to suggest a more deliberate strategem on Henry's part than Elton intended. In my view Henry selected More as his lord chancellor in part because it was one of the best means available to bolster his propaganda campaign, in that it publicized how serious he was about promoting humanist ideals at his court. Despite the fact that More would do what he could in the coming years to oppose Henry's divorce, I suspect that Henry considered More still to be playing an important role in that propaganda campaign right up until his resignation in 1532. In More's published writings while chancellor, as we shall see, he attempted to undermine that role that Henry scripted for him, by exploiting the official image of the king in ways designed to thwart the royal will.

II

Thomas More's promotion reflected well on Henry because of More's fame at home and on the Continent as the leading humanist in England. He was a friend of Erasmus, and according to Erasmus's recently published praise of him More was a man of broad learning and personal integrity, and a very "Socrates in wisdom."[9] Because, too, More's latest

---

[8] Elton, "Sir Thomas More, Councillor," in *St. Thomas More: Action and Contemplation*, ed. Richard S. Sylvester (New Haven: Yale University Press, 1972), p. 110; reprinted in Elton, *Studies in Tudor and Stuart Politics and Government*, vol. 1, p. 147.

[9] Erasmus's most famous portraits of More appear in two letters, one to Ulrich von Hutten and the other to Guillaume Budé (see *The Collected Works of Erasmus*, ed. R. J. Schoeck and B. M. Corrigan [Toronto: Toronto University Press, 1974–], vol. 7, no. 999 and vol. 8, no. 1233; the numbering is that of the standard modern Latin edition, *Opus epistolarum Des. Erasmi Roterodami*, ed. P. S. Allen, M. H. Allen, and H. W. Garrod, 12 vols. [Oxford: Oxford University Press, 1906–58]). Three

publications were anti-Protestant polemics – the *Responsio ad Lutherum* (1523) and *A Dialogue concerning Heresies* (1529) – his appointment contributed to Henry's public image as defender of the faith, a champion of the Church whose allegiance the pope would not want to lose over such a matter as a request for a divorce.

Thomas More was also the author of *Utopia* (first printed in Louvain, 1516), an internationally acclaimed work of moral and political philosophy. It is, however, a book that contains a powerful condemnation of kings, a fact that would seem to qualify its author's propagandistic value to Henry. In Book Two Raphael Hythlodaeus describes the state of Utopia because he has been challenged to provide an alternative to what he sees is the inherently flawed system of monarchy, a form of government that naturally leads, as he had asserted in Book One, to tyranny and social injustice. The More-character in *Utopia* (Morus) does somewhat resist Hythlodaeus's judgment, but rather lamely, as critics have always remarked. Even so, by hiring its author, Henry VIII could make the book *Utopia* do him service. It models the kind of inquiry into a general question (What would be the best state of a commonwealth?) that Henry is requiring of oppositional discourse, and as critical of Henry as their sub-texts *might* be, books like *Utopia* are too general and indirect to be challenging any of his specific actions. Moreover, it reflects very well on Henry that the author of such a persuasive case against entering a king's service would agree to enter into his.

We can most fully appreciate the basis of this flattering implication for Henry by examining that crucial exchange at the end of *Utopia*'s Book One in which Hythlodaeus and More put forth their opposing philosophies of counsel. This passage has been at the center of the debate over More's sincerity or irony in voicing (through Hythlodaeus) an attack on the system of monarchy and (through Morus) a defense of the counselor's duty to serve under tyrants.[10] The scene is set within the private garden of a house in Antwerp, where Morus is residing while on break from his diplomatic duties. He is in conversation with his friend Peter Giles and a new acquaintance, a world traveler and student of Greek

---

editions of Erasmus's letters were printed in the 1520s, including Froben's monumental *Opus epistolarum* of 1529, the year of More's appointment.

[10] See, for example, J. C. Davis, "More, Morton, and the Politics of Accomodation," *Journal of British Studies* 9 (1970): pp. 27–49; J. H. Hexter, "Thomas More and the Problem of Counsel," in *Quincentennial Essays on St. Thomas More: Selected Papers from the Thomas More College Conference*, ed. Michael J. Moore (Boone, North Carolina: Albion, 1978), pp. 55–66; Quentin Skinner, "Sir Thomas More's *Utopia* and the Language of Renaissance Humanism," in *The Languages of Political Theory in Early Modern Europe*, ed. Anthony Pagden (Cambridge: Cambridge University Press, 1987), pp. 123–57.

philosophy, Raphael Hythlodaeus.[11] Giles expresses surprise that Hythlodaeus is not already in some fortunate king's service, and Hythlodaeus explains that if he were, he would either have to tell lies in order to win his master's favor or give frank advice that he knows would be resented, and since his soul abhors all falsehood and flattery he knows he must stay away from the courts of kings. To this Morus replies:

> To tell the truth, I do not think that such ideas should be thrust on people, or such advice given, as you are positive will never be listened to. What good could such novel ideas do, or how could they enter the minds of individuals who are already taken up and possessed by the opposite conviction? In the private conversation of close friends this academic philosophy is not without its charm, but in the council of kings, where great matters are debated with great authority, there is no room for these notions. (p. 99)

Hythlodaeus answers that this is "just what [he] meant . . . by saying there is no room for philosophy with rulers," a conviction that will lead him to describe Utopia, which like Plato's model republic flourishes because its rulers are philosophers.[12] How much happier that land will appear to us, he promises, than the tyrannies of Europe. But before inviting Hythlodaeus's monologue on Utopia, Morus tries again to defend the office of a court counselor, by offering a philosophy that allows an honest man to serve his king whatever his king's faults:

> There is another philosophy, more practical for statesmen, which knows its stage, adapts itself to the play in hand, and performs its role neatly and appropriately. This is the philosophy which you must employ. Otherwise we have the situation in which a comedy of Plautus is being performed and the household slaves are making trivial jokes at one another and then you come on the stage in a philosopher's attire and recite the passage from the *Octavia* where Seneca is disputing with Nero. Would it not have been preferable to take a part without words than by reciting something inappropriate to make a tragicomedy? You would have spoiled and upset the actual play by bringing in irrelevant matter – even if your contribution would have been superior in itself. Whatever play is being performed, perform it as best you can, and do not upset it all simply because you think of another which has more interest.

---

[11] Hythlodaeus, says Peter Giles, is "most learned in Greek" and has "devoted himself unreservedly to philosophy": "His sailing has not been like that of Palinurus but that of Ulysses or, rather, of Plato" (*CW*, vol. 4, pp. 49 and 51, with the Latin text on facing pages; the translated passages from this volume that follow have been slightly adjusted).

[12] *Republic* 5.473c–e.

So it is in the commonwealth. So it is in the deliberations of monarchs. If you cannot pluck up wrongheaded opinions by the root, if you cannot cure according to your heart's desire vices of long standing, yet you must not on that account desert the commonwealth. You must not abandon the ship in a storm because you cannot control the winds.

On the other hand, you must not force upon people new and strange ideas which you realize will carry no weight with persons of opposite conviction. On the contrary, by the indirect approach you must seek and strive to the best of your power to handle matters tactfully. What you cannot turn to good you must at least make as little bad as possible. (pp. 99–101)

Morus's conception of a counselor's duty, we note, does not contest Hythlodaeus's claim that kings tend to be tyrants. He seems to accept tyranny as a given, as we gather from the aesthetic and rhetorical principle of *decorum* that lies behind his advice to Hythlodaeus. The rules of decorum prescribe that each element of an artwork or persuasive speech be appropriate to its context.[13] So, the counselor guided by the rules of decorum will take into account particularities of place and time and audience, judge how much good he can do and by what means, and in the long run accomplish the most good for king and commonwealth through his circumspection. There is not much room for a Henry VIII, philosopher-king, in this picture, because Morus acknowledges that straightforward admonishments to wise policy and virtuous actions are not the ordinary (because they are the least efficable) mode of counsel. The wise counselor must use discretion, adapt himself to the play at hand, hold his tongue at one moment and at another dissemble, in order to make things "as little bad as possible" (*quam minime malum*) in serving a king inclined to follow his own will.

The implications of this passage's classical sources prove even more critical of monarchy, because the drama analogy that is the vehicle for Morus's advice to Hythlodaeus is itself equivocal and, in Arthur Kinney's words, adds "a darker undercurrent to the witty disputation on the surface" of Book One.[14] Interrupting a Plautine comedy, an actor speaks the lines of Seneca's disputation with Nero in the Roman history

---

[13] Though of course a commonplace, Renaissance exhortations to speak, write, and act "suitably to the occasion" typically had their source in Horace's *Ars poetica* and Cicero's rhetorical works (e.g., *De oratore* 3.55.210–60.225).

[14] *Humanist Poetics: Thought, Rhetoric, and Fiction in Sixteenth-Century England* (Amherst: University of Massachusetts Press, 1986), pp. 70–2. The "tragic irony" of this analogy is also discussed by John Crossett in "More and Seneca," *Philological Quarterly* 40 (1961): pp. 577–80.

play, *Octavia*.[15] Though these lines may be "more superior" in themselves, as Morus suggests, they are ill-timed and ineffective "in the play at
hand." But the allusion to Seneca's disputation with Nero functions
more complexly than just as a piece of tragic drama contaminating the
aesthetic coherence of a comedy (producing a *tragicomoediam*). This
particular example is ironic because even within *Octavia* Seneca's words
fail to abide by the rules of decorum. Like Hythlodaeus Seneca can only
speak his mind, and his persistence in dissuading Nero from doing what
he has already made up his mind to do – banish his wife from Rome –
only provokes the emperor's anger:

> Have done at last; you are already growing too burdensome to me.
> One may still be permitted to do what Seneca disapproves.
>
> (lines 588–9)

Renaissance readers were familiar with Seneca's career through *The
Annals* of Tacitus, whose account makes Nero's anger in this scene even
more chilling and makes the stronger argument in the debate between
Hythlodaeus and Morus all the more difficult to call. Seneca and
Afranius Burrhus were charged with training and counseling the young
Nero, or as Tacitus puts it, their task was "to ensure that the sovereign's
years of temptation should, if he were scornful of virtue, be restrained
within the bounds of permissible indulgence" (13.2). In other words, they
had to try to make Nero as little bad as possible. But Seneca was
eventually accused of conspiring against the emperor, and Nero ordered
him to commit suicide (15.61). For this reason Seneca was to Renaissance humanists a hallowed martyr, illustrating like the fates of Socrates
and Cicero the end to which good men come in times of tyranny. In a
passage devoted to the importance of decorum in Thomas Starkey's
Dialogue between Pole and Lupset, for instance, Pole illustrates his point
that "a man must regard time and place if he will handle matters of state"
with the case of Seneca, who, "if [he] had not been in the time of Nero, so
cruel a tyrant, but in the time of Trajan, so noble a prince, his virtue
should have been otherwise esteemed, and brought forth other fruit."[16]

Cicero had the same misfortune, according to Pole, because he lived in
the time of Pompey and Caesar, and appropriately enough the passage
from *Utopia* we are analyzing alludes to Cicero's writings and career as
well. The editors of the Yale edition compare Morus's advice for
Hythlodaeus to a repeated maxim in *De officiis:* "Of two evils choose

---

[15] The author of *Octavia* is unknown, but in More's time it was still attributed to
Seneca himself.
[16] *Thomas Starkey: A Dialogue between Pole and Lupset*, ed. T. F. Mayer, Camden
Fourth Series, vol. 37 (London: Royal Historical Society, 1989), p. 15.

the least" (*Primum minima de malis* [3.28.102, 3.29.105]),[17] while George Logan points to a longer passage in the same work in which Cicero states, "if at some time stress of circumstances shall thrust us aside into some uncongenial part, we must devote to it all possible thought, practice, and pains, that we may be able to perform it, if not with propriety, at least with as little impropriety as possible" (*si non decore, at quam minime indecore* [1.31.114]).[18] The Yale editors are right, too, in naming Plato as the source of Morus's ship-pilot metaphor, and in pointing out that this was a stock symbol of the statesman throughout antiquity and the Middle Ages;[19] but here More is probably recalling a specific passage in Cicero's letter to Publius Lentulus Spinther of December, 54 B.C., in which he defends himself for supporting the joint dictatorship of the First Triumvirs, Caesar, Pompey and Crassus:

> In sailing, it shows nautical skill to run before the wind in a gale, even if you fail thereby to make your port; whereas when you can get there just as well by tacking, it is sheer folly to court disaster by keeping your original course, rather than change it and still reach your desired destination. On the same principle in the conduct of state affairs, while we should all have as our one aim and object what I have so repeatedly preached – the maintenance of peace with honor – it does not follow that we ought always to speak in the same way, though we ought always to have the same goal in view (*non idem semper dicere, sed idem semper spectare debemus*).[20]

It would indeed be "sheer folly" for Cicero, now, to speak publicly in the manner that he could while consul (63 B.C.) and before the formation of the triumvirate, or as he may in this private exchange of letters with a friend. One's words "must agree with the times" (*temporibus assentiendum*), Cicero explains, and as More looks back to Cicero – to the tumultuous times in which the model statesman lived, and his horrible end at the hands of Mark Antony – he found both an authority and a case in point for Morus's argument in *Utopia*: since Trajans are few and far between, men must adapt themselves to living and effecting good under tyrannies.

[17] *CW*, vol. 4, p. 374 n. 100/1–2.
[18] George M. Logan, *The Meaning of More's "Utopia"* (Princeton: Princeton University Press, 1983), p. 116 n. 73.
[19] *CW*, vol. 4, p. 373 n. 98/27, citing *Republic* 6.488a–489a.
[20] *Ad familiares* 1.9.21.

III

When Henry offered *Utopia*'s author the position of lord chancellor, he certainly did not intend that the world would interpret the appointment as More's opportunity to effect good under a tyrant. If readers believed that Hythlodaeus was More's real spokesman in the dialogue, and Morus was what his name means in Latin (*fool*), then More's acceptance of the great seal would have indicated that he had found in Henry an exception to Hythlodaeus's claim that kings are by nature tyrants and that only flatterers serve them. It would demonstrate by example that a good man, in this reign, could with a clear conscience serve his king. But as far as Henry's image was concerned it did not matter whether one took Hythlodaeus's or Morus's views to be the author's own, for in either case, More's appointment could only be the decision of a Trajan. Only a true philosopher-king would seek out a man so committed to speaking the blunt truth as a Hythlodaeus; only a king who wanted the best for himself and his realm would employ a man who had publicly espoused a policy of covert opposition as the usual method for serving kings. This is why I suggest More's appointment was conceived as one more element in the king's propaganda program. The new lord chancellor contributed, in a material way, to Henry's construction of a philosopher-king public image, whether or not Henry planned in practice to heed or even invite More's counsel.

Nonetheless, More used his appointment to put Morus's advice into practice, to test that "more civil philosophy" that attempts to make things as little bad as possible according to one's means in a given time and place. As lord chancellor, More hoped he would be well placed to defend the Church in England against the Protestants at home and abroad, against the religious and political reformers in Parliament, and – indirectly, of course – against the king.[21] The importance of the cause outweighed the personal risk.

More's words and deeds in this period are especially interesting when we consider how great that risk must have seemed to him, for he would soon have become aware that it went beyond the physical dangers attending opposition to Henry. He had reason to perceive he risked spiritual dangers as well. During the spring and summer of 1530, as we know, Henry's agents were collecting opinions against the validity of his marriage from the faculties of various universities in Europe. The court was preparing to present these opinions to Clement VII and to publish

---

[21] On More's efforts to protect the Church in England see, especially, Guy, *The Public Career of Sir Thomas More*, chapters 6–9; Alistair Fox, *Thomas More: History and Providence* (New Haven: Yale University Press, 1982), pp. 167–98.

them in the form of the *Censurae* (and in its English version, *The Determinations of the Most Famous and Most Excellent Universities*). These activities alarmed the papal court, and in an effort to stop them Clement issued a breve of excommunication against anyone who, "tempted by hope of reward, or by request, hatred, fear or favor," should "against his conscience" speak or write anything concerning Henry's matrimonial case.[22] In its own way, this breve is another example of delicate reticence. The pope specifically addresses neither the advocates nor opponents of Henry's cause; he prohibits people in general from selling their pens to the highest bidder or submitting their voices, against the dictates of conscience, to whichever authority tries to coerce them. Just as Elton remarks about Henry's message in the *Determinations*, no one would have mistaken Clement's intended referents in his breve, the theologians signing their names to the university decisions. But by adopting this neutral stance Clement avoids making any public accusation that Henry, behind the scenes, is not behaving as a disinterested seeker after truth. At the same time, he leaves its proscription open enough both to imply his own neutrality, and to discourage, anywhere, the writing of any more pamphlets.[23] But it also put Henry's lord chancellor in a very tight spot. As the king's orator, it was More's role to speak for Henry in Parliament and in public. Impossibly, More would have to perform the duties of his office and at the same time maintain his own policy of reticent delicacy, attempting as best he could to obey the pope's breve and follow his conscience.

For a time, in his writings, More pulled it off. From 1529 to 1532 he published religious polemics that reinforced the image of Henry's court as a bastion of the faith: *A Supplication of Souls* (1529), *A Dialogue concerning Heresies* (1529 and 1530), and *The Confutation of Tyndale's Answer* (1532). In these More praises Henry as a virtuous and learned prince, obliging him with confirmations of his philosopher-king image. But to a greater extent More stresses Henry's image as a committed defender of the faith and pious champion of Rome. In *A Dialogue concerning Heresies*, for example, More celebrates Henry's "blessed zeal," and he cites passages from the "noble book" against Luther written by his "most faithful, virtuous and most erudite prince" right

---

[22] ". . . mandamus ne, in dicta matrimoniali causa contra conscientiam, spe præmii aut prece, odio vel timore aut gratia ducti, verbo aut scriptis aliquid allegare" (my translation). The full Latin text of this breve, issued May 21, 1530, is in Pocock, *Records of the Reformation*, vol. 2, pp. 633–4.

[23] On the Continent there were scores of these pamphlets. According to one report, "Fresh books appear daily in English, French, and Latin, part in favor of the king and part for the queen" (*SP, Venetian*, vol. 4, no. 823). A discussion of tracts written "for the queen" is Maria Dowling's "Humanist Support for Katherine of Aragon," *Bulletin of the Institute of Historical Research* 57 (1984): pp. 46–55.

alongside citations from Augustine, Jerome, and other Church fathers.[24] At the same time, More declares as heresy not only the reformers' unorthodox theological doctrine, but the arguments for limiting the Church's jurisdiction within England that Henry himself, though behind the scenes to be sure, was promoting in Parliament.

One of *A Dialogue*'s primary themes is the danger heretical opinions pose to the commonwealth, because heresy, More believes, arises out of malice and leads to riot and sedition. Naturally, then, Henry is enlisted against Tyndale's latest treatise, the "book of obedience, or rather disobedience,"[25] for More's voice is that of the state against rebellion. Its original title page emphasizes this point:

> A dialogue of sir Thomas More knight: one of the council of our sovereign lord the king and chancellor of his duchy of Lancaster. Wherein be treated divers matters, as of the veneration and worship of images and relics, praying to saints, and going on pilgrimages. With many other things touching the pestilent sect of Luther and Tyndale, by the one begun in Saxony, and by the other labored to be brought in to England.[26]

This summary of the contents indicates polemic on strictly religious doctrine, but because it also implies that the opinions are sanctioned by the king, of whose council the author is a member, we are led to believe Henry is as much determined to defend the Church against her enemies as he was in 1521. In 1530 this implication of the king's approval would be strengthened when the statement, "Newly overseen by the said sir Thomas More chancellor of England" was appended to the title page. *A Dialogue*'s representation of the king seems legitimated, because its author is now Henry's right-hand man. In addition, the reference to the "pestilent sect of Luther and Tyndale" – the first "begun in Saxony" and the other "labored to be brought in to England" – hints at something like an infiltrating, foreign enemy. This implication foregrounds More's purpose in the text to emphasize the martial aspect of Henry's role as

---

[24] For examples see *CW*, vol. 6, pp. 183, 318, 344, 351, 362, 402. *A Dialogue* was first printed shortly before More's promotion to lord chancellor but after the crisis over the divorce arose.

[25] *CW*, vol. 6, p. 349. More and other enemies of Tyndale recognized and advertised that his ideas on kingship were derived from Luther, but it is also true that similar ideas were held by reformist thinkers within the Church itself, such as Erasmus. See for example the speeches of Eusebius in *Convivium religiosum*, translated by Craig R. Thompson as "The Godly Feast" in *The Colloquies of Erasmus* (Chicago: University of Chicago Press, 1965), pp. 57–9; the Latin text is in *Opera omnia Desiderii Erasmi Roterodami* (Amsterdam: North Holland Pub. Co., 1972–), vol. 3, pp. 242–3.

[26] *CW*, vol. 6, p. 3.

joint defender of England and defender of the faith, by defining attacks against the Church as jointly sedition and heresy. If More could get his readers to accept this definition, and just as importantly if Henry could then perceive that his subjects accepted it, Henry just might be led to believe that the paradox of his public image and private actions was too dangerous to sustain.

More's *Supplication of Souls*, a reply to Fish's *Supplication for the Beggars*, similarly defends orthodox theology, in this case the doctrine of purgatory. It also labels as heretical Fish's idea of the supremacy of kings and his call for limiting Church privileges. The speaker of the tract is a soul in purgatory who at first laments that the living have forgotten him in their prayers, but then he turns to refute Fish's claim that the Church has ruined the commonwealth and bankrupted the king. One way he does this is by charging Fish with plagiarism. Noting the way Fish "roll[s] in his rhetoric from figure to figure," the soul then asserts: "surely the man cannot fail of such eloquence: for he hath gathered these goodly flowers out of Luther's garden almost word for word without any more labor but only the translating out of the Latin into the English tongue."[27] If we recall the rumor that Henry carried around *A Supplication for the Beggars* in his bosom for several days, enticed as he was by its ideas of royal supremacy, we must appreciate the audacity of More's charge even if that rumor stayed within court circles. Here is the lord chancellor pointing out that Fish's ideas have been acquired from the very arch-heretic Henry himself "refuted and confounded" just eight years before, in his *Assertio adversus Lutherum*.

IV

We are witnessing in these passages a much more sophisticated rhetorical strategy than that age-old gambit of attributing to one's king "the virtues which one wishes him to acquire," that indirect approach whereby "under the appearance of praise" the counselor will "paint the perfect prince" so that "in comparing himself with the model" the real prince "will shamefacedly realize his deficiencies."[28] Since it is again the principle of decorum that gives this strategy its promise of success, Morus's philosophy of counsel supplies useful terms to give it explication. When Morus advises Hythlodaeus to adapt his

---

[27] *CW*, vol. 7, pp. 127–8.

[28] Quoting the Yale editors' note to Morus's recommendation of the "indirect approach," *CW*, vol. 4, pp. 373–4 n. 98/30; Erasmus, they point out, describes this strategy in *Opus epistolarum*, nos. 397 and 399.

words to "the play at hand" in order not to "spoil and upset" the situation "by bringing in irrelevant matter," he is assuming the presence of an audience with power. In the theater, the audience judges whether decorum has been violated and the play spoiled; it has the power to laugh at what is incongruous, to boo the players, or to walk out.[29] At court, "in the council of kings where great matters are debated with great authority," the audience is comprised of the "actors" themselves – that is, the king and his counselors – all of whom would pose a threat to a Hythlodaeus who indecorously speaks his mind at the wrong time. But in the early 1530s this formula was modified. With the start of Henry's propaganda campaign, the audience was now extended to include the public.

This extension is significant, in the context of my study, not because there existed a wide reading audience in England that itself put pressure on the king to conform to the play at hand and to follow particular courses of action. Rather, what gave whatever audience there actually was the power to influence discourse was the king's perception that it was out there and that it needed swaying, and More's perception that it could be invoked in his attempts to sway the king. In theatrical terms, More's tactic was not just to stage an idealized king by whom Henry could measure himself, but to place that ideal king within a real context, to spotlight him against the religious schisms forming the contemporary political backdrop, "the play at hand," in order to encourage the king to sense that it would be indecorous – or rather, dangerous – to continue on his course.[30]

But how could More have hoped this indirect approach might actually work? It is one thing to define, on paper, what it means for Henry to act "neatly and appropriately" within given circumstances, and something else to put constraints on Henry's behavior in real life. My answer is that the nature of Henry's propaganda campaign put More in a position to hope. According to his public image, Henry was eager to hear the opinions of "wise men," to weigh the advice of the counselors, judges, and scholars whom his propaganda indicated were guiding his steps. He had hired More, in part, to bolster that image. If Henry now perceived that in his subjects' eyes More's opinions were the wisest ones, though they conflicted with his own he might still feel compelled to heed them.

[29] It is likewise in the case of oratory, says Cicero: the public (*multitudo*) has more say than the experts (*docti*) in judging a speech's success or failure (*Brutus* 49.184–6).

[30] This is not to say that More's polemics against heresy were "really" aimed at Henry rather than the heretics or the weak of faith. They were aimed at both because both threatened the Church. I call More's arguments against Tyndale "backdrop," therefore, only in speaking of his rhetorical strategy to sway the king.

Thus, Thomas More was indirectly, though quite publicly, attempting to steer the ship of state. He was acting according to Morus's advice rather than in the manner of a Hythlodaeus pleasantly proved wrong. It could not last. We have already seen, in our examination of the rhetoric of the royal dialogues, that Henry increasingly demanded more concord from his subjects. It was not long before the king overcame his reputed reluctance to put More "in ruffle of his conscience" by requiring him to speak for his cause. During the 1531 session of Parliament, Henry sent More first into the House of Lords and then into the House of Commons to present the texts of the university determinations against the king and queen's marriage. Hall reports the tense occasion:

> While the Parliament sat, on the 30th day of March, at afternoon there came into the common house the lord chancellor and divers lords of the spirituality and temporality to the number of twelve and there the lord chancellor said, you of this worshipful house I am sure be not so ignorant but you know well that the king our sovereign lord hath married his brother's wife, for she was both wedded and bedded with his brother prince Arthur, and therefore you may surely say that he hath married his brother's wife, if this marriage be good or no many clerks do doubt. Wherefore the king like a virtuous prince willing to be satisfied in his conscience and also for the surety of his realm hath with great deliberation consulted with great clerks, and hath sent my lord of London here present to the chief universities of all Christendom to know their opinion and judgment in that behalf. And although that the universities of Cambridge and Oxford had been sufficient to discuss the cause, yet because they be in his realm and to avoid all suspicion of partiality he hath sent into the realm of France, Italy the pope's dominions, and Venetians to know their judgment in that behalf, which have concluded, written and sealed their determinations according as you shall hear read.
>
> (p. 775)

At this point, More presented Sir Brian Tuke, who read "word by word" the determinations of the universities of Orleans, Paris, Angiers, Bourges, Bologna, Padua, and Toulouse (taking up four and half folio sheets in Hall's *Chronicle*), and "after these determinations were read," continues Hall, "there were showed above an hundreth books drawn by doctors of strange regions, which all agreed the king's marriage to be unlawful, which were not read, for the day was spent." At last More instructed his audience, "Now you of this common house may report in your countries what you have seen and heard and then all men shall openly perceive that the king hath not attempted this matter of will or pleasure, as some strangers report, but only for the discharge of his conscience and surety of the succession of his realm" (p. 780).

More's duties on this day are typically cited as the most "embarrassing" or "mortifying" in his public career.[31] At least that. More must have known that he was treading dangerously close to the injunction of Clement VII's 1530 breve of excommunication. More was only reading a script, it is true, not voicing his own thoughts, but his role in the day's proceedings surely grazed close to going "against his conscience," and he was speaking – as the breve prohibits – "by request," out of "fear or favor." Chapuys reports that after the determinations had been read in the house of Lords, "some one asked the chancellor for his opinion; on which he said that he had many times already declared it to the king; and he said no more."[32] The author of *Utopia* was caught in just the conflict Hythlodaeus vowed to avoid, between a life dedicated to truth and speech suited to the moment.

On May 16, 1532, More defied Morus's admonishment that "you must not abandon the ship in a storm because you cannot control the winds," and resigned the chancellorship. The Submission of the Clergy, in which Convocation agreed to Henry's demand that it relinquish its power to make laws, occurred just the day before and proved to More unequivocally that the Church in England was beyond any protection he could offer it while in Henry's employ. I said before that More's appointment as lord chancellor had been a victory for Henry's propaganda. Now More's abrupt resignation must have dealt a humiliating blow. It said that England's "Socrates in wisdom" would have nothing more to do with this so-called philosopher-king. The next year More further damaged Henry's image by skipping Anne's coronation ceremony and entering into a propaganda battle against Christopher St. German. After the *Doctor and Student* dialogues St. German had continued to write in favor of a parliamentary supremacy, which at the time Henry found useful. In 1532 Berthelet printed four editions of *The Division of the Spirituality and Temporality*, and in 1533 he printed another dialogue, *Salem and Bizance*, in which St. German elaborated on his earlier arguments for the primacy of state law over ecclesiastical privileges. More attacked St. German's position in his *Apology of Sir Thomas More, Knight* and *The Debellation of Salem and Bizance* (both published in 1533).[33] John Guy suggests that More's polemics against St. German had

---

[31] See, for example, Guy, *The Public Career of Sir Thomas More*, pp. 156–9; Parmiter, *The King's Great Matter*, p. 160.

[32] *LP*, vol. 5, no. 171.

[33] St. German responded in *The Additions of Salem and Bizance* (1534). This exchange is treated in John Guy, *The Public Career of Sir Thomas More*, pp. 151–6; Guy, "Thomas More and Christopher St. German: The Battle of the Books," in Fox and Guy, *Reassessing the Henrician Age*, pp. 95–120; Fox, *Thomas More*, pp. 167–98; Rainer Pineas, *Thomas More and Tudor Polemics*, pp. 192–213; and the introduction to *CW*, vol. 10.

much to do with his eventual arrest on April 17, 1534. Henry's "affection" for More "turned to malice and hatred," says Guy, in part because of Henry's "mental association of More and Fisher as equal partners in the Catholic press campaign against 'his' jurisdictional revolution." When More resigned he swore he would not meddle in state affairs, but "Henry VIII believed that his ex-chancellor had broken his trust."[34]

As damaging to Henry's image as More's resignation and subsequent activities were, however, we have seen that even while More held office he made only a qualified contribution, at best, to Henry's campaign to represent himself as a philosopher-king. His published writings rather resisted the campaign's aim to prepare people for Henry's defiance of Rome. But Henry's disappointment in More did not discourage him from trying again. As the next chapter argues, Henry simply accepted the services of England's second most renowned humanist, who stepped up to play the role that Thomas More would not.

---

[34] Fox and Guy, *Reassessing the Henrician Age*, pp. 118–19.

3

Thomas Starkey, Thomas Elyot, and Henry VIII's Republic of Letters

The dimension of the royal propaganda that publicized Henry as a philosopher-king and advertised that learned counselors were present at his court, deliberating and advising him on the issues of the day and on personal morality, required that the court's flesh-and-blood counselors behave in a manner that did not raise doubts about whether or not Henry was really listening to them. Thomas More's conspicuous lack of participation in the business of Henry's divorce, and the indirect pressure that his religious polemics were putting on Henry to defend the Church, raised those doubts. Yet for Henry to dismiss such a prominent figure as More would only put that image further into question. This chapter shows how the court bolstered its propaganda campaign by patronizing humanist books that would attest to the integrity of Henry's philosopher-king image. Not only this, it will be seen that these tracts from Berthelet's press counter the advice of Hythlodaeus and Morus, and refute the premises behind *Utopia*'s criticism of monarchy. They challenge Hythlodaeus's view of kings by upholding monarchy as the best form of government, but most tellingly, they also deny the possibility that in the reign of Henry VIII there could be any need for the advice of a Morus, by conceiving of decorum in ways other than as a means for restraining the will of a tyrant.

Possibly Thomas Cromwell commissioned these works, but he hardly needed to take so much trouble. Elton points out that as Cromwell rose in the king's favor "the prophets of reform" – Protestants and humanists alike – "naturally flocked to him." Elton also shows that though Cromwell encouraged some humanists to support the divorce and the royal supremacy, building a corps of these writers was a low priority for him because the assistance he most required was supplied not by classicists but by "the real experts, the common lawyers," who collaborated with him in drafting bills for Parliament.[1] Even lacking an

---

[1] Elton, *Reform and Reformation*, pp. 172–3. Elton treats this topic at more length in "The Political Creed of Thomas Cromwell," *Transactions of the Royal Historical Society*, Fifth Series, 6 (1956): pp. 69–92; reprinted in *Studies in Tudor and Stuart*

outright request from Cromwell for a certain type of treatise, humanist suitors eager for patronage would have been sufficiently keen to recognize the kinds of tracts Henry would appreciate and patronize: namely, those that speculate on the best state of a monarchy (or of a monarch, in the *speculum principis* tradition), and that conceive of the principle of decorum only in ways that are flattering to kings who are philosophers.

I am not suggesting that we should revalue the authors of these treatises as merely propagandists. They offered their words more in the spirit of counsel than outright flattery, for they warn against the dangers of tyranny and they lament many of the same evils plaguing the nobility that More voices through Hythlodaeus. No doubt they hoped their compositions would be as effective in counseling the king as in achieving their promotion, and that thereby they would attain the ideal of "applied humanism" which has been described in our classic accounts of the English humanist movement.[2] Nevertheless, in my view the two authors who are the subject of this chapter were careful to meet the rhetorical guidelines established by the king's public image, and they strove to counter the philosophies of Hythlodaeus and Morus because they knew they needed to affirm Henry's fiction in order to gain Henry's favor and ear. They treat the behavior of kings as a general question, according to the conventions of the *speculum principis* genre and to Henry's terms for the conduct of "open" debate and counsel that he was ostensibly encouraging. More than this, their four tracts on the question of kings and counsel all devote lengthy sections to conceiving of decorum in a manner that, at the very least, accepts the possibility of philosopher-kings, while three explicitly praise Henry for being one.

II

The first of these works was written by Thomas Starkey. A student of philosophy and civil law in Italy in the late 1520s and early 1530s, Starkey was in the entourage of Cardinal Reginald Pole until shortly before Pole's defection over the divorce issue. Cromwell gave Starkey employment, and the most important of his first tasks, though a futile

Politics and Government, vol. 2, pp. 215–35. Studies of Cromwell's broader sponsorship of government and religious reform include Elton, *Policy and Police*; Elton, *Reform and Renewal: Thomas Cromwell and the Common Weal* (Cambridge: Cambridge University Press, 1973); Riegler, "Printing, Protestantism, and Politics."

[2] F. Caspari, *Humanism and the Social Order in Tudor England*, chapter 1; Arthur Ferguson, *The Articulate Citizen and the English Renaissance*, chapter 7; and James McConica, *English Humanists and Reformation Politics under Henry VIII and Edward VI*, chapter 5.

one, was to urge Pole back into Henry's service. By 1535 Starkey was appointed chaplain to the king, and while in this position he wrote a number of religious and political tracts. The one for which he is best remembered is an untitled dialogue that exists only in his own hand, usually referred to as *A Dialogue between Pole and Lupset*.[3] This manuscript has been of greatest interest to students of Tudor political thought, whose attention is especially given to Starkey's radical proposal that kings should be elected (though elected, to be sure, out of the ranks of the nobility, by the nobility).[4] Until recently scholars put the date of the *Dialogue*'s composition sometime between 1533, when Starkey was studying law and acquiring ideas of civic humanism in Avignon, and 1538, the last year of his service at court and the year that he died. But the current authority on Starkey's career, Thomas Mayer, has used paleographical and diplomatic evidence to establish an earlier date. Mayer shows that Starkey finished the *Dialogue* before the end of 1532, and that he began writing it as early as the end of 1529, though more likely in 1530 after he had returned to England in the company of his patron, Reginald Pole, from a mission to Paris to sound out the French theologians on the divorce question.[5] Given the earlier date of 1530, Mayer argues that during the early stages of its composition Starkey shifted his purpose for the *Dialogue*. At first designed to praise Pole and persuade him back into public life, it became by late 1530 "the centerpiece of Starkey's own credentials, no longer an advertisement for

---

[3] Citations of the *Dialogue* are from *Thomas Starkey: A Dialogue between Pole and Lupset*, ed. T. F. Mayer. I also make use of *A Dialogue between Cardinal Pole and Thomas Lupset, Lecturer in Rhetoric at Oxford*, printed in *England in the Reign of King Henry the Eighth*, Pt. 2, ed. J. M. Cowper, Early English Text Society, Extra Series, no. 32 (London: EETS, 1871).

[4] See Baumer, *Early Tudor Theory of Kingship*, pp. 116 and 209–20; Zeeveld, *Foundations of Tudor Policy*, pp. 128–56; Skinner, *The Foundations of Modern Political Thought*, vol. 1, pp. 222–5; G. R. Elton, "Reform by Statute: Thomas Starkey's *Dialogue* and Thomas Cromwell's Policy," *Proceedings of the British Academy* 54 (1968): pp. 165–88, reprinted in Elton, *Studies in Tudor and Stuart Politics and Government*, vol. 2, pp. 236–58; T. F. Mayer, "Thomas Starkey's Aristocratic Reform Programme," *History of Political Thought* 7 (1986): pp. 439–61.

[5] "Faction and Ideology: Thomas Starkey's *Dialogue*," *Historical Journal* 28 (1985): pp. 1–25. This evidence is also presented in Mayer's full length study, *Thomas Starkey and the Commonweal: Humanist Politics and Religion in the Reign of Henry VIII*, Cambridge Studies in Early Modern British History (Cambridge: Cambridge University Press, 1989), pp. 93–6, as well as the preface to Mayer's edition of the *Dialogue*, pp. x–xii.

For a time Thomas Lupset was with Pole and Starkey on the mission to France, which was the last that Pole performed for Henry; see Mayer, "A Mission Worse than Death: Reginald Pole and the Parisian Theologians," *English Historical Review* 103 (1988): pp. 870–91. On this period in Pole's career see Wilhelm Schenk, *Reginald Pole, Cardinal of England* (London: Longmans, 1950), pp. 19–48.

Pole.''[6] Thus, just as the first tracts of Henrician propaganda began to appear from Berthelet's press, Starkey redirected the *Dialogue* to catch the eye of the king. As I purpose to show, Starkey deliberately offered his vision of the ideal monarchy as an alternative to More's Utopia.

In the previous chapter I cited Lupset's observation in Starkey's *Dialogue* that Socrates, Cicero, and Seneca all suffered because they were living in bad times. That passage occurs in the tract's first invocation of the decorum principle. The fates of these three great men, says Lupset, prove that the prudent courtier "must regard time and place if he will handle matters of state" (p. 15). Fortunately for England, he goes on to say, the present time is fit for men of wisdom and virtue to enter into the service of their king:

> *Lupset:* Master Pole, what so ever regard be of wise men to be had either of time or of place, this to us is certain, that now, in our time, when we have so noble a prince, whom we are sure nothing to have so printed in his breast as the cure of his common weal, both day and night remembering the same, we should have no such respect. For this I dare affirm, there was never prince reigning in this realm which had more fervent love to the wealth of his subjects than hath he; there was never king in any country which bare greater zeal to the administration of justice and setting forth of equity and right than doth he; after he is thereof informed and surely instruct by his wise counselors and politic men. (pp. 16–17)

The praise Lupset gives to Henry in this passage explains the motive for his and Pole's discussion. Because a philosopher is king, and because this king wants other good men to help him improve the realm, the time is ripe for "wise counselors and politic men" like Pole and Lupset (and Starkey) to engage in fruitful dialogue and action: "The time exhorteth us," says Lupset, "seeing that now our most noble prince hath assembled his Parliament and most wise counsel, for the reformation of this his common weal" (p. 17).

Starkey argues this thesis by applying the principle of decorum according to the character of an entire reign. Under a bad ruler good men either suffer or avoid affairs of state; under a good ruler good men take advantage of the time and work to better the realm. In comparison to that in *Utopia*, one might object, this conception of decorum simplifies

---

[6] Mayer, *Thomas Starkey*, pp. 89–90. The manuscript of the *Dialogue* is prefaced by a dedicatory letter to Henry, most likely written, says Mayer, "hard on the heels of the completion of the *Dialogue*'s first draft no later than the end of 1532" (ibid., p. 96). The letter is reprinted in *Starkey's Life and Letters*, in *England in the Reign of King Henry the Eighth, Pt. 1*, ed. Sidney J. Herrtage, Early English Text Society, Extra Series, no. 32 (London: EETS, 1878), pp. lxxiii–lxxv.

things drastically. There is no need, as there is in *Utopia*, of a moral imperative to take risks, to try through indirect means to make matters under a tyrant "as little bad as possible." For most of the dialogue Pole and Lupset take decorum on such easy terms.

The one point at which decorum is conceived in a different sense occurs after Lupset and Pole have agreed on the subject of their disputation and on an outline for the order of topics to be covered. At this point Lupset makes one stipulation. He requests that Pole not fall into the "great frantic folly" of patterning his talk after Plato's *Republic*, but stick to the reality of the present state of England:

> Sir, this process liketh me well; but hear of one thing, I pray you, take heed, that in this your device of your communication you follow not the example of Plato, whose order of common weal no people upon earth to this day could ever yet attain. Wherefore it is reputed of many men but as a dream and vain imagination, which never can be brought to effect . . . Therefore look you to the nature of our country, to the manner of our people, not without respect both of time and of place, that your device hereafter, by the help of our most noble prince, may the sooner obtain his fruit and effect. (p. 18)

Lupset requests Pole, in other words, not to take Plato's *Republic* for inspiration, as everyone knows Thomas More did when he wrote *Utopia*, because it will only result in a "dream."[7] This admonishment is Starkey's way to declare that his inquiry into the best state of a commonwealth will be useful, and so do real service to his king. Pole grants Lupset's request, promising that his will be a vision of a "restored" commonwealth, not anything like More's "vain" imaginings in Book Two of *Utopia*, for Starkey means to provide practical and realistic solutions to the country's problems.[8] That is what observing decorum means in this passage: sticking to practical answers, having "respect both of time and of place" when proposing changes. Decorum so conceived has nothing to do with maneuvering through the shifting winds of court politics and intrigue, as it does in *Utopia*, for Starkey has already settled the question, though it is

---

[7] Among the many comparisons that have been made between More's *Utopia* and Plato's *Republic*, the most detailed are Colin Starnes, *The New Republic: A Commentary on Book I of More's Utopia, Showing its Relation to Plato's Republic* (Waterloo, Ontario: Wilfrid Laurier University Press, 1990); and George M. Logan, *The Meaning of More's "Utopia,"* chapter 3 and epilogue.

[8] In *Il principe* (which Starkey may well have read), Machiavelli similarly states that, "since my intention is to say something that will prove of practical use to the inquirer, I have thought it proper to represent things as they are in real truth, rather than as they are imagined. Many have dreamed up republics and principalities which have never in truth been known to exist" (*The Prince*, trans. George Bull [Harmondsworth: Penguin, 1961], pp. 90–1).

reiterated here, that Henry is a virtuous king listening to the advice of his wise and virtuous counselors. Everyone can get right to work, therefore, addressing the specific social problems that trouble the kingdom "here and now."

The problems that Pole and Lupset identify, we discover, are for the most part those that Hythlodaeus catalogues in his conversation at Cardinal Morton's. Pole and Lupset lament the enclosure of land for sheep pasturage (pp. 65–6), the wasted, untilled land and decayed cities and towns (pp. 49–50), the overly harsh treatment of thieves (pp. 80–1), the exportation of corn, wool, and tin in exchange for such luxuries as silk and wine (pp. 62–4), and the abundance of idle servants schooled in foppish graces rather than useful trades (p. 87).[9] But in addition, Pole and Lupset condemn the payment of annates to the Church (p. 84), and in a clear reference to the pope's avocation of Henry's case to Rome they agree that it is intolerable that causes other than schism are sued out of the realm (pp. 84, 132–3).

Despite this support of Henry's position, no one has ever suggested that Starkey intended *A Dialogue between Pole and Lupset* for the king's propaganda campaign. This would be curious but for Starkey's radical proposals for the future election of kings and the constraint of their powers. As Pole observes, however virtuous is the present king the virtue of future kings cannot be guaranteed, so he suggests that "after the decease of the prince" the next one should be chosen "by election of the common voice of the Parliament assembled." Furthermore, this king "should not rule and govern at his own pleasure and liberty," says Pole, but be "ever subject to the order of his own laws," acting only in conjunction with his council and Parliament (p. 112). We have seen that Henry was at this time advertising his reliance on the wisdom of his council and Parliament, but Pole's plan goes too far – though not, it seems to me, because it favors the supremacy of law over the royal will. Rather, Starkey undercuts one of Henry's most persuasive reasons for the necessity of divorcing Catherine and marrying Anne Boleyn: to secure a male heir. If the next king is simply to be elected by Parliament, Englishmen need not feel anxiety at their barren queen. In sum, Starkey's dialogue was right for Henry's campaign in several ways, in that it argues for less Church interference in the life of England, it is a work of moral and political philosophy that attests to Henry's nurturing of humanism at his court, and it provides alternative conceptions of decorum that flatter Henry rather than embarrass him; but it was incompatible with a key tactic in the divorce propaganda. *A Dialogue*

---

[9] Andrew M. McLean identifies these correspondences between *Utopia* and *A Dialogue between Pole and Lupset* in "A Note on Thomas More and Thomas Starkey," *Moreana* 11 (1974): pp. 31–5.

between Pole and Lupset, therefore, was not one of the dialogues printed by Thomas Berthelet. It remained, instead, among the papers of Thomas Cromwell.[10]

III

The story is different for Sir Thomas Elyot. Over fifteen of his works were printed by Berthelet in the 1530s and 1540s, including several of the earliest translations of Greek texts into English and the first Latin-English dictionary.[11] After printing in 1530 *Plutarch's Education, or Bringing up of Children* (translated, according to the title page, by "Sir Thomas Elyot, one of the king's counsel"), Berthelet published in the next few years all of Elyot's original English compositions. The first was *The Governor* (1531), appearing just before Elyot's departure on the most important government appointment of his career, as Henry's ambassador to the court of Charles V (from 1531 to 1532). Like *Plutarch's Education*, *The Governor* sets out to describe the proper training of youth, and is in this respect a kind of modern day version of Quintilian's *Institutiones oratoriae*. But because *The Governor* offers a training program for male children of the nobility – specifically, potential future kings – the work is also in the tradition of the *speculum principis*. Such a work entails for Elyot defining the commonwealth that his ideal prince will rule, and he does so in a manner that, like Lupset's protest in Starkey's *Dialogue*, makes it clear *The Governor* will not go in for any unrealistic and foolish notions. Scorned abovemost is the absence of personal property, a characteristic of Plato's ideal republic and the land of Utopia. "It seemeth that men have been long abused in calling *rempublicam* a common weal," says Elyot; but "they which do suppose it so to be called for that, that every thing should be to all men in common, without discrepance of any estate or condition, be thereto moved more by sensuality than by any good reason or inclination to humanity."[12] Etymology, Elyot explains, teaches us that *common* "signifieth estate, condition, substance, and profit," not shared property, and he promises that those who err on

[10] Calendared in *LP*, vol. 8, no. 216.

[11] The standard biographies are Stanford E. Lehmberg, *Sir Thomas Elyot: Tudor Humanist* (Austin: University of Texas Press, 1960), and Pearl Hogrefe, *The Life and Times of Sir Thomas Elyot, Englishman* (Ames: Iowa State University Press, 1967). A study of Elyot's literary career is by John M. Major, *Sir Thomas Elyot and Renaissance Humanism* (Lincoln: University of Nebraska Press, 1964).

[12] *A Critical Edition of Sir Thomas Elyot's* The Boke named the Governour, ed. Donald W. Rude (New York: Garland, 1992), p. 15; subsequent references are given in the text.

this point will soon, in their reading of *The Governor*, be "satisfied either with authority or with natural order and example" (p. 15).

Just as *Utopia* has been viewed as More's Christian revision of Plato's *Republic*, John Major calls *The Governor* "a kind of latter-day *Republic*" that strives, like Starkey's *Dialogue*, to be a more "worthy guide" than More's because of its fitness for practical application.[13] Major suggests that *The Governor* may even be Elyot's "refutation" of More's ideas, being "in part at least, the semiofficial reply, by a spokesman for Tudor policy, to the more daring claims set forth in *Utopia* regarding the best form of government for men."[14] I agree with this statement, but believe, too, that we can be more specific about the nature of Elyot's "semiofficial reply" than Major ventures. We know that Hythlodaeus prefers Utopia's shared rulership to monarchy because kings (he insists) are by nature tyrants. Elyot sets out to disprove this claim. The very subject of his book, after all – the education of princes – is founded on the premise that princes can be taught. The aim of this teaching, as Pearl Hogrefe summarizes it, is the governor's "private morality and ethical government." Through his studies he will acquire the accomplishments not only of the courtier and warrior, but of the scholar, becoming "a man of learning because knowledge leads to virtue."[15]

The Governor is dedicated to Henry VIII as the living pattern of an ideal prince, but that is only the first way in which Elyot obliges his patron. His definition of the practice of court decorum deflects any issues that could bring into question the integrity of Henry's philosopher-king image. We see this first in the chapter on "majesty in speech":

> Toward the acquiring of majesty, three things be required to be in the oration of a man having authority: that it be compendious, sententious, and delectable, having also respect to the time when, the place where, and the persons to whom it is spoken. For the words perchance apt for a banquet or time of solace be not commendable in time of consultation or service of God. That language that in the chamber is tolerable, in place of judgment or great assembly is nothing commendable. (p. 118)

This explanation is satisfactory insofar as *The Governor* is devoted to the education of rulers. It can be expected to urge a prince's observance of

---

[13] *Sir Thomas Elyot and Renaissance Humanism*, p. 7.

[14] Ibid., p. 139. Pearl Hogrefe counters Major's suggestion in her study of Elyot's life and work, rightly reminding us that the concept of "Christian sharing" was widely current among humanist writers of the period (she cites Erasmus, Colet and Vives); but her claim that "detailed discussion of Elyot's possible intention to refute *Utopia* seem futile" (*Life and Times of Sir Thomas Elyot*, p. 119), this chapter refutes.

[15] *Life and Times of Sir Thomas Elyot*, p. 130.

decorum rather than his counselors'. But this shift of focus from counselor to prince is also a means for Elyot to sidestep the implicit condemnation of kings embedded in Morus's advice to observe decorum at court. Similarly, his illustrations are just too obvious. The manner of speaking that is appropriate at the dining table, we are told, is not suitable for prayer; bedroom talk is not suitable in a court of law. Such admonishments supposedly apply to the actual speech of kings, but they are little more useful as a guide to real behavior than are their classical sources, aimed as *they* are at aspiring poets: "A subject for comedy refuses to be handled in tragic verse," says Horace; "the banquet of [King] Thyestes disdains to be narrated in lines suited to everyday life."[16] True enough that this is long-hallowed commonplace wisdom, and viewed as such it would be odd to find fault with it. But as an alternative to Morus's philosophy of counsel we might interpret it as just so much smoke.

I think it likely Elyot recognized this too, for later in *The Governor* he returns to elaborate on the question of decorum. When he does it appears at first that he will confront the delicate matter of offering counsel to a king after the manner of Morus. Asserting that "the end of all doctrine and study is good counsel" (p. 257), Elyot acknowledges that rivalry, avarice, and dissembling among court counselors are common problems. But in the end the focus of this section is the king who knows how to benefit from counselors who possess these vices:

How necessary to a public weal it shall be to them that do remember that in many heads be divers manners of wits, some inclined to sharpness and rigor, many to pity and compassion, divers to a temperance and mean between both extremities; some have respect to tranquillity only, other more to wealth and commodity, divers to much renown and estimation in honor. There be that will speak all their mind suddenly and perchance right well; divers require to have respect and study, wherein is much more surety, many will speak warily for fear of displeasure; some more bold in virtue will not spare to show their minds plainly, divers will assent to that reasons wherewith they suppose that he which is chief in authority will be best pleased. These undoubtedly be the diversities of wits. And moreover, where there is a great number of counselors, they all being heard needs must the counsel be the more perfect. For sometime perchance one of them, which in doctrine, wit, or experience is in least estimation, may hap to express some sentence more available to the purpose wherein they consult than any that before came to the others' remembrances; no one man being of such perfection that he can have in an instant remembrance of all thing. (p. 258)

---

[16] *Ars poetica*, lines 88–91.

Speaking plainly or staying one's tongue, boldness or fear, these are merely a matter of character and temperament – of "the diversities of wits." Rivalry, avarice, and dissembling are naturally failings of certain counselors, because after all they are traits common among men. Elyot makes a reasonable point, but one that buries Hythlodaeus's contention that kings, by nature, foster these vices in their counselors. Instead he presumes that his educational program has produced the ideal ruler, one who tolerates a diversity of wits because he knows that good ideas occasionally spring from where one least expects them, and whose moral and politic wisdom lies in his ability to judge objectively the best policy from the choices that his counselors present him, whatever their motives.

IV

Stanford Lehmberg, in his biography of Thomas Elyot, notes that *The Governor*, on the whole, advocates an absolute monarchy, and like Major he speculates on the possibility that it could have been printed to support the royal supremacy. Recalling "the government's eagerness to secure a propagandist in 1531," which included Cromwell's attempt to entice Tyndale into the king's service, Lehmberg suggests that there may be some truth to "the hypothesis that Elyot's political views were put forth at Cromwell's request," and that it may be significant that Thomas Berthelet was Elyot's publisher. Lehmberg stresses the tentativeness of his suppositions. He admits that it "may have been only a coincidence" that the royal press printed *The Governor*, and he drops the subject by saying that "the idea that these chapters are the earliest example of Cromwellian propaganda is intriguing but unprovable."[17] Despite Lehmberg's caution, Pearl Hogrefe objects strongly to any suggestion that Elyot was connected to a propaganda campaign. "The printing of *The Governor* by Berthelet does not seem significant, nor does [Lehmberg] make much of that point," she writes. "Perhaps Berthelet as the king's printer did set up in type every book or pamphlet that Henry wished to have printed, but it does not follow that every book printed by Berthelet was ordered by the king."[18] Hogrefe further insists that *The Governor*, rather than advocating absolute monarchy, "sharply restrict[s] the power of the king by demanding of him reason, equity, and unusual understanding, by emphasizing his duty to rule for the welfare of his

---

[17] *Sir Thomas Elyot*, pp. 49–51.
[18] "Sir Thomas Elyot's Intention in the Opening Chapters of *The Governour*," *Studies in Philology* 60 (1963): p. 133.

inferiors, and by stating that his rewards should be in proportion to the use of these standards."[19]

Hogrefe's argument regarding the royal press seems a valid one, in that it does appear unlikely that every book published by Thomas Berthelet was ordered by the king. In 1531, for example, Berthelet printed the usual selection of popular law books, as well as a variety of works that Henry would seem to have had little stake in: *The Table of Cebes*, translated from the French by Sir Francis Pointz; a sermon by Colet; and a *declamatio* by Erasmus on the subject of suffering the death of a friend. *The Governor* could well belong with these books in a category of miscellaneous works of a learned and moral nature that Berthelet and other prestigious presses ordinarily printed. And, if we accept Hogrefe's view that Elyot's intention in *The Governor* is to "restrict" the king's power, then it would be hard to imagine how the book could serve as propaganda for an "absolute monarchy." The same reasoning Hogrefe applies to Elyot's two 1533 dialogues, *Pasquil the Plain* and *Of the Knowledge which Maketh a Wise Man*, which "were undoubtedly efforts to warn the king against his policies," she says. "These would not knowingly have been issued by the order of Henry VIII."[20]

But what are we to make of the fact that Elyot's *The Governor* and his two 1533 dialogues are the only works ever to appear from Berthelet's press that are even subtly critical of Henry VIII? Would Berthelet have jeopardized his appointment as the king's printer by printing a book that attempts to "restrict" the king's power? Would he have printed *Pasquil* and *Knowledge*, if they really contain the thinly veiled criticism of Henry's policies that scholarly consensus since Hogrefe ascribes to them?[21] I suggest Berthelet printed these books because they were useful to Henry despite their criticisms. They may very well warn and accuse Henry, that is, but they do so strictly according to Henry's guidelines for published counsel, with the result that Elyot's criticism is so general and framed by flattery as to be neutralized even while he praises the king for admirably deigning to hear it. To my mind, therefore,

---

[19] Ibid., p. 136. Similarly admiring characterizations of Elyot's design are in F. W. Conrad, "The Problem of Counsel Reconsidered: The Case of Sir Thomas Elyot," in *Political Thought and the Tudor Commonwealth: Deep Structure, Discourse, and Disguise*, ed. Paul A. Fideler and T. F. Mayer (London: Routledge, 1992), pp. 75–107; John Guy, "The Rhetoric of Counsel in Early Modern England," in *Tudor Political Culture*, ed. Dale Hoak (Cambridge: Cambridge University Press, 1995), pp. 293–4; Greg Walker, *Persuasive Fictions*, pp. 107–11.

[20] "Sir Thomas Elyot's Intention," p. 133.

[21] Hogrefe and most other critics have assumed that Elyot was defending More in these works, but Alistair Fox has recently argued that Elyot was protesting what he perceived was his own mistreatment by the court; see "Sir Thomas Elyot and the Humanist Dilemma," in Fox and Guy, *Reassessing the Henrician Age*, pp. 52–73.

any absolute denial that Elyot was engaged in government propaganda, or in refuting More's *Utopia*, is based on a misunderstanding of Henrician propaganda. Part of that campaign was designed to demonstrate Henry's commitment to nurturing philosophy and philosophers at his court, to show that he was receiving advice on the issues of the day and on personal morality for his own and the realm's welfare. It was perfectly acceptable to "restrict" the power of kings so long as those restrictions were in books of philosophy published by the king's printer. This is where Elyot fit in. The publication of all his books by Berthelet coupled with his various government posts (like More's appointment as chancellor), told readers that the voice of humanist virtue was being heard and rewarded by the king. Henry welcomed admonitions against tyranny, provided those admonitions were expressed by his counselors and in the general terms that he demanded that they use, because in this way he advertised his own commitment to just and thoughtful rulership.

Elyot's participation in Anne Boleyn's lavish coronation ceremony, in 1533, was one more instance of his role in delivering this message.[22] Sydney Anglo describes this public spectacle in detail, working mainly from ambassadors' accounts, the description in Hall's *Chronicle*, and a contemporary pamphlet memorializing the event.[23] He remarks that "the pageant series presented in London for the coronation entry of Anne Boleyn was an affirmation of the breach with Rome,"[24] and that it relied on overtly humanistic themes in its accolade for the new queen. Such a "show of humanism" must have been precisely what Henry had in mind for the event, because the charge of planning and conducting the pageant went to John Leland, an antiquary employed in the royal libraries, and Nicholas Udall, the Latinist who is best known today for his comedy *Ralph Roister Doister*. Leland and Udall designed classical sets – the nine Muses singing at the fountain of Helicon, for example – and they

---

[22] According to Roper, More bravely refused to take part in this event (*Life of Sir Thomas More*, p. 229), and he is not mentioned in the list of participants in *LP*, vol. 6, no. 562. Elyot is listed twice.

[23] *Spectacle, Pageantry, and Early Tudor Policy*, pp. 243–61. The eyewitness accounts and official rolls of the participants are calendared in *LP*, vol. 6, nos. 561–3, 585, 653; *SP, Spanish*, vol. 4, pt. 2, nos. 704, 1100, 1107. See also Hall, pp. 798–805; and *The Noble Triumphant Coronation of Queen Anne, Wife unto the Most Noble King Henry the VIIIth*, reprinted in *An English Garner: Ingatherings from our History and Literature*, 8 vols., ed. Edward Arber (Westminster: A. Constable, 1893–97), vol. 2, pp. 41–51, a tract printed by Wynkyn de Worde for John Gough, under the king's privilege. Gough is credited for printing only a few books, but half of these had a government connection; he printed a description the previous year, for instance, of *The Manner of the Triumph at Calais and Boulogne*, also with the king's privilege (reprinted in Arber, *An English Garner*, vol. 2, pp. 33–40).

[24] Anglo, *Spectacle, Pageantry, and Early Tudor Policy*, p. 247.

composed and recited along the procession route verses celebrating Anne's beauty and fertility (she was three months pregnant) and the Golden Age to come, using Latin in classical meters with frequent echoes of Horace and Vergil.[25]

Anglo finds this pageant aesthetically disappointing. He contrasts it with the previous two in the century, the first marking Catherine of Aragon's entry into London in 1501 and the second honoring Charles V's visit in 1522. In 1501 especially "the whole series had been mathematically symmetrical with almost every allusion relating to a carefully devised scheme," and "the basic concepts employed had been strongly rooted in medieval cosmology, and the imagery had been drawn from medieval pageant tradition . . . Now in 1533 two classical scholars devised both pageants and speeches so that for the first time England witnessed a pageant series which seemed truly classical." But, says Anglo, "the humanism was superficial": it had only a "self-conscious Latinity" and "thin veneer of commonplace literary allusions," and with its "indigestible mass of eulogistic Latin verse extolling the beauty, virtues, and excellences of Anne Boleyn," it was, essentially, "a dull, trite, and lamentably repetitious pageant series."[26]

If, however, we turn from the question of artistic merit to its function in Henry's propaganda campaign, we can see that this celebration would have been most effective in its public association of Henry's court with the intellectual and ethical fruits of humanism. In Henry, so the public sees, England has an enlightened prince, a philosopher-king who has surrounded himself with this chorus of humanists who now in the streets of London sing his and Anne Boleyn's praises, and presumably provide him not only with the imaginative luggage of their classical learning but with the moral and political wisdom they have acquired. Among this chorus's number, and affirming the message of this humanist spectacle, the author of *The Governor* is also on hand, performing the office of servitor for the Archbishop.[27] Elyot, that is, attended Archbishop Thomas Cranmer, who just weeks before the coronation had declared Henry's marriage to Catherine invalid, and then performed the wedding ceremony that made Anne queen.

[25] The manuscript of these verses is calendared in *LP*, vol. 6, no. 564, and printed in Furnivall, *Ballads from Manuscripts*, vol. 1, pp. 378–413; Udall's English verses only are in Arber, *An English Garner*, vol. 2, pp. 52–60.

[26] *Spectacle, Pageantry, and Early Tudor Policy*, p. 248.

[27] *LP*, vol. 6, no. 562 (p. 247).

V

In the same year as Anne Boleyn's coronation the king's printer published *Pasquil the Plain* and *Of the Knowledge which Maketh a Wise Man. Pasquil* is a dialogue between three men espousing three different philosophies of counsel: Pasquil, who will only speak plainly;[28] Gnatho, who will only say whatever he thinks his prince wants to hear; and Harpocrates, who tries to remain silent as long as possible. Now that the duty of counselors is the subject of discussion rather than the forming of good governors, we cannot expect that Elyot will simply repeat the discussion of decorum from his earlier *speculum principis.* It even appears that Elyot will treat in plain words the dilemmas posed in *Utopia*, when we see that Gnatho closely paraphrases Morus's advice to Hythlodaeus:

> Well Pasquil, thou wilt never leave thine old custom in railing, yet hast thou wit enough to perceive what damage and hindrance thou hast thereby sustained: and more art thou likely and with greater peril, if thou have not good await [i.e., take good heed], what, and to whom, and where thou speakest.[29]

Elyot raises the issue of decorum in this passage in a way that promises to lead toward the touchy topic of how to serve bad kings, but it will not happen. Elyot's first evasive move is to define the principle of decorum as he did in *The Governor*, according to the commonplace advice given to aspiring poets. Gnatho defends his commitment to flattering his prince by citing "Aeschylus's counsel" for how one may "soonest come to promotion," which, reports Gnatho, is "holding thy tongue where it behooveth thee" and "speaking in time that which is convenient" (pp. 48–9). Pasquil tells Gnatho that he misunderstands ·Aeschylus, and explains that the playwright did not mean counselors should only speak when they see that it will please their prince and lead to their promotion, but that they ought to speak on the subject that is appropriate to the occasion. He then cites overly obvious, and so not very helpful, examples of times to refrain from discoursing on certain subjects:

> Where two hosts be assembled, and in point to fight, if thou be among them, though thou be a great astronomer, it behoveth thee to hold thy

---

[28] For a discussion of the Roman "Pasquil tradition," which once a year allowed anyone of any rank to lampoon anyone else by means of "attaching his comments [*pasquinate*] to the old statue of Pasquil," see Hogrefe, *Life and Times of Sir Thomas Elyot*, p. 189; Major, *Sir Thomas Elyot and Renaissance Humanism*, p. 98.

[29] *Pasquil the Plain*, in *Four Political Treatises*, ed. Lillian Gottesman (Gainsville, Florida: Scholars' Facsimiles and Reprints, 1967), p. 47.

tongue, and not to talk of conjunctions and of the trine or quartile aspects but to prepare thee to battle. Where a good fellowship is set at dice or at cards, though thou be learned in geometry, hold thy tongue and speak not of proportions or figures. (p. 52)

Elyot marvelously mixes time-honored commonplace wisdom and humor in this passage, and again, taken on these terms it would be perverse to make objections to it. As a rebuttal of Morus's philosophy of counsel, however, it is disappointing, because it is hardly more helpful than the *The Governor*'s reminder that "bedroom talk is not suitable in a court of law."

Shortly afterwards, though, Pasquil does offer examples of appropriate speech for an occasion, and these admittedly are more applicable to the duty of counselors because they exhibit one person's effort to sway another toward wise action. He advises, for example, that "if before battle joined, thou beholdest thy side the weaker, and thine adversaries more puissant and stronger, speak then of policy, whereby thou hopest to obtain victory"; and, "before that thy friend sitteth down to dice, if thou dost perceive that he shall be overmatched, discourage him betime, or he repent him in poverty" (p. 54). Pasquil is now ready to consider the question of how best to warn a king that he is on a dangerous path, and he appeals to the principle of decorum:

Where thou seest thy lord or master in the presence of many, resolved into fury or wantonness, though thou hast all ready advertisements, how he shall refrain it, yet hold thy tongue then, for troubling that presence . . . When thou perceivest thy master to be resolved into wrath or affections dishonest, before wrath be increased to fury, and affection into beastly enormity, as opportunity serveth thee, reverently and with tokens of love toward him, speak such words as shall be convenient. (pp. 53–5)

Elyot is at last treating decorum in the context of the moment, rather than according to the diverse temperaments of men or to the character of a whole reign. As Pasquil says, "Opportunity and time for a counselor to speak do not depend of the affection and appetite of him that is counseled: marry, then counsel were but a vain word, and every man would do as him list. For if he listed not to hear any counsel, he should never be warned of his own error" (pp. 55–6). Scholars have uniformly read these passages to be Elyot's defense of More's or his own dedication to truth and plain counsel, whether Henry wants it or not. But they do not take into account the passage that directly follows. After Gnatho compliments Pasquil for his good reason, which he admits he is surprised at because "men have always reputed thee but for a babbler and railer," Pasquil responds by railing for several pages against those men who do so accuse him – that is, the avaricious popes and prelates of the Church, the Protestants by whom "saints [are] blasphemed and miracles reproved for jugglings," and the "emperors and princes" who are "in perpetual discord and often times in peril" (pp. 56–8). In his mind Elyot may well have been including Henry among this last group, but considering this dialogue's printing by the royal press it appears that Elyot is pointing his finger at *those other* rulers, the emperors and princes who, like the papists and Protestants, detest Pasquil's plain speaking because they only want to hear what accords with their appetites. That, by implication, leaves Henry, the one king who listens to the plain truth.

Yet curiously, we are warned not to read *Pasquil the Plain* allegorically. Elyot tells us in the preface that, "in this book, [Pasquil] useth such a temperance, that he noteth not any particular person or country" (p. 42),[30] and Pasquil makes the same claim when he concludes the dialogue: "I have said nothing, but by the way of advertisement, without reproaching of any one person, wherewith no good man hath cause to take any displeasure. Judge what men list, my thought shall be free" (p. 100). That is an odd final assertion. He says "I dare to speak the truth" right after admitting that his words apply to no one in particular. But it is this generalizing that allows Elyot and Henry both to get, to some extent, what they want out of *Pasquil.* For Elyot it is the veil that he casts over criticism. For Henry it is what makes that criticism too vague to be an open remonstrance on a specific issue. And because *Pasquil* abides by Henry's rules for debate and counsel on general questions, it is not only safe but valuable to the king's cause. It represents the king's willingness to hear and publish wisdom, and it provides a pattern for the discourse of others on the topic of kings, counselors, and commonwealths.

The same claim applies to Elyot's *Of the Knowledge which Maketh a Wise Man.* This is a dialogue between Plato and Aristippus of Cyrene (a teacher of rhetoric and courtier to Dionysius I), which teaches that a wise man is he who best knows himself. When the two speakers meet, Plato has just returned home after having been imprisoned and then sold into slavery for speaking too plainly to Dionysius.[31] By mistreating him in this manner, Plato concludes, Dionysius not only "put away" Plato, he put away himself (lost the opportunity to know himself, that is), because why else would he have summoned Plato in the first place, unless it was to help him discover the wisdom – the self-knowledge – that he lacked?[32]

---

[30] In the proem to *The Governor* Elyot makes the same protest, that he dispraises vice "without any other particular meaning to the reproach of any one person" (p. 6).

[31] Elyot may deliberately be recalling to readers' minds Hythlodaeus's reference to Plato's unhappy encounter with the Syracusan tyrant (see *CW*, vol. 4, p. 87).

[32] *Of the Knowledge which Maketh a Wise Man*, ed. Edwin J. Howard (Oxford, Ohio: Anchor Press, 1946), pp. 230–1.

Of the Knowledge which Maketh a Wise Man is generally considered Elyot's most forthright protest statement against Henry's mistreatment of Thomas More. The exception is Alistair Fox, who makes a good case that in *Knowledge* Elyot protests Henry's neglect of Elyot.[33] In any event, Elyot's criticism of Henry seems barely beneath the surface. Consider the following passage in which Plato condemns Dionysius's hypocritical encouragement of open debate and philosophy, which is surely a transparent allusion to Henry's own hypocritical self-representation as a philosopher-king:

> *Aristippus:* I do not a little marvel of this that thou tellest me, for when I went from King Dionysius, he mought not suffer that thou moughtest be one hour from him . . .
> *Plato:* Soon after that thou haddest obtained license of the king to go unto Athens, he became wonderful sturdy, in so much as no man mought blame any thing wherein he delighted, nor praise any thing which was contrary to that that he used. And that sober and gentle manner in hearing sundry opinions reasoned before him, whereto of a custom he was wont to provoke thee and me, was laid apart, and supposing that by hearing of sundry philosophers dispute and reason, he himself had attained to a more perfect knowledge than any other that spake unto him, began to have all other men in contempt. And as it were Jupiter, who (as Homer saith) with a wink made all heaven to shake, he would with a terrible countenance so visage them, whom he knew would speak their opinions freely, that they should dread to say anything, which they knew should be contrary to his appetite.
> (pp. 18–21)

Undoubtedly Elyot intended us to equate Dionysius with Henry in this passage, but at the same time we cannot but keep in mind that this equation occurs in a work framed by explicit praise for England's king. In his preface Elyot even praises Henry for valuing the open counsel his books provide. Henry VIII, says Elyot, is a true philosopher-king:

> Ne the sharp and quick sentences, or the round and plain examples set out in the verses of Claudian the poet in the second book [of *The Governor*], or in the chapters of Affability, Benevolence, Beneficence, and of the diversity of flatterers, and in divers other places, in any part offended his highness: but (as it was by credible persons reported unto me) his grace not only took it in the better part, but also with princely words full of majesty commended my diligence, simplicity and courage in that I spared none estate in the rebuking of vice: which words full of very nobility brought unto my remembrance the virtuous Emperor Antonine, called for his wisdom Antonine the philosopher. (pp. 6–8)[34]

---

[33] Fox and Guy, *Reassessing the Henrician Age*, pp. 63–73.
[34] Elyot also professes to admire Henry for recognizing the contribution *The*

In the last sentence Elyot is referring to Marcus Aurelius Antoninus, Roman Emperor from A.D. 161 to 180 and one of the model philosopher-rulers whose biographies appears in the *Historiae Augustae.* Elyot also mentions Antoninus in *The Governor*, where he observes that "the Emperor Antoninus was surnamed philosopher, for by his most noble example of living and industry incomparable he during all the time of his reign kept the public weal of the Romans in such a perfect state that by his acts he confirmed the saying of Plato, that blessed is that public weal wherein either philosophers do reign, or else kings be in philosophy studious" (p. 41).[35] As we see in the passage from *Knowledge*, Elyot means by his reference to Antoninus to confirm that kings have been philosophers, and that Henry is one now.

There is additional evidence of Henry's dedication to just rule in Elyot's report that the king commended his "courage" in "rebuking vice." But then we have to ask, exactly which vices did Elyot rebuke? Not any that were identified specifically as Henry's, but only vices in general in people in general. All the same, says Elyot, Henry is to be admired for "taking it in the better part." This curious balancing act continues as Elyot on the one hand praises Henry for his tolerance of "sharp" and "quick sentences" (by which we might think he means "biting criticism"), while on the other hand he declares, just as he had in *Pasquil the Plain*, that no one man is being singled out for censure:

> In like wise our most dear sovereign lord perfectly knew that no writer ought to be blamed, which writeth neither for hope of temporal reward, nor for any private disdain or malice, but only of fervent zeal toward good occupation and virtue. Perdie man is not so yet conformed in grace, that he can not do sin. And I suppose no prince thinketh himself to be exempt from mortality. And for as much as he shall have more occasions to fall, he ought to have the more friends or the more instruction to warn him. And as for my part I eftsoons do

Governor had made to the English language: "His highness benignly receiving my book, which I named *The Governor*, in the reading thereof soon perceived that I intended to augment our English tongue," says Elyot, and "His grace also perceived, that throughout the book there was no term new made by me of a Latin or French word, but it is there declared so plainly by one mean or other to a diligent reader that no sentence is thereby made dark or hard to be understand" (pp. 5–6).

[35] Translating "Sententia Platonis semper in ore illius fuit, florere civitates si aut philosophi imperarent aut imperantes philospharentur," from "Marcus Antoninus Philosophus Iulii Capitolini," in *Scriptores Historiae Augustae*, vol. 1, 26.13. Five Italian editions of this work, plus one prepared by Erasmus (Basel: Froben, 1518), were available by the 1530s (*Scriptores*, p. xxxvii). However, Henry H. S. Croft, in his edition of *The Governor*, points out Elyot's likely use of second-hand sources in references to Antoninus (*The Boke Named the Governour, Devised by Sir Thomas Elyot, Knight*, 2 vols. [London: Kegan Paul and Co., 1880], vol. 1, p. 46 n. a).

protest that in no book of my making I have intended to touch one man more than another. For there be Gnathos in Spain as well as in Greece, Pasquils in England as well as in Rome. Dionyses in Germany as well as in Sicily, Harpocrates in France as well as in Egypt, Aristippus in Scotland as well as in Cyrena; Platos be few, and them I doubt where to find. (p. 9)

So, says Elyot, *Knowledge*'s admonishments toward virtue are really offered for all who need them, wherever they may be – in Spain, Greece, Germany, or France – for indeed, those who can use wise counsel are everywhere. Fortunately for England (and Rome, interestingly, where the Pasquil tradition arose), it contains plain-speaking Pasquils. Platos, meanwhile, are hard to find (and now we are talking about Plato the wise philosopher, not the "vain dreamer"), although this book advertises that Elyot and Henry know where one Plato is. As the author of this dialogue Elyot speaks for and through Plato, as Plato did Socrates. He is England's modern-day Plato, and even if he feels "put away" in real life, officially he is not. His books are published by the printer to the king; he is participating in the queen's coronation; he is, on paper anyway, "one of the king's counsel."

Once we understand how Elyot's English works served the royal propaganda campaign in this manner, we might reconsider the publishing circumstances of those other tracts of moral and political philosophy that Berthelet printed in the same period. It is possible Henry did direct Berthelet to issue them, if Henry perceived that he had a stake in their reflection on him and his court. Given, that is, that one of the uses of the royal press was to represent Henry VIII as an enlightened king who valued and patronized humanists, Berthelet could well have been encouraged, even commissioned, to print the kinds of books that enlightened men read. Surveying his output during this period reveals a good many such books. Several are in dialogue form and in the *speculum principis* tradition, reinforcing the impression of a corps of Pasquils on hand to advise their king. Some of these are translations known or thought to be Elyot's, such as Lucian's *A Dialogue between Lucian and Diogenes* (1532; *STC* 16894), and Isocrates's *The Doctrinal of Princes* (1533; *STC* 14278). Other translations include *Precepts Teaching a Prince his Duty* by Agapetus (1529; *STC* 193); Erasmus's *De contemptu mundi* (1532–33; *STC* 10470.8, 10471); Ulrich von Hutten's *De morbo Gallico* (1529; *STC* 14024); and the *Economicus* by Xenophon (1532; *STC* 26069). The last is a dialogue between Socrates and his disciple Critobulus on the subject of managing one's estate, a work that Cicero famously claimed proves there is "nothing more befitting royalty than zeal in husbandry."[36]

---

[36] *De senectute* 59.

The royal press also printed Nicholas Udall's *Flowers for Latin Speaking selected out of Terence* (*STC* 23899), dated the same year Udall helped to design and perform the pageant series for Anne's coronation. Thomas Lupset, who in Starkey's *Dialogue* is Pole's companion in conversation, wrote books of his own in the 1530s and these were published by Berthelet. In addition to *A Treatise of Charity* (1533; *STC* 16939) and *A Fruitful Treatise Teaching the Way of Dying Well* (1534; *STC* 16934), there is Lupset's translation of *How a Man May Flee Vices* (1534; *STC* 14270), a treatise by St. Isidore that contains advice for princes as well as ordinary men. In a chapter titled "On Sovereignty," for instance, we discover admonishments like Elyot's for a ruler to observe decorum: "Both in punishing and cherishing, keep a mean" says Isidore. "Behold certainly, what is covenable for the time, where, when, how, and wherefore thou biddest any thing to be done" (sig. 15^r).

In short, the king's propaganda was in good company. Alongside *The New Additions to Doctor and Student*, *A Dialogue between a Soldier and a Clerk*, and *A Glass of the Truth*, there issued from the press of Thomas Berthelet this chorus of humanist books attesting to Henry's serious interest in the new learning, to his patronage of learned men, and ultimately, to the wisdom that would guide his steps in such uncertain times as these, when, as Elyot says in a letter to a friend, "we have hanging over us a great cloud,"[37] and people need to be reassured that their king is receiving counsel from the experts.

[37] To Sir John Hackett (April 6, 1533), in *The Letters of Sir Thomas Elyot*, ed. K. J. Wilson, *Studies in Philology* 73 (1976): no. 5.

4

Competition Between Printers and the Business of Representing the King

Whether Henry's subjects saw the words *Thomas Berthelet, printer to the king* on a royal proclamation or at the end of a dialogue by Thomas Elyot, I have argued, they would have understood that the text was doing official service: proclaiming new laws, stating the king's views, representing the king as he wanted others to see him. But however effective Berthelet's press was in communicating Henry's mind and philosopher-king image, the job of representing king and commonwealth was a more ambiguous and contested business than is revealed by an examination of the royal press's output alone. Berthelet was, in fact, vulnerable to competition, both in the usual sense of market competition and in the sense of speaking for the government. Indeed, the distinction between these two types of competition was not as clear as the king's printer would have liked. As this short chapter explains, the Rastells in particular were in a position to claim a share of Berthelet's special status.

The first point to be made is that the king's printer was in certain cases liable to interpret business competition as something more serious than just a challenge for market share. He was just as protective of his role as the official *representer* of the king and government. This first becomes evident in the case of Richard Pynson, Berthelet's predecessor who held the title *impressor regni* from 1508 until his death in 1530. Pynson printed new statutes and proclamations as they were issued by Parliament and the court, and he was also the primary publisher of court records and law texts, as well as re-editions of statutes from past years. Yet for the most part the royal printer's business went unprotected by the law, and a consequence was the room for a rivalry that arose in the mid-1520s between Pynson and Robert Redman, when Redman began reprinting Pynson's law books. One of Redman's piracies was an edition of the *Magna Carta* (1525; *STC* 9269) in which Redman states that his shop is at the sign of the George in St. Clement's Parish, just outside Temple Bar. Apparently he was occupying Pynson's old shop and using Pynson's old sign, even though Pynson himself was still using the sign of the George at his new location, also near Temple Bar.[1] In other words, Redman seemed to be advertising his shop in such a way as to invite confusion between his press and Pynson's.

We can presume, too, that about the same time as his publication of *Magna Carta* Redman must also have brought out an edition of Littleton's *Tenures* (though no copy has survived), because Pynson responded by printing another edition of his own in 1525 that included, at the end, a note to readers pointing out that his is printed "not only more correctly, but embellished with a finer type than that which slipped out of the hands of Robert Redman, or more rightly, Rudeman." "And yet," Pynson continues, "the buffoon has dared to promise by his own pains to imprint all the reverend and sacred laws of England skillfully and correctly. Whether this is truthful speaking or just hot air, you may perceive instantly by reading the *Littleton* printed with his brand of attention and diligence."[2]

Although Pynson was protective of his official business, he did not betray any indignation when other printers reissued other types of books that had originally appeared from his press. Whenever his competition published one of his school books, for instance, or an almanac, a work of literature or philosophy, or any other tract not of a legal nature, Pynson seems never to have bothered to respond with an edition of his own.[3] Yet Pynson was likely to reprint a law book even when he was not, so it appears, the original publisher, as was the case with a number of yearbooks published by Redman in 1527. Yearbooks consist of selected court cases from the rolls of Common Pleas (usually only of one term per edition, Easter or Michaelmas), and in the early part of the century these

---

[1] E. Gordon Duff, *Westminster and London Printers*, pp. 172–3, and *A Century of the English Book Trade* (London: Bibliographical Society, 1905), pp. 126 and 132. Duff's account of the Pynson-Redman rivalry remains accurate, even after the updating of the *STC*. Also on this subject see Johnston, "A Study of the Career of Richard Pynson," pp. 133–4 and 172–5.

[2] . . . mea non solum emendatior, verum etiam elegantioribus typis ornatior prodeat in lucem: quem elapsus est e manibus Rob. Redman, sed verius Rudeman . . . tamen ausus est scurra polliceri, sua cura reverendas ac sanctas leges Angliæ scite vereque: omnes imprimere. Utrum verba dare usus, an verax sit, tu Littiltono legendo sua cura ac diligentia excuso, illico videas (from Littleton's *Tenures*, *STC* 15722.5; my translation). Redman was neither intimidated by these insults nor cowed by Pynson's official status; he continued to publish law books and statutes formerly printed by the royal press.

[3] Examples of unanswered publications of works printed beforehand by Pynson include the *Tractatus secundarum* (*STC* 15574), *Accidentia* (*STC* 23148.8) and *Vocabula* (*STC* 23182.5) by John Stanbridge, printed by Peter Treveris around 1527; John Skot's edition of the morality play *Everyman* in 1528 (*STC* 10606); and in the same year *The Destruction of Jerusalem by Vaspazyan and Tytus* (*STC* 14519), the *Shepherd's Calendar* (*STC* 22411), and Thomas a Kempis's *Imitation of Christ, Books 1–3* (*STC* 23960), all printed by Wynkyn de Worde.

were almost exclusively printed by Pynson. From the start of his career Redman reprinted Pynson's yearbooks, but of the eight that he published in 1527 only one is known to have appeared in a previous Pynson edition.[4] It did not matter. Pynson obviously felt that Redman was trespassing on his territory again, because within a year he printed his own editions of six out of the eight.[5]

The sense of proprietorship that this reveals on Pynson's part, not only of the particular legal works that he had printed but of the whole category of law books, again indicates that he was motivated by something other than just resentment of his competition's piracy. His "note to the reader" quoted above suggests that he believed the function of the king's printer was to represent *properly* – not only accurately but ornately – the king, the government, and the "reverend and sacred laws" of the realm.[6] This role of representing the king and his government with editions befitting their majesty will become all the more critical when the next royal printer finds himself responsible for publishing an increasing amount of royal propaganda. Neither printer nor king will want that majesty diluted by the crudely done reprints of rude men.

When Pynson died in 1530, his title was granted to Thomas Berthelet, a former apprentice in Pynson's shop. Berthelet also inherited the rivalry with Redman, which lasted to the end of the 1530s. Each time Redman brought out an edition of Fitzherbert's *Diversite de courtz*, Littleton's *Tenures*, or the *Natura Brevium*, Berthelet published an edition of his own within a year, and for the whole decade the two printers took turns bringing out the same issues of statutes and yearbooks. But now that Berthelet had the additional responsibility of being the king's printer at this time of the most extensive royal propaganda campaign that had been seen in England, so there was an even greater imperative to assert, and to reassert, his press as the one representer of Henry's government, image, and interests.

One of the ways this prestige and privilege was signified was in the superior quality of his publications. Berthelet did not inherit Pynson's old types (Redman did), but purchased new sets, and in the words of

---

[4] 3 Henry VI, *STC* 9632; first printed by Pynson in 1510, *STC* 9631.

[5] These are: 13 Edward IV (Redman, *STC* 9840; Pynson, *STC* 9840.3), 14 Edward IV (Redman, *STC* 9846; Pynson, *STC* 9845), 16 Edward IV (Redman, *STC* 9856a; Pynson, *STC* 9856), 18 Edward IV (Redman, *STC* 9866; Pynson, *STC* 9865), 19 Edward IV (Redman, *STC* 9872; Pynson, *STC* 9871), and 14 Henry VIII (Redman, *STC* 9944.5; Pynson, *STC* 9945). The dating of these editions is discussed in the headnote to Yearbooks in *STC*, vol. 1, pp. 434–5.

[6] Neville describes the increasingly improved design of Pynson's editions of the statutes over the years, which imply, as she argues, his efforts to reflect the authority of king and parliament in the appearance of his books ("Richard Pynson, King's Printer," pp. 39–64).

E. Gordon Duff his "printing and beautiful type were alone in England able to rival the work of the foreign printers."[7] In addition, Berthelet seems to have had his books bound only in materials that were attractive and expensive, such as calf and deerskin rather than the usual sheep or goat.[8]

Superior workmanship and materials would have gone far to distinguish Berthelet's books as products befitting the prestige of the royal press. He was also not slow to exercise the authority of his special status against competitors through legal action. In 1533 he successfully petitioned to have one of his publication privileges enforced, when Thomas Cromwell fined Robert Redman 500 marks for pirating *The Division between the Spirituality and Temporality* by Christopher St. German.[9]

II

A different sort of problem was the overtly political competition that Berthelet met with from the Rastell family, which acquired with Thomas More's promotion a legitimate role in representing government policy, since every one of More's works from 1529 to 1533 was printed by John or William Rastell. To some degree, it must be expected, More's authority as lord chancellor would have extended beyond his own

---

[7] *Westminster and London Printers*, p. 181.

[8] In *Thomas Berthelet: Royal Printer and Bookbinder to Henry VIII, King of England* (Chicago: The Caxton Club, 1901), Cyril Davenport described numerous fine bindings of books that had been in the royal library – most in expensive grades of leather, some in satin or velvet – which he took to be Berthelet's on the grounds that Berthelet was printer to the king. But it has since been shown that Berthelet did not do his own binding, and the court patronized at least five different binderies during the reign of Henry VIII. See Howard M. Nixon, "Early English Gold-Tooled Bookbindings," in *Studi di Bibliografia e di Storia in onore de Tammaro De Marinis*, 4 vols., ed. Romeo De Maio (Verona: G. Mardersteig, 1964), vol. 3, pp. 283–308; Nixon and Mirjam M. Foot, *The History of Decorated Bookbinding in England* (Oxford: Clarendon Press, 1992), pp. 25–42; Geoffrey D. Hobson, *Bindings in Cambridge Libraries* (Cambridge: Cambridge University Press, 1929). All that is important to my analysis, however, is that Berthelet's books were offered, either for presentation to the king or for sale, in bindings that were almost certainly of better quality than other London printers'.

[9] This is the first recorded penalty for the infringement of the royal privilege in England (see Duff, *Westminster and London Printers*, p. 175), and it is calendared in *LP*, vol. 6, no. 480 ("Cromwell's Bonds"): "Of Rob. Redman in 500 m. that he shall not sell the book called *The Division of the Spirituality and the Temporality*, nor any other book privileged by the king." In 1531 Redman had reprinted with impunity the first and second dialogues of *Doctor and Student* (*STC* 21567 and 21568), but these were not originally printed by Berthelet.

writings to the presses from whence they came, and so to other books printed by the two Rastells. Until Henry's assertion of personal authority became explicit in the 1534 supremacy legislation, as we have seen, his public image allowed such a space for multiple voices. So long as Henry posed as an impartial seeker after truth and justice, and so long as the king's discursive rules were followed, More and the Rastells could offer their counsel and attempt to make matters "as little bad as possible," as Morus says and as the remaining two chapters of this study document. Yet before we examine their attempts at "prudential counsel," we need to see how the Rastell name, through what probably amounts to a fluke of timing, became associated with the government on even stronger grounds than its connection to More's.

Through the first quarter of the sixteenth century John Rastell was, foremost, a prominent London lawyer. His printing business, which began as early as about 1510, was devoted mainly to the publication of law books, but probably because he produced only a few per year until 1525 Pynson never regarded him as a serious business rival. In the late 1520s Rastell started to branch out. Besides his abridgments of statutes and other legal texts he printed Latin grammars, poetry, and Thomas More's *A Dialogue concerning Heresies* (*STC* 18084). Then, in early 1530, Rastell was apparently commissioned to print the statutes passed by Parliament in its first session (from November 3 to December 17, 1529).[10] It seems Berthelet's appointment as printer to the king, on February 15,[11] came too late for this job. Once that appointment was made Berthelet certainly went straight to work, because during the remainder of 1530 he printed the original Latin version of the *Determinations of the Most Famous Universities*, as well as three editions of a royal proclamation against vagabonds (*STC* 7774–6). But Berthelet's monopoly was compromised. Rastell's name, too, was now associated with government business.

John Rastell reinforced this association by continuing through 1530 to print abridgments of statutes and legal works, such as the *Expositiones terminorum legum anglorum* (*STC* 20703.3). After his religious conversion the elder Rastell switched political allegiances, even offering his services to Thomas Cromwell, but his son William carried on the press battle in support of the Catholic cause. William had started his printing career in 1529 with two editions of Thomas More's *Supplication of Souls* (*STC* 18092 and 18093), and he printed the second edition of *A Dialogue concerning Heresies* in 1530 (*STC* 18085). The quasi-official status of John Rastell's name would have passed to his son William not just because of name association, therefore, but because William Rastell

[10] 21 Henry VIII (*STC* 9363.6 and 9363.8), in *Statutes*.
[11] Duff, *Westminster and London Printers*, p. 178.

Chapter Four

published Lord Chancellor More's works during 1531 and 1532, alongside law books and editions of the statutes.[12]

Thus we may observe that just at the moment Henry was initiating his
propaganda campaign against Rome and for his divorce, a rivalry
emerged between Thomas Berthelet, printer to the king, and the Rastells,
printers to the king's orator. Both parties were associated with legal and
government publications, and both had a legitimate claim to represent
the interests of king and commonwealth. On the strength of this position,
so I will argue in the next two chapters, first John and then William
Rastell attempted to make the logic of Henry's philosopher-king image
work for them. Their books encouraged readers to expect that a true
philosopher-king would take a very different course of action than the
one Henry was pursuing behind the scenes. The Rastells pressured the
king, in this way, to change his policies before his own propaganda had
prepared the way to take them public. Or to repeat my characterization
of More's strategy in his polemical writings, the Rastells printed works
that they hoped Henry would read, and would sense that his subjects
interpreted as the best advice he had available to him. In this event,
claiming as he was to be soliciting and following good counsel, Henry
might just feel constrained to heed it.

[12] The Rastells were also the first printers of law books in English; on this subject
see Howard Jay Graham, "The Rastells and the Printed English Law Book of the
Renaissance," *Law Library Journal* 47 (1954): pp. 6–25; Graham and J. W. Heckel,
"The Book that 'Made' the Common Law: The First Printing of Fitzherbert's *La
graunde abridgement*, 1514–1516," *Law Library Journal* 51 (1958): pp. 100–16; and
Graham, "'Our Tong Maternall Maruellously Amendyd and Augmentyd': The First
Englishing and Printing of the Medieval Statutes at Large, 1530–1533," *UCLA Law
Review* 13 (1965–66): pp. 58–98.

5

Keeping the Faith and Keeping the Peace:
Henry VIII's Divorce and his
Obligations as a Christian Prince

Like More's *Dialogue concerning Heresies*, the two prose dialogues
that are the subject of this chapter most obviously are religious polemics
in support of the orthodox faith. My interest here, however, is to
elucidate a neglected dimension of these tracts, to show not only how
they contrived to persuade their readers, Henry VIII included, to remain
firm in their Catholic beliefs and loyal to the Church, but how they
pressured Henry to reverse his government's anti-clerical policies and to
give up his own quarrel with Rome over the divorce. The first is *A New
Book of Purgatory*, a treatise defending Church doctrine that was written
and published by John Rastell the year before his religious conversion.[1]
The second is William Barlow's *A Dialogue describing the Original
Ground of these Lutheran Factions*, printed by William Rastell in 1531.

John Rastell's *A Book of Purgatory* elicited criticism from Tyndale and
even a point-for-point rebuttal from John Frith, but on the whole
contemporaries considered the tract misguided if not damnable, while
scholars today tend to view it with bemusement. The dialogue's inter-
locutors are a Turk and an Almain (a German) who use only "natural
reason and good philosophy" – meaning the process of logical argu-
mentation – to prove through disputation the existence of God, the
immortality of the soul, and the existence of purgatory.[2] "With reasons

---

[1] The classic account of Rastell's career is A. W. Reed, *Early Tudor Drama:
Medwall, the Rastells, Heywood, and the More Circle* (London: Methuen, 1926),
pp. 1–28. A recent study is Albert J. Geritz and Amos Lee Laine, *John Rastell*,
Twayne's English Authors Series (Boston: Twayne Publishers, 1983).
[2] Rastell printed three editions that year (*STC* 20719, 20719.5, and 20720).
References are to Albert Geritz's modern critical edition: The Pastyme of People
and A New Boke of Purgatory *by J. Rastell with a facsimile of* The Pastyme: *A
Critical Edition*, The Renaissance Imagination, vol. 14 (New York: Garland, 1985).
On the contemporary pamphlet war over the doctrine of purgatory into which
Rastell's dialogue entered, see the introduction to More's *Supplication of Souls* in
CW, vol. 7, pp. lxv–cxvii; Clebsch, *England's Earliest Protestants*, pp. 88–94; and
Birch, *Early Reformation English Polemics*, pp. 63–8.

and arguments made *pro et contra*, and on both parts answered, replied, and objected," we are promised, "the truth of every proposition shall sooner and better be known" (p. 410). This statement gives a fairly accurate indication of the sort of scholastic language and argumentative process, complete with appeals to the authority of Aristotle (*ipse dixit*), by which John Rastell ventures his dialectical proof of purgatory. It also gives a fair idea why readers tend to find *A Book of Purgatory* somewhat tedious. For the same reason that Cardinal Morton is reluctant to hear his lawyer guest refute one by one Hythlodaeus's criticisms of the English penal system, one must have patience and stamina to read Rastell's dialogue to its end.

Yet the feature that most undermines *A Book of Purgatory*'s persuasiveness is the two speakers' agreement not to appeal to their respective holy scriptures, the Bible and the Koran. In one sense this ground rule is only logical, for neither one could ever grant the self-evident truth of the other's authoritative text. But as a result Rastell must pay scant attention to the theological issues relevant to the controversy, most significantly the doctrine of justification by faith alone, which, because it concerns the fundamental question of where souls go and why, was strenuously debated by More and Tyndale in their dispute over purgatory.[3] And remembering that this polemic is aimed at religious reformers, whose challenges to orthodoxy were based in large part on the notion of *sola scriptura*, we are right to wonder how Rastell thought he would ever be taken seriously. John Frith did publish a rebuttal within a year, it is true, but before he answers Rastell's particular arguments he admits he is baffled that anyone, "now since we have the light declared unto us," would yet "proceed in blind ignorance and not confer and examine these juggling mists [i.e., complicated religious questions] with the light of God's word." Rastell's *Book of Purgatory*, says Frith, "lieth already in the dirt."[4] A modern appraisal by E. J. Devereux is only somewhat less dismissive: "*A New Book of Purgatory* is a remarkable book because of its peculiar emphasis on 'natural reason and good philosophy' and its

---

[3] See especially More's *A Dialogue concerning Heresies* (*CW*, vol. 6, pp. 377–402), and Tyndale's *The Parable of the Wicked Mammon* (*Doctrinal Treatises*, pp. 29–126). Edward Surtz, S. J., treats this controversy in his study of Bishop Fisher's career, *The Works and Days of John Fisher: An Introduction to the Position of St. John Fisher (1469–1535), Bishop of Rochester, in the English Renaissance and the Reformation* (Cambridge, Mass.: Harvard University Press, 1967), pp. 194–213.

[4] John Frith, *A Disputation of Purgatory* (1530; *STC* 11386.5), in *The Work of John Frith*, ed. N. T. Wright, The Courtenay Library of Reformation Classics, vol. 7 (Appleford, Berkshire: Sutton Courtenay Press, 1978), pp. 86 and 96. Frith's *Disputation* contains three parts: the first refutes Rastell's *Book of Purgatory*, the second More's *Supplication of Souls* (1529), the third Fisher's *Assertionis Lutheranae confutatio* (1523).

frequently inexplicable ideas about religions other than Christian, not to mention its misunderstanding of the nature of reformed theology."[5]

I would not wish to defend Rastell's logic or theology, and neither would I downplay Rastell's intention to establish the existence of purgatory in the minds of his readers. But I do propose to show that he was up to more than his modern readers recognize or than his contemporaries, if they did, betray in their rebuttals. We have seen already how Thomas More, in his apparently state-sponsored invectives against heresy and heretics, tried to influence Henry's actions by stressing the king's image as a defender of the faith, thereby counseling him, indirectly, to protect the Church in England rather than continue his attacks on it. I believe John Rastell was imitating his brother-in-law's strategy in *A Book of Purgatory*. That is, Rastell, too, was using More's "indirect approach" to counsel Henry to stand firm in his religious and political allegiance to Rome. As the previous chapter demonstrates, Rastell was in a position to make this attempt because of the quasi-official status of his press. Readers would have noted that *A Book of Purgatory* came from the same house that had published not only the lord chancellor's works but Parliament's latest set of statutes. Rastell was in the business of representing the government, and appropriately this dialogue presents itself as just that sort of dialectical discovery of truth – with "reasons and arguments made *pro et contra*" – supposedly being conducted at court. Rastell's book thus presumes to offer a sample of the wise debate that Henry claims to be soliciting and heeding. If Henry could be led to believe that his subjects interpret it as such, consequently he should feel obligated to act in accordance with that wisdom, to strive harder, that is, to be more like the Christian philosopher-king that his propaganda says he is.

As for Rastell's decision to write on the topic of purgatory, he was probably inspired by Thomas More's *Supplication of Souls*, which as we recall counters Fish's *Supplication for the Beggars* and is written in the voice of a soul lamenting that his still-living friends and family, who no longer believe in purgatory, are depriving him of the prayers that would speed him into heaven. It was probably More, too, who gave Rastell the idea of staging a *sine scriptura* debate between a Christian and a Turk.[6] At one point in *A Dialogue concerning Heresies*, More posits a hypothetical debate between himself and a pagan on the subject of miracles:

> Now if I were in this matter to dispute with a paynim, that would make the question between their miracles and ours, albeit I should have

---

[5] "John Rastell's Press in the English Reformation," *Moreana* 49 (1976): p. 35.
[6] Cf. Geritz's discussion of More's influence on Rastell's *A New Book of Purgatory*, in The Pastyme of People *and* A New Boke of Purgatory, pp. 35–6.

a clear matter in the end, yet must it needs be a long matter and much entricked [ere] it should come at the end. And whole books would it hold, both the confuting of theirs, and unto them the assertation of our own, specially for that they receive not our scripture, and between them and us nothing common to ground upon but reason.[7]

We can well imagine how Rastell might have read this as something like a challenge, and yet, he seems to have reversed More's meaning. In *his* hypothetical debate it is Gyngemyn the Turk who convinces Comyngo the Christian of purgatory's existence. The irony of this arrangement is not that a Turk believes in purgatory, however, for that assertion is found also in More's *Supplication of Souls*.[8] As Albert Geritz points out, the irony is rather that "a non-Christian . . . seems to understand the divine truth better than a so-called follower of Christ."[9] Gyngemyn, a "paynim," has to go to the trouble to persuade a Christian of something Christians should already believe.

At one level, then, we are seeing an early version of that popular topos in religious satire, the pagan who turns out to be more virtuous than the nominal Christian, which is a story devised to evoke shame (as do More's suffering souls in purgatory) in the nominal Christian reader.[10] It is towards this end that Rastell has Gyngemyn decline to embrace Comyngo's Christianity, even though Gyngemyn concedes Christ's teachings should be followed:

> *Comyngo:* Now I thank thee with all mine heart, and I shall love thee while I live, and would to God that thou were of our holy sect and Christian belief, and so I will counsel thee and require thee to be.

---

[7] *CW*, vol. 6, p. 102.

[8] More claims in *Supplication of Souls* that "not only among Christian people and Jews, of whom the tone hath, the tother hath had, the perceiving and light of faith, but also among the very miscreant and idolaters, Turks, saracens, and paynims, except only such as have so far fallen from the nature of man into a brutish beastly persuasion as to believe that soul and body die both at once: else hath always the remnant commonly thought and believed, that after the body is dead and deceased, the souls of such as were neither deadly damned wretches for ever, nor on the tother side, so good but that their offenses done in this world hath deserved more punishment than they had suffered and sustained there, were punished and purged by pain after the death ere ever they were admitted unto their wealth and rest" (*CW*, vol. 7, pp. 172–3). Gyngemyn's claim is only a bit more sweeping than this, when he says that the existence of purgatory is a doctrine embraced by "all people in the world of what country so ever" (p. 408).

[9] The Pastyme of People *and* A New Boke of Purgatory, p. 36.

[10] The exemplary life of the Utopians serves a similar function, as the marginal glosses to *Utopia* remind us: e.g., "How Much Wiser the Utopians Are than the Common Run of Christians!" (*Quanto plus sapiunt Vtopiani, quam Christianorum uulgus*) (*CW*, vol. 4, pp. 156–7).

> *Gyngemyn:* I thank you for your good counsel, but as to that request I will not show thee my mind at this time, because I have now no time nor space, how be it I know well that Christ of whom ye Christian men believe, was a very holy man and a good and hath taught you so many good lessons of virtue, that there can be no better, which I will advise thee to observe and keep. And another time peradventure I shall meet with thee again, and show to thee my mind, but now I pray thee pardon me for I must needs depart from thee: therefore yet again I say now farewell. (p. 487)

Gyngemyn reveres Christ but declines to commit himself to the Christian faith, though not illogically. It is reasonable that he should excuse himself from Comyngo's invitation to convert, for Comyngo is the representative of a "holy sect and Christian belief" that he fails to grasp. What sort of people can these Christians be, Gyngemyn must wonder, when they need a paynim to remind them to "observe and keep" Christ's "many good lessons of virtue"?

The irony of the Gyngemyn character is working at still other levels. For one thing, he turns out to be a very westernized infidel, which may go far toward explaining why *A Book of Purgatory*'s readers have not known what to make of him. The fact that he is a spokesman for Church doctrine and yet (being an infidel) clearly an ambiguous hero has been cited as evidence of the *Utopia*'s influence on Rastell's dialogue. But this influence has not been made clear. Gyngemyn has been called "a combination of the rational Utopians and the great Arabs who had influenced scholastic logic, while Comyngo is a partly Lutheran Hythlodaeus,"[11] but these analogies do not hold up. Comyngo is the somewhat dim questioner in the dialogue, not the teacher, and he voices the reformers' objections to purgatory.[12] He is literally the *morus*, or fool, and Gyngemyn is the wise outsider, the philosopher who does the teaching. Gyngemyn's tone and role much more closely resemble Hythlodaeus's.

But though Gyngemyn is "rational" like Hythlodaeus or the Utopians, he is certainly not like "the great Arabs who had influenced scholastic logic." In fact Rastell writes as though he were unaware of the long scholastic tradition in the Near East, by deliberately stressing its absence. At the end of the second dialogue, after Gyngemyn's logical demonstration of the soul's immortality, Comyngo says to Gyngemyn, "I marvel much where thou hast learned and had all this cunning knowledge of all

---

[11] Devereux, "Rastell's Press," p. 37.

[12] In this respect, Comyngo is similar to the "messenger" in More's *Dialogue concerning Heresies*, who reports to More the "perilous and pernicious opinions" he has picked up in the company of entrenched heretics.

these things . . . for I hear say that in thy country there is but a little learning or study of philosophy [and] that the common people there shall not be suffered to study any manner of subtle science or art, nor that ye have no manner of places ordained by your heads and governors," meaning "divers places of studies and universities," such as in Christendom, where "the people [may] resort together for the learning thereof." Gyngemyn does not contradict Comyngo. "I assure thee," he replies, "the learning that I have gotten, hath not been all in mine own country, for in my youth I had good parents and friends" who "put me forth to the intent I should learn some other strange languages, by whose help and means I was in divers cities and universities in Christendom long time abiding and sojourning where I learned part of my philosophy and of other science" (pp. 454–5).

Gyngemyn, then, is adept at logical disputation because he has trained at the same universities that Comyngo and his fellow Christians attend. But as the very progress of this dialogue is meant to demonstrate, that schooling is going to waste on Christians like Comyngo. Heresies are blinding nominal believers to the light of reason and God's truth, or, put another way, a declaration such as Comyngo's that one will use "good philosophy and right reasoning" to arrive at truth is only paying lip service to the process if the methods are not properly learned and applied, as Gyngemyn has accomplished to Comyngo's amazement.

II

One might begin to perceive, just on this evidence, that these two messages – that a man should be a true Christian if he is going to call himself a Christian, and a true philosopher if he is going to call himself a philosopher – are aimed, though by necessity more vaguely, at Henry VIII as well as at the members of the new sects and their polemicists. The likelihood of such an intention on Rastell's part appears stronger when we see that, in the manner of Thomas More, Rastell has placed his fictional discourse within a portion of real context – indeed, for many in Europe within the context of its biggest crisis – with the result that readers are encouraged to measure the actions of the king not merely against the just-stated moral lesson, but against their consequences within that portion of the contemporary religious and political scene. By "that portion of the scene" I am referring to the Turkish invasions of Europe, which Rastell invokes right at the start of the dialogue in order to introduce purgatory as the topic of Comyngo and Gyngemyn's discourse:

In the beginning of their said communication Comyngo the Almain asked of Gyngemyn the Turk, what tidings or news were in his country, which Gyngemyn showed him of the great wars which the great Turk had lately had in divers places, as well of the great siege of Rhodes, as of the great battles, which he had lately had in Hungary. But yet the said Gyngemyn was not so glad to tell the tidings and news in and about his country, as was desirous to know of some strange news in other places in Christendom. And oft times required this Comyngo to show him some new tidings of his country. To the which Comyngo the Almain answered and showed him that there was a new variance in Christendom and a schism begun of late among the people there, concerning their faith and belief, and said that there was a new opinion sprung among the people, that there is no purgatory, nor that the soul of man after it is separate from the body, shall never be purged nor purified of no sin that remaineth therein, but that it shall immediately after it is separate from the body, go to heaven to eternal joy and salvation, or else to hell to eternal pain and damnation.

(pp. 407–8)

While Gyngemyn's countrymen are invading the West, Comyngo's are preoccupied with divisive heresies, including this opinion that purgatory does not really exist. We might be tempted to say about this passage that Rastell is only providing a case in point for a theme found often in More's polemics, that heresy makes nations weak. To deny the existence of purgatory is to "increase vice and sin and also utterly destroy the common wealth and quiet living of the people" says Gyngemyn (p. 485), which in turn makes commonwealths more vulnerable to attack. But Rastell's readers would not have taken Gyngemyn's reminder of Turkish victories in Hungary and Rhodes so blandly as the phrase "a case in point" is likely to imply. The "great Turk" had been invading the West without serious resistance off and on throughout the decade of the 1520s, and by 1530 Europeans justly feared that their lands were on the verge of being overrun by the Turkish army.

Just as John Rastell indicates by coupling the Turkish peril with religious schism, furthermore, orthodox Catholics conceived of these as parallel problems. They were both a threat to the "Common Corps of Christendom,"[13] and reflected the failure of Christian kings to protect

---

[13] The concept of a *Corpus Christianum*, by which orthodox Catholics such as More not only measured the threat of Turks, heretics, and the rise of the powerful nation-state, but conducted their own lives, has been the subject of numerous studies of the history and thought of the period. See Franklin le van Baumer's early articles: "The Church of England and the Common Corps of Christendom," *The Journal of Modern History* 16 (1944): pp. 1–21; "England, the Turk, and the Common Corps of Christendom," *The American Historical Review* 50 (1944): pp. 26–48; and "The Conception of Christendom in Renaissance England," *Journal of the History of Ideas* 6 (1945): pp. 131–56. Studies that treat the power of this concept in More's life and

their subjects in a united defense against heretics and infidels, the common foes of the faith. Gyngemyn's and Comyngo's exchange at the start of *A Book of Purgatory* therefore seems deliberately couched to invoke people's fears for the Church's and their personal safety, not to mention their resentment at the tardiness of Europe's rulers to take action. John Rastell would counsel Henry VIII to be different, reminding him of his special obligation as defender of the faith.

That specific relevance to Henry becomes clear after reviewing the circumstances of the Turkish invasions during the 1520s and examining the impact of Henry's great matter on England's response to this crisis. The place to begin is with the Turkish victories that Gyngemyn himself mentions: the capture of Belgrade and the island of Rhodes by the Ottoman Sultan, Suleiman the Magnificent, in 1521 and 1522. With these defeats Europe's conception of war against the Turk was transformed from a religious crusade for the recovery of Constantinople and Jerusalem to the preservation of western civilization. As Robert Adams tells it, the pope considered the loss of Rhodes that of "the 'key of Christendom,'" and, Adams continues,

> thereafter the invasion of a helpless Italy seemed merely a matter of time and the Turk's convenience. Promptly the papal legate to England pointed out to Henry and Wolsey that . . . "the rest of Christendom and England itself are in the greatest danger." He spoke but common sense.[14]

As it happened, the next few years (from 1523 to 1525) were inconvenient for Suleiman to invade Hungary, because he had to put down a rebellion by the former Mamluks in Egypt. But in 1526 the Sultan attacked the West again, and at the battle of Mohács the Turks overwhelmed the greatly outnumbered Hungarian army and killed Hungary's King Louis II while he was making his retreat. England and Europe soon received graphic reports of the disaster, of the Turk's looting and spoiling of the region, and of the prisoners they took with them as they withdrew for the winter.[15] With Louis II dead without an heir most of the Hungarian

---

writings are Stephen Greenblatt, "At the Table of the Great: More's Self-Fashioning and Self-Cancellation," in *Renaissance Self-Fashioning*, chapter 1; and Brian Gogan, *The Common Corps of Christendom: Ecclesiological Themes in the Writings of Sir Thomas More*, Studies in the History of Christian Thought, ed. Heiko A. Oberman, vol. 26 (Leiden: E. J. Brill, 1982).

[14] Robert P. Adams, *The Better Part of Valor: More, Erasmus, Colet, and Vives on Humanism, War, and Peace, 1496–1535* (Seattle: University of Washington Press, 1962), p. 273. For an account of the Turkish invasions, and of European reactions and inaction, see Dorothy M. Vaughan, *Europe and the Turk: A Pattern of Alliances, 1350–1700* (Liverpool: Liverpool University Press, 1954), pp. 104–86.

[15] See *LP*, vol. 4, pt. 2, nos. 2496, 2588, 2589, for example. After each summer

nobility chose John Zápolya, Voivode of Transylvania, as their new king, and in September, 1526, Zápolya agreed to recognize Ottoman suzerainty and to pay Suleiman yearly tribute. But many of the nobles rejected Zápolya and instead backed the brother of Charles V, Ferdinand of Austria, who had married Louis II's sister and so claimed a hereditary right to the throne. Civil war over the dispute broke out in 1527 when Ferdinand invaded Hungary and besieged the capital at Buda. Zápolya fled to Poland and from there arranged a deal with Suleiman to be restored. The Turks invaded Hungary again in 1529, put Ferdinand's forces to flight, but then kept on going, until by the end of the summer they were at Vienna. Suleiman's army laid siege to the city for three weeks and then withdrew, returning home unpursued. He left Zápolya king of his vassal state and Europe humiliated at its impotence.

In the minds of those Europeans who had been calling for unified preparation and resistance against the Turkish threat, the war between Ferdinand and Zápolya, and Zápolya's scandalous alliance with Christendom's common enemy, gave further proof to their princes' self-absorbed ambition for private gain and glory despite the threat of universal destruction. Zápolya and Ferdinand were not, after all, the only Christian kings preoccupied with fighting between themselves in the face of imminent attack from the Turks. Charles V and Francis I had been at war with one another since 1515 over territories in France and Italy. In the same years that Suleiman took Belgrade and Rhodes, Francis layed siege to Navarre (in 1521) and Charles captured Milan (1522). In 1524 Francis even encouraged Suleiman to attack Charles in the East, because he hoped to have fewer of Charles's forces to contend with in the West. Meanwhile Charles entered into a treaty with the Duke of Bourbon, who had defected from Francis, and with Henry VIII. The three agreed to conquer France and divide it equally, even as the inevitable Turkish invasion loomed nearer.

The wars between the princes continued into the second half of the decade. The Duke of Bourbon attacked Francis in 1525, but at Marseilles he was forced to retreat into Italy, where Francis followed him. During the French siege of Milan Francis was captured, and while he lay prisoner in a castle in Madrid alliances shifted. Francis's mother, Louise of Savoy, convinced England to join with France in a mutual defensive and offensive pact. In early 1526 Francis was freed after agreeing to give up to Charles all the territory he had won plus two million gold *écus* and his two sons as hostages. Yet once he was safely

campaign Suleiman withdrew to Istanbul to replenish his armies (see Stanford Shaw, *History of the Ottoman Empire and Modern Turkey, Volume I: Empire of the Gazis: The Rise and Decline of the Ottoman Empire, 1280–1808* [Cambridge: Cambridge University Press, 1976], p. 88).

home Francis prepared to retrieve his losses. He joined Henry and Pope Clement VII in the League of Cognac, which included the city-states of Milan, Genoa, Florence and Venice. In retaliation, Charles sent against them an imperial army, comprised partly (but most notoriously) of German mercenaries, and in May of 1527 this army descended on Rome and sacked the city. The reports of its destruction of churches, libraries, and art treasures, and of the torture and slaughter of thousands of the city's citizens, shocked Europeans to much the same degree, and in much the same language, as the previous reports of Turkish atrocities in Eastern Europe.[16]

Historians concur Suleiman never planned to occupy Europe. His intention was to ensure Hungary would remain a vassal buffer state between himself and the Habsburg Empire, and, while he was at it, to give the West a demonstration of his military invincibility. But at the time Europeans feared worse. Suleiman's march to Vienna and sub-sequent invasions of Hungary kept many people, even in far-off England, steeling themselves for the sack of Christendom. And as they watched their own kings persist in short-sighted wars for one another's territories the menace of the great Turk grew more ominous. Their anxieties were voiced in the countless pamphlets, many written by the most prominent humanists of the day, protesting the failure of Europe's princes to unite against the Turks.[17]

Publicly, of course, the princes declared their desire for universal peace, and they took turns calling on one another to put aside their differences and to join in an alliance against the Turks. They were urged, too, by the three popes of the decade, Leo X (to 1521), Adrian VI (1522–23), and Clement VII. Henry VIII received numerous requests from Rome to provide aid and even take the lead against Suleiman. A month

---

[16] Wolsey confirms for Henry the news of Rome's fate in *LP*, vol. 4, pt. 2, no. 3147. More describes the event with horror, referring to it as an example of the German Lutherans' malice in *A Dialogue concerning Heresies*, *CW*, vol. 6, pp. 370–2 (on his sources see appendix C, pp. 773–7). See André Chastel, *The Sack of Rome, 1527*, trans. Beth Archer, The A. W. Mellon Lectures in the Fine Arts, Bollingen Series, vol. 35, no. 26 (Princeton: Princeton University Press, 1983), p. 92 (figs. 55a and 55b), for a photograph and tracing of the graffito "V.K. Imp. Martinus Lutherus," scratched onto Raphael's *Triumph of the Holy Sacrament* during the imperial army's occupation of Rome.

[17] See the last chapters of Robert Adams's *The Better Part of Valor*, which document how Erasmus and Vives, especially, responded to the crisis with impas-sioned pleas for a general peace between the princes and a united defense against Christendom's common enemy. For discussions of the image of Turks in early modern Europe, see C. A. Patrides, "'The Bloody and Cruell Turke': the Back-ground of a Renaissance Commonplace," *Studies in the Renaissance* 10 (1963): pp. 126–35; and Robert Schwoebel, *The Shadow of the Crescent: The Renaissance Image of the Turk, 1453–1517* (New York: St. Martin's Press, 1967).

after the battle of Mohács in 1526, for instance, Cardinal Campeggio sent a letter to Henry telling him that "All Christendom is in danger from the Turk, now that Hungary has been defeated and slain," and that all Clement's hope is in the English king, the defender of the faith.[18] Over the next two years Ferdinand, Charles V, King Sigismund of Poland, and Zápolya added their frantic pleas to the pope's.[19] But Henry prudently put them off. He would not rush into battle against the infidel while other Christian princes battled against each other, he insisted. As a message from Henry to Clement after the defeat at Mohács professed,

> [The king] greatly regrets the evils of the times. Could not help shedding tears on reading the pope's breve of 22 September. Wept over the loss of Hungary, which is owing to the dissensions of Christendom. When other princes have agreed, he will not be behind-hand in joining the crusade.[20]

And while Vienna was under siege Henry told Chapuys, "I think it is a great shame that whilst the Turk is in Austria, the patrimony of the emperor, he should not rescue it, but make war upon Christians."[21] "As to himself," he said on another occasion,

> he was a small king in the corner [of Europe], far away from the rest of the Christian princes, and almost powerless to help in such enterprises, for even if he did assist on this occasion to the utmost of his ability, the emperor would find that without concurrence of some other Christian princes his succor would be of little or no avail. Besides, on no account would he be the first in an undertaking of this sort; though when other princes joined he would certainly not be the last.[22]

Then, beginning in 1528, we see a sudden change in the substance of Henry's refusals. His replies were motivated by something other than wise discretion or (in accordance to his 1524 agreement with Charles) a plan to obtain territories from a defeated France. Charles and Clement were asking for Henry's help, and he wanted something from them, a divorce from Charles's aunt, Catherine of Aragon. From this point on Henry exploited the Turkish threat in order to obtain his divorce, linking promises to cooperate in a united war against the Turk with

---

[18] *LP*, vol. 4, pt. 2, no. 2515; also see no. 2466, and Pocock, *Records of the Reformation*, vol. 2, no. 260.

[19] See *LP*, vol. 4, pt. 2, nos. 3096, 3102, 3231; vol. 4, pt. 3, nos. 5474, 5981, 6056; vol. 5, no. 374.

[20] *LP*, vol. 4, pt. 2, no. 2584. Cf. the "king's answer" to the same effect in Hall, p. 720.

[21] *LP*, vol. 4, pt. 3, no. 6026.

[22] *SP, Spanish*, vol. 4, pt. 1, no. 224; a similar declaration is made in no. 248.

their cooperation in his great matter. In his instructions for the ambassadors to Charles V (dated November, 1529), for example, Henry says the emperor should be told not to "make difficulty to persuade the queen" regarding her course of action during the divorce proceedings, given Charles's need for Henry's "amity in consequence of the state of affairs in Italy and Turkey."[23] We hear of the strategy again in a 1530 report to Charles from the Imperial ambassador to Rome, Micer Miguel Mai, stating that "the king of England in answer to the emperor's request has answered that he will gladly help in this enterprise of the Turk if the divorce trial is remitted to England, or at least to France."[24]

III

We can only assume the More circle observed the incongruity between the king's self-representation and his diplomatic maneuvers. Henry was claiming to be above the self-interest that prevented amity between the other princes, but like them he was placing his private aims before the safety of Christendom, because he was making his divorce a prerequisite to his involvement in Europe's defense. Henry's great matter, as much as any other dispute in Europe, was contributing to the dissension among princes that prevented their formation of a united front against the Turks. Gyngemyn's reference to the Turkish invasions thus reflects as badly on Henry as it does on other princes, so long as he continues to be distracted from his obligations as a Christian prince. And in 1530 Henry was very concerned not to have anything "reflect badly" on him, as the initiation of his propaganda campaign in that year attests. *A Book of Purgatory*, for this reason, challenges Henry to put his duty as defender of the faith before his divorce.

That duty, to be sure, did not have to be defined so specifically as an expedition led by Henry against the Turk. As Thomas More saw it, Henry could accomplish an equivalent defense of Christendom by supporting rather than attacking the Church, and rejecting rather than flirting with the reformist ideas circulating within his court. Rastell implies the same thesis, for by pairing a Turk and a Lutheran, as *A Book of Purgatory* does, he exploits the conceptual parallel between these two threats and thereby makes Henry – so long as he is opposing rather

[23] *LP*, vol. 4, pt. 3, no. 6069. Also see *LP*, vol. 5, nos. 274 and 792, in which Henry promises to lead a crusade against the Turks once his cause has been returned to England.
[24] *SP, Spanish*, vol. 4, pt. 1, no. 537.

than defending the Church – appear as the moral equivalent of the great Turk.

This parallel between Turks and Lutherans was not only figurative. First of all, Lutherans were then associated with what is sometimes called a doctrine of non-resistance against the Turk. In 1518 Martin Luther declared that "plagues, wars, insurrections, earthquakes, fires, murders, thefts, as well as the Turks, Tartars, and other infidels" were all but "the lash and rod of God," so that the "big wheels" in the Church who "now dream of nothing else than war against the Turk," want "to fight, not against iniquities, but against the lash of iniquity, and thus they would oppose God who says that through that lash he himself punishes us for our iniquities because we do not punish ourselves for them."[25] This statement was specifically condemned in the papal bull of 1520 excommunicating Luther, and in 1529 Luther published two treatises defending his original point that a Christian prince's duty is to protect his subjects, not to wipe out false religions.[26] But by then the change in circumstances worked against him. The Turks were no longer a past and distant enemy symbolizing the scourge of God but a present one on Europe's doorstep. William Tyndale was also adamant about the distinction between non-resistance and making sure one's own house is in order rather than making war on non-Christians.[27] For polemical purposes, however, More and others in the Catholic press campaign fed the misconception that the reformers favored quick surrender to the invading Turks.[28]

It was all the harder for the Lutherans to shake off this stigma because of the notoriety of their insistence, beginning in 1526, to link their military aid to Ferdinand with religious concessions. Stephen A. Fischer-Galati concludes his study of the development and success of this strategy over four decades of the sixteenth-century with the observation that "almost all major concessions wrested from the Habsburgs since 1526 were connected with Ottoman activities in Eastern and

---

[25] *Explanations of the Ninety-five Theses*, in *Luther's Works*, ed. Jaroslav Pelikan and Helmut T. Lehmann, 55 vols. (Philadelphia: Muhlenberg Press and Fortress Press, 1955–86), vol. 31, pp. 91–2. The original Latin text is in *D. Martin Luthers Werke*, 64 vols. (Weimar: H. Bohlau, 1883–), vol. 1, p. 535.

[26] These treatises are *Vom Kriege wider den Turken* and *Heerpredigt wider den Turken*, in *Luthers Werke*, vol. 30, pt. 2.

[27] *The Obedience of a Christian Man*, in *Doctrinal Treatises*, p. 204.

[28] In *A Dialogue concerning Heresies*, for example, More refutes what he calls the Protestant position that "Christ so far abhorred all such violence that he would not any of his flock should fight in any wise, neither in the defense of themself or any other, not so much as in the defense of Christ himself, for which he blamed Saint Peter, but that we should all live after him in sufferance and patience, so farforth that . . . we should not fight in defense of ourself against the Turks and infidels" (*CW*, vol. 6, p. 406).

Western Europe, and the all-important Lutheran campaign for legal recognition in Germany exploited the insoluble Habsburg-Ottoman conflict over Hungary."[29] Ferdinand could not count on assistance from Charles once the League of Cognac had formed against Spain, and so he turned to Germany for troops. On August 27, 1526, the German estates agreed to send 24,000 men, but only after the Habsburgs promised that at least for the foreseeable future they would tolerate Lutheranism by allowing German leaders to "live, act and rule their subjects in such wise as each one thought right before God and his Imperial Majesty."[30] But the commitment to send troops came too late for Hungary's aid. The defeat at Móhacs occurred just four days later. To all appearances, the Lutherans got what they wanted at other Christians' expense.

To be fair, in the 1520s both Catholics and Lutherans in Germany opposed providing Ferdinand with the massive assistance that he was demanding. This opposition increased when Zápolya and Ferdinand redefined the "Hungarian Crisis" as a dispute over which of them would be king, rather than as an immediate need to fortify Europe's eastern outpost against future Turkish attacks. It is also true that on several occasions the Protestants and Catholics compromised for the sake of mutual defense.[31] But just as the participation of Spaniards at the sack of Rome was forgotten in accounts of the carnage appearing in anti-Lutheran propaganda, the Lutherans were perceived to be the ones dragging their feet and undermining what efforts were being made toward Christendom's defense. Accordingly, reformers and Turks become analogous to one another, as readers of Thomas More's polemics see when the threat of Protestantism is repeatedly measured against that of the Turks. In *A Dialogue concerning Heresies*, for instance, More compares the relative barbarity of the Turks and Lutherans in his description of the sack of Rome, where, he says, it was the false Christian who proved "more hot and more busy than the great Turk" in the destruction of Europe. Indeed, the Lutherans have surpassed the Turks in savagery, says More, and are now instructing the devil:

> Thus devised these cursed wretches so many divers fashions of exquisite cruelties, that I own they have taught the devil new torments

---

[29] *Ottoman Imperialism and German Protestantism, 1521–1555*, Harvard Historical Monographs, vol. 43 (Cambridge, Mass.: Harvard University Press, 1959), p. 116; also see Kenneth Setton, "Lutheranism and the Turkish Peril," *Balkan Studies* 3 (1962): pp. 133–68.

[30] Fischer-Galati, *Ottoman Imperialism*, p. 26.

[31] As in the case of the Augsburg Confession of 1530; see Fischer-Galati, *Ottoman Imperialism*, pp. 43 and 46.

in hell, that he never knew before, and will not fail to prove himself a
good scholar, and surely render them his lesson when they come there,
where it is to be feared that many of them be by this. For soon after
that they had in Rome exercised a while this fierce and cruel tyranny,
and entered in to the holy churches, spoiled the holy relics, cast out the
blessed sacrament, pulled the chalice from the alter at mass, slain
priests in the church, left no kind of cruelty or spite undone, but from
hour to hour imbruing their hands in blood, and that in such wise as
any Turk or saracen would have pitied or abhorred, our lord sent soon
after such a pestilence among them that he left not of them the third
part alive.[32]

As anti-Protestant propaganda this is directed at a public seduced by
Tyndale and his false religion. But as counsel for Henry VIII, it is a
confirmation that just as the duty of a Christian prince is to defend his
realm against the cruel Turk, so Henry is obliged to defend from a crueler
enemy not only the churches and everything in them denounced by the
Protestants – the holy relics, the sacrament, the priests themselves – but
just as vigorously, the Church and all its sacred laws.

When *A Book of Purgatory* appeared in the same year as the second
edition of More's *Dialogue*, it naturally took its place with it in this
context of public alarm and controversy in which Turks, Protestants
and princes were interconnected politically and imaginatively. This is

---

[32] *CW*, vol. 6, p. 37. Thomas More's most elaborate equation between Turks and
Lutherans occurs in *A Dialogue of Comfort against Tribulation*, which he wrote from
1534 to 1535 while a prisoner in the Tower (first published by Richard Tottel in
1553). The fictional setting of this dialogue is in Hungary, the year before the 1529
Turkish invasion. A young Hungarian man, Antony, visits his uncle Vincent and
shares his fear of the suffering that he, his family, and his fellow countrymen are
facing at the hands of the Turks, from enslavement and religious persecution to
torture and death. The work is primarily in the *Consolatio* tradition, written as a
means for More to secure personal comfort at the prospect of his own torture and
death, but like *A Dialogue concerning Heresies* it was also meant to warn readers
against enemies within the fold:
> *Vincent:* [The great Turk] sends his people hither and his false faith therewith,
> so that such as are here and remain still, shall either both lose all and be lost to,
> or forced to forsake the faith of our savior Christ, and fall to the false sect of
> Mahomet. And yet which we more fear than all the remnant, no small part of
> our own folk that dwell even here about us, are (as we hear) fallen to him, or all
> ready confederate with him, which if it so be, shall happily keep this quarter
> from the Turk's incursion, but then shall they that turn to his law, leave all
> their neighbors nothing, but shall have our goods given them, and our bodies
> both, but if we turn as they do, and forsake our savior too, and then (for there
> is no born Turk so cruel to Christian folk, as is the false Christian that falleth
> from the faith) we shall stand in peril if we persevere in the truth, to be more
> hardly handled and die more cruel death by our own countrymen at home,
> than if we were taken hence and carried into Turkey. (*CW*, vol. 12, pp. 6–7)

why Gyngemyn's opening reference to the Turkish capture of Rhodes, Hungary, and "divers" other places, in the same paragraph as Comyngo's statement that Christendom is in a state of religious schism, suggests that Rastell is using that indirect approach modeled by the polemics of his brother-in-law to influence the king. Because *A Book of Purgatory* was written and printed by John Rastell, a public figure with court connections, like More's *Dialogue concerning Heresies* it represents the government in two ways. It speaks, first, in a spokesman's voice, confirming the king's role as defender of the faith through its confirmation of an orthodox theological doctrine. Second, it portrays an "inquiry into a general question," that form of fruitful debate and wise counsel that Berthelet's press is modeling and that oppositional discourse must adopt in order to be tolerated. As such, it is advice that Rastell would hope his readers, Henry among them, might interpret as the wisest counsel available on the connected matters that it concerns. After the model of More's polemics, we can also observe, Rastell's counsel is based on the principle of decorum. The setting of Gyngemyn and Comyngo's debate is the looming threat to Christendom posed by infidels and reformers now in this particular "time and place." That obligates a Christian king to take certain actions, at the very least to discontinue certain others, if he means to remain in the eyes of his subjects a defender of the faith, and of the faithful in his realm.

IV

Not long after the third edition of *A Book of Purgatory* appeared, John Rastell's son William published *A Dialogue describing the Original Ground of these Lutheran Factions* by William Barlow (1531; *STC* 1461). The circumstances of Barlow's authorship of this religiously orthodox tract are obscure and troublesome, for in the years to follow he distinguished himself as one of the most zealous reformers in the reigns of Henry VIII and Edward VI. He was appointed to several bishoprics after 1535, in Scotland, Wales and England, and effected sweeping and radical reforms in his sees until under Mary's reign he was arrested. Released after recanting his Protestantism, Barlow fled into exile, then returned to England with the accession of Elizabeth I to become Bishop of Chichester. This is all well-documented, but three questions concerning Barlow's early career have divided scholars: Was William Barlow the same man as Jerome Barlow, author of several Protestant tracts including, with William Roy, the anti-Wolsey satire *Read Me and Be Not Wroth*? If Jerome and William Barlow were not the same men, was *A Dialogue on the Lutheran Factions* actually written by

Jerome rather than William? And, if William Barlow is the book's author and not Jerome, did he write it because he truly had recanted his Protestant beliefs for a while, or because he perceived it would gain him the favor of More or the king?

So contested are the answers to these questions that our modern critical edition of the dialogue contains two different essays on the identity and motives of William Barlow – one by the dialogue's editor, Andrew M. McLean, and an "alternative view" written by the series editor, G. E. Duffield.[33] McLean agrees with those who say that Jerome and William were not the same men, and in his view William Barlow wrote *A Dialogue on the Lutheran Factions* to curry favor with Chancellor More at a time that he was disillusioned with Protestantism and intent on giving his career a boost.[34] Duffield, in contrast, thinks it more likely that Jerome was William Barlow's pen-name, and that he only wrote *A Dialogue on the Lutheran Factions* because he had no choice, being arrested on his return to England and then coerced, by Thomas More, to write this "conversion story" as the price for his liberty.[35]

The evidence for both versions is sparse, as McLean and Duffield acknowledge, but whatever the truth about Jerome and William Barlow, and whether or not Barlow's dialogue was written for the sake of self-promotion or "under duress," the matter of importance to this study is that *A Dialogue on the Lutheran Factions* appeared as the work of William Barlow from William Rastell's press in 1531, and as an unmistakable contribution to the More and Rastell press campaign against heresy. It is true that George Joye, among others, assumed More himself had written the book.[36] But More responded by praising

---

[33] Andrew M. McLean, ed., *The Work of William Barlowe, including Bishop Barlowe's Dialogue On the Lutheran Factions*, The Courtenay Library of Reformation Classics, ed. G. E. Duffield, no. 15 (Appleford, Berkshire: Sutton Courtenay Press, 1981). All citations from *A Dialogue on the Lutheran Factions* are to this edition.

[34] Ibid., pp. 156–77. McLean cites for support Anthea Hume, "A Study of the Writings of the English Protestant Exiles, 1525–35" (Ph.D. dissertation, University of London, 1961); and E. Gordon Rupp, *Studies in the Making of the English Protestant Tradition, Mainly in the Reign of Henry VIII* (Cambridge: Cambridge University Press, 1947), pp. 61–72, although Rupp concludes that Jerome Barlow wrote *A Dialogue on the Lutheran Factions*, not William.

[35] *A Dialogue on the Lutheran Factions*, pp. 178–95. Cf. A. Koszul, "Was Bishop William Barlow Friar Jerome Barlow?" *Review of English Studies* 4 (1928): pp. 25–34.

[36] Duffield thinks it quite possible that George Joye (who makes the accusation in *Supper of the Lord*) is correct in believing More wrote the work; see *A Dialogue on the Lutheran Factions*, pp. 189–91, 195 nn. 21 and 22. The Yale editors of More's *Confutation* (*CW*, vol. 8) note numerous parallels between it and Barlow's dialogue, but do not address the issue of Joye's accusation.

it as William Barlow's in his next work, *The Confutation of Tyndale's Answer.*[37] Officially, *A Dialogue on the Lutheran Factions* was not More's, but it had his explicit sanction.

To all appearances, it also had the blessing of the king. According to the colophon, it was printed by William Rastell "with the privilege of our sovereign lord king Henry the VIII, that no man print the same again within the space of seven year next ensuing." Rarely was a printer's rights to a work so clearly specified among publications of the early 1530s. But in 1531 Henry was intent to demonstrate his orthodoxy – his "defense of the faith," as we have seen – so in one sense Barlow's book was just the kind of polemic against Lutheran heresies that Henry would wish to link with his name, and which we might expect him to endorse by means of the royal privilege.

However, to say *A Dialogue on the Lutheran Factions* is a book against Lutheran heresies is not strictly accurate, for it attacks several sects besides Luther's, and hardly argues at all against any of their theological positions. Instead, Barlow stresses the social unrest that has followed the spread of the different sects on the Continent. That is a strategem familiar to us in Thomas More's works, but past studies of Barlow's book have seemed to take it for granted that his alarming descriptions were intended to discourage only Henry's subjects from lapsing in their faith. As the following analysis of Barlow's dialogue should make clear, his concern with the keeping of good order in the realm, and with the qualities of good governance that will preserve that order, make *A Dialogue on the Lutheran Factions* equally a work of counsel for the king.

V

Like the preface of John Rastell's *A Book of Purgatory*, Barlow's preface assures readers that his dialogue will proceed according to good reason and without prejudice. "I have perceived the fashion, manner, and order of all states" in which the different sects thrive, Barlow says, so now he intends "plainly to show the verity" of those sects, "without hatred of them or favor of any other persons" (p. 35). Past reports have mistakenly portrayed the Lutherans, Zwinglians and Anabaptists as commencing a new golden age of Christian living in Europe, but those reports, he explains, have come from men "having little learning, less

---

[37] Published by William Rastell in 1532. More states that readers may learn of the "unmannerly manners and lawless laws" of the "sundry manner sects" in Saxony and Almain in "the book of M. William Barlow, that long was conversant in the country" (*CW*, vol. 8, pt. 2, p. 663).

discretion, small devotion, and scant a courtesy of wisdom" (p. 36). In contrast, this book promises to show that the "new prophets" are "destitute of reason, void of good arguments, and without any sense of truth" (p. 30); their "enormities," furthermore, will seem "half impossible to be used among reasonable people endued with any wisdom or learning" (p. 36).

Barlow touches not at all on the sects' "arguments" or "sense of truth" underlying their doctrine, as I noted, but rather devotes his energy to the "enormities." In the preface he emphasizes one in particular – that Luther and the other reformers "worry men with words of convicious maledictions and seditious slanders," so that their followers are "not afraid to despise their sovereigns without regard of their power, condemning all authority contrary to the doctrine of St. Peter" (p. 30). In a book that comes from the quasi-official press of William Rastell and with royal privilege, this warning against sedition has behind it the specter and authority of Henry VIII. But it is also a warning *for* Henry VIII, who behind the scenes had been urging reformation legislation through Parliament, trying to recruit reformers to his propaganda campaign and tolerating their pamphlets at court, and sending hints to Rome that he was growing increasingly attracted to Lutheran ideas the longer his divorce was delayed. After the model of More and Rastell, one of Barlow's aims in *A Dialogue on the Lutheran Factions* is to advise the king against such risky games.

In fact, the warning of sedition and social unrest is the most prominent theme of Barlow's dialogue. Right from its opening, when Nicholas welcomes William home "from parts off beyond the sea," and exclaims that "we have sore longed for your safe return, hoping to hear some news from our evangelic brethren of Germany and in what manner the gospel doth prosper there and go forward" (p. 43), William only has news of the social discord wrought by the new religion.[38] He reports that Luther has made "princes and temporal governors in contempt of their subjects" (p. 49), and that his followers "took such a stomach" that they "arose up with open sedition in divers parts of Germany above the number of an hundred thousand persons, in such a furious fashion, that every man almost stood in fear of his life" (p. 50). Returning to the subject of this "unquietness" in Germany later in the dialogue, William tells Nicholas (very likely referring to the title page of Ulrich von Hutten's *Gesprächbüchlin* [1521]), that it was with "heavenly wisdom" that Luther had been "portrayed with a book in his hand, and by him Hutten his protector in complete harness holding a drawn sword, with certain texts underneath

---

[38] The interlocutor "William" is of course so named to represent William Barlow, but for the sake of clarity I will keep a distinction between William, one of the speakers in the dialogue, and Barlow, the dialogue's author.

provoking sedition" (p. 75).[39] What begins as rebellion against the Church, an "intolerable variance between secular people and the clergy" (p. 55), Nicholas learns, leads inevitably to rebellion against the state.

With a growing number of the reformers' "defamous libels and slanderous writings everywhere disperpled abroad,"[40] Barlow continues, the sects have multiplied, so that "whereas was but one faction before, only of the Lutherans," there has since sprung up the "Oecolampadians or Zwinglians," who "are as one with the Lutherans in railing against the clergy, and in condemning the authority of the church"; while the Zwinglians themselves have "issued also the third faction named Anabaptists," who alone contain "above forty sects of divers heresies and sundry opinions" (pp. 55–6). William goes on to identify some of these opinions in the course of his conversation with Nicholas, but it remains clear that religious differences between the myriad sects are not the most serious concern, either for Barlow or for Christian kings. It is rather the threat to social order, and to the safety of those who keep order. After all, says William, the Anabaptists do even "affirm that it is impossible for kings, princes, justices, and other governors of the commonweal to be Christian men" (p. 57).

To underscore the danger of tolerating the spread of religious sects William cites the example of the "earl" of East Friesland (Count Edzard I),[41] who "first receiving Martin Luther's doctrine, and afterward Oecolampadius's opinion, suffered his people to read all manner of books, and to be of whatsoever sect or opinion they would without any restraint." Soon neighbor was fighting neighbor, "one condemning another with deadly hatred"; "then was it a wonder to see what murmuration, grudge, and rumor of sedition was among the people, not without likelihood of falling together by the ears, and insurrection against their prince, had not he sought provident means to pacify them" (pp. 63–5). Certainly, passages like this are meant to disabuse Nicholas and readers like him who entertain idyllic fantasies about the evangelic lives of their "brethren" abroad. But they also impress upon the king his need to curb these factions that breed sedition. For one of the lessons of East Friesland, says William, is that "the bridle of sensuality is set at large" not only by "the sturdy frowardness of seditious subjects," but also "by the effeminate tenderness of princes" who so "negligently"

---

[39] See McLean's n. 52 in *A Dialogue on the Lutheran Factions*, pp. 147–8, and the facsimile of Hutten's book on p. 42.

[40] McLean bases his text on the second edition of *A Dialogue on the Lutheran Factions* (1553); I follow the 1531 edition for *defamous* in this sentence. McLean glosses *disperpled* as "dispersed," but see *dispeple* in the *OED*: "to publish."

[41] See *A Dialogue on the Lutheran Factions*, p. 142 n. 40.

disregard danger "that afterward their fearful rigor is scant able to redress it" (p. 66).

And what precisely *is* the "original ground of these Lutheran factions," as the full title of Barlow's dialogue promises to reveal? Not clerical abuses, says William, nor even "malice," as More charges, but rather, a wayward king who seeks to justify his and his people's fall from the Church and God:

> Was not the original ground and cause of M. Luther's heresy to do pleasure to his prince, and to purchase favor among the people? . . . When princes and commonalties are first bent upon affection against the Church, or conceive any strange purpose contrary to scripture, then immediately they find at hand such learned persons that can endeavor their brains in approving their lusts, making that which is unlawful lawful, which say that good is evil and evil is good, calling light darkness and darkness light. (pp. 95–6)

Barlow is shaving very close to Henry VIII here – few readers could have missed this. A staple of the royal propaganda was that Henry had surrounded himself with "learned persons," so our drawing the analogy that Barlow invites points to those persons who were then "endeavoring their brains" to justify the royal divorce, and to limit the Church's jurisdiction in England. Here they are cast by Barlow as dangerous sophists leading their king to chaos. Furthermore, for Barlow to say that these "learned persons" are laboring to approve their princes' "lusts" is an especially damning and daring suggestion, because we know how intent Henry was to discourage this interpretation of his motives.

Yet, all the while we must also keep in mind that *A Dialogue on the Lutheran Factions* is feigning not to be an attack on Henry at all. It is a book from the Rastell press, graced with the royal privilege, offering counsel from a true "learned person" for the benefit of king and country. So while on the one hand Barlow's descriptions of rebellion and his definition of the "original ground" of the Lutherans challenges Henry to abandon his "strange purpose," and to show no "effeminate tenderness" to anyone "bent upon affection against the Church," on the other hand it is implied that Henry all along has made it his mission to defend the faith and his faithful subjects from the threats that William reports to Nicholas.

On two occasions in the dialogue Barlow affirms the latter message by defining Henry's position on Henry's behalf. The first instance repeats a tactic of Thomas More's. At one point William refers to "the outrageous treatise" that Luther "wrote against the king's highness both in Latin and Dutch, so shameless and seditiously" (pp. 49–50). The content of Luther's tract is not discussed, for as in More the reference alone does the work, reminding us of the king's press battle with Luther in the previous decade. Henry's subjects are assured, and Henry advised, that the court will remain loyal to the Catholic Church and continue to put down heresy and sedition.

The second example is much subtler, and quite clever in the way it adapts one of Tyndale's tactics to a different end. In *The Practice of Prelates*, we saw, Tyndale claimed that Cardinal Wolsey had planted the idea of divorce in the king's head, and this put Henry in the difficult position of appearing still to be guided by the advice of his former and unpopular lord chancellor. Barlow, interestingly, has William recall the late cardinal when he is describing the seizure of Church property by the Lutheran estates in Germany. There were some there, William reports, who "gave counsel that it should be necessary to deprive the clergy of their goods, and to distribute their possessions, lands, and rents among lay people," and also "to throw down all monasteries and churches, making coin of crosses, chalices and other sacred jewels" (p. 89). This plan won the assent of "certain princes" who foolishly hoped "a golden world or a time of felicity" would result from the sudden abundance of wealth. But as William relates, instead "the goods are wasted, and no man can tell how" (p. 90). Referring perhaps to those in the Commons protesting against tithes and other Church exactions, William then observes that many now in England "wish full heartily after such a ruffling change." But he does not, as we should expect, repeat at this point his claim that such thievery is the work of heretics. Instead, William closes the matter by saying, "I let pass my Lord Cardinal's act in pulling down and suppressing of religious places, our Lord assoil his soul. I will wrestle with no souls: he knoweth by this time whether he did well or evil" (p. 91).

As McLean points out, William refers here to Wolsey's dissolution of Bromehill and other religious houses in order to found colleges at Oxford and Ipswich.[42] Since Barlow was Prior of Bromehill at the time, we might not be surprised that he finds an opportunity to voice the resentment he still harbors. But that is not all he is doing. By linking the dissolution of monasteries with Cardinal Wolsey just after condemning the Lutherans for their seizure of Church goods, Barlow in a sense confirms for Henry that he can keep a middle ground between two unflattering images. Henry does not want to look the "effeminate" king who winks at his subjects' heresy and sedition; and neither does he want to appear the pawn of the Church, as the polemics by Tyndale and other reformers had characterized him when Cardinal Wolsey was lord chancellor. As king of England and defender of the faith Henry must stamp out sedition and heresy, but in doing so, Barlow indicates, he need not be concerned that

---

[42] *A Dialogue on the Lutheran Factions*, p. 91 n. 4.

he will appear to have subjugated himself to the pope. For as Barlow reminds him, Henry has demonstrated that he has the power and the will to correct abuses such as Wolsey's when he sees them in the English clergy.

The conclusion to *A Dialogue of the Lutheran Factions* adds urgency to Barlow's challenge for Henry to fulfill the duties of his title and public image, for despite William's description of social upheaval in Europe Nicholas is not dissuaded from his beliefs. The last topic of discussion is whether the Bible ought to be made available in English, and Nicholas insists that it should. William echoes Thomas More's arguments against this plan, conceding that in principle an English Bible is a good idea, but then he says that "for the time that now is, the people being disposed as they now be," it is not worth the risk of planting "such fruit as we find grown thereof in Almain." Nicholas replies: "Well, I shall bethink me till we meet again, and then will I be so bold also to take Tyndale's part in defense of his translation and other books which he hath put forth in English" (p. 123). Amicably enough William and Nicholas then bid each other farewell. Their continued disagreement, however, does not just leave the door open for a sequel, and in terms of its larger message to the king and his subjects the specific issue of whether the Bible should be made available in translation is not as important as the fact of disagreement.

William's main point throughout the dialogue, we must keep in mind, is that views such as Nicholas's ultimately lead to violence. Their friendly parting and promise to meet again can only augur good, therefore, if we are optimistic that through dialogue Nicholas will be won round to the Catholic faith and the wisdom of the government's prohibition against Tyndale's books. At some point, William's lessons argue, continued dialogue – especially of the "disinterested," philosophical kind – would be too much "tenderness" on the part of the king. Barlow thereby encourages his readers to expect that Henry will not tolerate for long those of his subjects who are resistant to reason. He will use his power as king to protect the beliefs and legislative powers of the Church. This would, of course, require Henry to desist in his confrontation with Rome over the divorce. A long shot to be sure. But among the More circle it was nevertheless a goal that building such expectations in Henry's subjects would translate into pressure on Henry's actions.

6

Re-Staging Henry VIII:
Skelton's *Magnificence* and
Heywood's *The Play of the Weather*
in 1530 and 1533

In the history of English literature the Rastells are remembered primarily for their contributions to drama. John Rastell, in addition to hosting dramatic performances in his home and occasionally producing pageants at court,[1] wrote and printed *The Play of the Four Elements*, and was the publisher of *Gentleness and Nobility*, *Calisto and Melibea*, *Love and Riches*, and John Skelton's *Magnificence*.[2] His son William Rastell printed the anonymous play *Pater, Filius, et Uxor*, or *The Prodigal Son*, Henry Medwall's *Goodly Interlude of Nature*, and several of John Heywood's plays, including *The Play of the Weather*.[3]

In *Plays of Persuasion: Drama and Politics at the Court of Henry VIII*, Greg Walker argues persuasively that Skelton wrote *Magnificence* in 1519 or early 1520, and that Heywood wrote *The Play of the Weather* in 1529, although as I shall discuss below, a later date for *Weather* has been suggested by Richard Axton and Peter Happé in their critical edition of Heywood's plays. Walker explicates the likely

---

[1] The fullest discussion of Rastell's involvement in court revels and pageants is in Anglo, *Spectacle, Pageantry, and Early Tudor Policy*, pp. 164–7 and 188–97. See, too, Richard Axton's introduction to *Three Rastell Plays: Four Elements, Calisto and Melebea, Gentleness and Nobility*, Tudor Interludes (Cambridge: D. S. Brewer, 1979); Reed, *Early Tudor Drama*, pp. 17–20; and Pearl Hogrefe, *The Sir Thomas More Circle: A Program of Ideas and their Impact on Secular Drama* (Urbana: University of Illinois Press, 1959), pp. 254–6, in which Rastell's home entertainments are described.

[2] *Magnificence* was printed by Rastell partly in Treveris's type (see the headnote to its entry in *STC* [22607]).

[3] *STC* 13305. The others are *Johan Johan, Tib, and Sir Johan* (*STC* 13298), *The Pardoner and the Friar* (*STC* 13299), *The Play of Love* (*STC* 13303), and probably *The Play of the Four Ps*, although no copy is extant. The earliest known edition of the *Four Ps* was printed about 1544 by William Middleton, the same year that he published an edition of *The Play of the Weather* (*STC* 13305.5). On the likelihood of a first edition of *The Four Ps* by William Rastell see *The Pardoner and the Friar, 1533; The Four Ps, ?1544*, ed. G. R. Proudfoot, Malone Society Reprints (Oxford: Oxford University Press, 1984), p. iii; and *The Plays of John Heywood*, ed. Richard Axton and Peter Happé (Cambridge: D. S. Brewer, 1991), p. 42.

political meanings of these two works according to his view of their composition and performance contexts, and he provides compelling accounts of their apparently original, intended implications. In this chapter, therefore, I refer frequently to Walker's analyses of *Magnificence* and *The Play of the Weather*, but do so in order to present what I see were changes in the plays' intended messages. For here I am less concerned with the first, acted performances and meanings of these plays, which is Walker's concern, than I am with the meanings they would have acquired when the Rastells printed them in 1530 and 1533.[4] Moreover, I propose that John and William Rastell were in large part motivated to print *Magnificence* and *A Play of the Weather* because they saw that these plays could do new work in a new age. Between the times that Walker argues these plays were written and the times they were printed obvious and important changes had occurred in their "political context," so that they could not mean what they once did. Thus, the Rastells were not only printing plays that they liked and thought would sell, they were printing plays alongside other works – Thomas More's polemics and the dialogues discussed in the preceding chapter – that they hoped would influence the king. The most obvious indication of this design is the circumstance that both *Magnificence* and *A Play of the Weather* stage a false philosopher-king, a counter-representation of the idealized image Henry was supplying of himself in his propaganda. In this way the Rastells called public attention to the distance (and, by implication, urged Henry to close the gap) between the actual and the ideal.

II

Skelton's *Magnificence* is a morality play about a king by that name, first duped by Folly and other vices into casting away Measure and Felicity but afterwards saved from Poverty, Despair and Mischief by Good Hope, Perseverance, and Redress. The consensus among critics before Greg Walker's study was that Skelton wrote *Magnificence* sometime in 1515–1516, and that it was the first of Skelton's satires against Wolsey, in the vein of *Colin Clout*, *Why Come Ye Not to Court?* and *Speak, Parrot*.[5] Walker shows instead that the play comments on an

---

[4] Again, as I explain in the second half of this chapter, it may prove that my analysis of *The Play of the Weather* will not so much explicate a "new printed meaning" of this play than support Axton and Happé's suggested later composition date of 1533.

[5] See H. L. R. Edwards, *Skelton: The Life and Times of an Early Tudor Poet* (London: Jonathan Cape, 1949), pp. 168–81; Ian A. Gordon, *John Skelton: Poet*

event now usually referred to as "the expulsion of the minions," which occurred in 1519.[6] In 1518 Henry had placed several of his young favorites in a new post within the royal household, "the gentleman of the privy chamber" (modeled on its French counterpart, *gentilhomme de la chambre*, at the court of Francis I).[7] Included among these suddenly-elevated gentlemen were Nicholas Carew, Francis Bryan, Edward Neville, Arthur Pole, Henry Norris, and William Coffin. Their primary official employment, other than attending Henry, was to serve as emissaries to France. But as Walker recounts, "in May 1519, within nine months of their promotion, four of them, Neville, Carew, Bryan and Coffin, in company with a number of other courtiers, Sir Henry Guildford, his half-brother Sir Edward, Sir John Peachy and Francis Pointz, were dismissed from the court and sent to posts elsewhere in

Laureate (Melbourne: Melbourne University Press, 1943), p. 137; A. R. Heiserman, *Skelton and Satire* (Chicago: Chicago University Press, 1961), pp. 69–73; Arthur F. Kinney, *John Skelton: Priest as Poet* (Chapel Hill: University of North Carolina Press, 1987), pp. 192–3; Maurice Pollet, *John Skelton: Poet of Tudor England*, trans. John Warrington (London: Dent and Sons, 1971), pp. 80–4. These essentially follow the argument in R. L. Ramsay's introduction to *Magnyfycence*, Early English Text Society, Extra Series, vol. 97 (London: EETS, 1908 for 1906), and Walker critiques most of them in *Plays of Persuasion*, pp. 61–6. Dissenting views have tended to rest on the supposed early date of the play (five years before the obviously anti-Wolseyan poems of the 1520s); see, for example, William O. Harris, *Skelton's* Magnyfycence *and the Cardinal Virtue Tradition* (Chapel Hill: North Carolina University Press, 1965), pp. 12–45; and David Bevington, who stresses that the play "deals with programs rather than with personalities," in *Tudor Drama and Politics: A Critical Approach to Topical Meaning* (Cambridge, Mass.: Harvard University Press, 1968), pp. 54–63.

[6] Walker first proposed this thesis in *John Skelton and the Politics of the 1520s*, pp. 88–9. He notes that Maria Dowling had earlier put forth the idea that *Magnificence* satirizes the court politics of 1519 in her "Scholarship, Politics and the Court of Henry VIII" (Ph.D. dissertation, University of London, 1981), but that in her view Wolsey was still the object of the satire. Dowling does not discuss *Magnificence* in *Humanism in the Reign of Henry VIII* (London: Croom Helm, 1985), a revision of her thesis. Walker cites other brief expositions of this reading of the play in I. Lancashire's introduction to *Dramatic Texts and Records of Britain: A Chronological Topography to 1558* (Cambridge: Cambridge University Press, 1984), p. 18, and Alistair Fox, *Politics and Literature in the Reigns of Henry VII and Henry VIII*, pp. 237–40 (see *Plays of Persuasion*, p. 66 n. 16). The view is also supported by John Scattergood in "Skelton's *Magnyfycence* and the Tudor Royal Household," *Medieval English Theatre* 15 (1993): pp. 21–48.

[7] The following account relies on Walker, *Plays of Persuasion*, pp. 66–72; Walker, "The Expulsion of the Minions Reconsidered," *The Historical Journal* 32 (1989): pp. 1–16; David Starkey, *The Reign of Henry VIII: Personalities and Politics* (London: G. Philip, 1985), pp. 69–80; and Starkey, "Intimacy and Innovation: the Rise of the Privy Chamber, 1485–1547," in *The English Court: from the Wars of the Roses to the Civil War*, ed. David Starkey, et al. (London: Longman, 1987), pp. 71–118.

disgrace."[8] Counter to the traditional interpretation of this event, Walker maintains that the minions were not dismissed simply because Wolsey feared they might "in due time have ousted him from the government."[9] Rather, he says, we find the real reason for the minions' removal in Hall's account of the disgraceful behavior they displayed while on a diplomatic mission to France and on their return to England. Says Hall,

> During this time remained in the French court Nicholas Carew, Francis Bryan and divers other of the young gentlemen of England, and they with the French king rode daily disguised through Paris, throwing eggs, stones and other foolish trifles at the people, which light demeanor of a king was much discommended and jested at. And when these young gentlemen came again into England, they were all French, in eating, drinking and apparel, yea and in French vices and brags, so that all the estates of England were by them laughed at: the ladies and gentlewomen were dispraised, so that nothing by them was praised, but if it were after the French turn, which after turned them to displeasure . . . and [they] so highly praised the French king and his court, that in a manner they thought little of the king and his court, in comparison of the other, they were so high in love with the French court, wherefore their fall was little moaned among wise men.
>
> (pp. 597–8)[10]

Thus, Walker notes, it was "the minions' extravagant behavior, their condescending, disparaging manner, and especially the overfamiliar way in which they treated their king," which "began to alarm the members of Henry's council" (p. 68). It was bad enough that the minions had, in David Starkey's words, "behaved rather like a visiting rugby team" while in France, but to make matters worse, when they returned to England they affected French mannerisms, prided themselves on their knowledge of French dances, "were rude about English fashion, food, and beer,"[11] and so, predictably, were resented by the elder nobles who felt this band of Frenchified fops was disgracing the majesty of the court. In short, Henry had a PR problem: by scorning their native court, the minions were damaging the king's image of magnificence.[12]

Walker believes the vices in Skelton's *Magnificence* exhibit the

---

[8] *Plays of Persuasion*, p. 66. Hereafter page references to Walker's book appear in the text.

[9] This is as the Venetian agent Sebastian Giustinian surmised; quoted in Starkey, *The Reign of Henry VIII*, p. 78.

[10] Quoted in Walker, *Plays of Persuasion*, pp. 67–8.

[11] Starkey, *The English Court*, p. 103.

[12] On the development and importance of the concept of *magnificence* at European courts during the fifteenth and sixteenth centuries, see Anglo, *Spectacle, Pageantry, and Early Tudor Policy*, pp. 98–123; Gordon Kipling, *The Triumph of Honour:*

extravagant behavior of the court minions, indicating Skelton's aim both to satirize them and to applaud Henry for their expulsion. They are vices in the roles of dissembling courtiers, each posing as a virtue and seeking a station within the king's household. Fancy, for example, calls himself Largess; Folly is Pleasure; Cloaked Collusion is Sober Sadness. The vices' pseudonyms appeal to Magnificence, winning them his trust and patronage, so that, as Folly boasts, those "come up of naught" are now "set in authority."[13] Having acquired their privileged positions – indeed, their "privy appointments," as they call them (line 1337) – the vices quickly squander Magnificence's health and wealth, bringing him to Poverty and Despair. This is what happens, says Adversity, to

> lords of realms and lands
> That rule not by measure that they have in their hands,
> That sadly rule not their household men.   (lines 1938–40)

These lines have the flavor of a maxim and the specificity, in the term "household men," of the topical reference Walker claims for the play. He finds additional support for his thesis in the pride the vice-courtiers have in their fancy French ways. Counterfeit Countenance, for example, advises:

> Counterfeit kindness, and think deceit;
> Counterfeit letters by the way of sleight;
> Subtly using counterfeit weight;
> Counterfeit language, *fayty bone geyte.*[14]   (lines 438–41)

And Courtly Abusion boasts:

> This new fonne jet [i.e., foolish fashion]
> From out of France
> First I did set;

Burgundian Origins of the Elizabethan Renaissance (Leiden: Leiden University Press, 1977), pp. 72–136.

[13] John Skelton, *Magnificence*, lines 1240–3, in *John Skelton: The Complete English Poems*, pp. 140–214. Hereafter line references are cited in the text.

[14] This is perhaps "a corruption of the French phrase *fait bon get* or *geste* meaning 'elegant' or 'finely fashioned'" (Scattergood's note, citing *The Poetical Works of John Skelton*, ed. Rev. Alexander Dyce, 2 vols. [London: Thomas Rodd, 1843], vol. 2, p. 242).

Leigh Winser shows the extent to which Skelton's depiction of French foolery is indebted to the Sottie, "a French dramatic form that flourished during Skelton's lifetime and provided him with at least three different models for his scheming knaves," in "*Magnyfycence* and the Characters of Sottie," *Sixteenth Century Journal* 12 (1981): 85–94. Peter Happé also writes on this topic in "Fansy and Foly: The Drama of Fools in *Magnyfycence*," *Comparative Drama* 27 (1993–94): pp. 426–52.

Made purveyance
And such ordinance,
That all men it found
Through out England.

All this nation
I set on fire;
In my fashion
This their desire,
This new attire.
This ladies have,
I it them gave.   (lines 877–90)

According to Walker, Skelton's depiction of the minions served a specific propagandistic purpose. Once it had been decided to expel the minions the court had to figure out a way to do it gracefully, because the expulsion was bound to be a delicate and potentially damaging move in itself. The sacking of so many and such recently-elevated members of the royal household was a step bound to reflect poorly on Henry, and indeed it was the talk of European court circles for a while (Walker cites some of the surviving "ambassadorial references to the rumors and controversy it excited, both in England and abroad" [p. 70 n. 32]).[15] An "authorized version" of the expulsion was required, and Walker is surely right in claiming that Hall's account preserves this version. As Hall reports the event, "the king's council secretly communed together" to discuss the problem of "certain young men" in Henry's privy chamber, who "not regarding his estate nor degree, were so familiar and homely with him, and played such light touches with him that they forget themselves." Because he had such a "gentle nature," Hall continues, Henry neither "rebuked nor reproved" the behavior of these young men; "yet the king's council thought it not meet to be suffered for the king's honor, and therefore they altogether came to the king, beseeching him all these enormities and lights to redress. To whom the king answered, that he had chosen them of his council, both for the maintenance of his honor, and for the defense of all thing that might blemish the same: wherefore if they saw any about him misuse themselves, he committed it to their reformation" (p. 598).

It was the circulation of such an authorized version "at court and elsewhere," says Walker, that "would seem to explain most satisfactorily Skelton's decision to write *Magnificence* in 1519" (pp. 69–71). If so, then it was Skelton's design to condemn the minions and advertise the salvation of the king. The generic conventionality of the morality play

---

[15] These references are calendared in *SP, Spanish*, vol. 2, nos. 1220 and 1235; *LP*, vol. 3, pt. 1, no. 246.

would have prevented the satire from too hotly scorching Henry, Walker explains, but more importantly it was performed *after the fact*: Henry had already expelled the vice-minions from his presence, so he corresponded to Magnificence in the final stage of the human drama, enjoying the grace and good counsel that come with Good Hope, Redress, Circumspection, and Perseverance. "Thus," Walker concludes, "in portraying Henry VIII as Magnificence, Skelton clearly fashioned a vehicle for praise of the king, rather than for criticism," because "the king who emerged from the play was strengthened by his experiences. His fall into folly was educational in its effects rather than corrupting" (p. 76).

In 1530, when John Rastell printed *Magnificence*, circumstances at court could not have allowed it to re-deliver that message, whether or not readers recalled the play's original political context and significance. If they did, they would know that the minions' "expulsion" was short-lived. They had nearly all regained court posts by 1520, and in 1530 most of them were helping in the business of Henry's great matter: serving as ambassadors to the pope, the emperor, and the King of France; testifying against the marriage at the legatine trial; and arguing for the king's cause in Parliament.[16] In other words, the courtiers whom *Magnificence* had satirized in 1519 were not only back in favor by 1529, but the king whom *Magnificence* had praised for expelling them was then relying on their service in his campaign to divorce the queen.

---

[16] In the late 1520s, the minions were employed as follows: Sir Francis Bryan, a cousin of Anne Boleyn's, was one of the ambassadors sent to Rome in 1528 to plead for the pope's consent to the divorce (see Parmiter, *The King's Great Matter*, p. 80; *LP*, vol. 5, nos. 427 and 454). Sir Nicholas Carew traveled to the court of Charles V in 1529 and 1530 before joining Bryan in France the following year (see *LP*, vol. 4, pt. 3, no. 6092). Edward Neville remained a royal favorite, receiving several grants from the king through the late 1520s (see *LP*, vol. 4, pt. 3, nos. 5516, 6301 [12], 6363 [1]). Sir Henry Guildford, controller of the household, was involved in the preparations for the arrival of Cardinal Campeggio when he came to preside over the legatine trial that was supposed to settle Henry's case, and in the trial Guildford testified as a witness to the twelve articles that challenged the validity of Henry's marriage to Catherine. Later in 1529, Guildford also served as a witness to the charter that created Anne Boleyn's father Earl of Wiltshire (see *LP*, vol. 4, pt. 3, no. 5774 [5 and 12]; Kelly, *The Matrimonial Trials of Henry VIII*, pp. 94–5). Henry Norris was made first a squire for the body and later a knight in the late 1520s, and he became one of Anne's strongest allies at court; on Henry and Anne's inspection tour of Wolsey's properties in 1529, they were attended only by Norris, who was employed in the absorption of Wolsey's estate by the court (see *LP*, vol. 4, pt. 3, nos. 6098, 6114, 6181–2). Sir William Coffin had also returned to service in the king's household, and his nearness to Henry enabled him to hold a seat in Parliament when it opened in 1529 (see S. T. Bindoff, *The History of Parliament: The House of Commons, 1509–1558*, 3 vols. [London: Secker and Warburg, 1982], vol. 1, p. 666); his name appears, too, with Thomas More's in a 1530 list of grants to the commission of the peace (*LP*, vol. 4, pt. 3, no. 6903 [8]).

Readers would not necessarily have to be aware of the play's original context and referents, however, to perceive its relevance to the situation at court in 1530. Henry was employing many men to assist him in his great matter – courtiers, clergymen, lawyers, and scholars – and all of these could easily be recognized as fitting targets of *Magnificence*'s satire.[17] They included, for instance, John Stokesley and Anne Boleyn's brother George Boleyn, sent in 1529 as ambassadors to Francis I to urge his alliance with Henry against Charles V in disputes that included above all the divorce question, and to collect opinions on the matter from French universities. They included England's foremost textual scholars hired by Henry to analyze the scriptural and canonical evidence pertaining to his case, such as Robert Wakefield, Henry's expert on oriental languages, lecturer in Hebrew at Cambridge and Oxford, and author, we recall, of the treatise in support of the divorce, *Kotser Codicis*. Henry's Greek scholar and tutor, Richard Croke, was another. He was dispatched on a mission to Italy in 1529, where he scoured the libraries and book shops for documents supporting Henry's case, and obtained, through request and purchase, as many signed opinions of experts as he could gather.[18]

---

[17] In addition to those listed below, I have cited many others who labored on behalf of the king's great matter previously but only in passing, so I offer a summary here: John Bell was Henry's proctor at the legatine trial in 1529 (as well as in the first, but secret, divorce trial of 1527 at Westminster; see Kelly, *The Matrimonial Trials of Henry VIII*, pp. 25 and 79). In 1530 Bell accompanied John Longland and Edward Fox to Oxford to request that university's opinion on the king's marriage (see *LP*, vol. 4, pt. 3, no. 6308). Fox traveled with Stephen Gardiner, Henry's secretary, to Cambridge for the same purpose, and the two served as ambassadors together at the papal court in Orvieto in 1528, securing agreement from a reluctant Clement VII to hold the legatine trial in England (see *LP*, vol. 4, pt. 2, no. 4120; Parmiter, *The King's Great Matter*, pp. 44–50). In 1529 Fox continued working on Henry's behalf, both in the trial itself and while on embassy to the French court (see Kelly, *The Matrimonial Trials of Henry VIII*, pp. 54–7; *LP*, vol. 4, pt. 3, no. 6022 [ii]). Fox accompanied Francis Bryan to the French court in 1531 (see *LP*, vol. 5, nos. 427 and 454). Gardiner was also engaged as an ambassador to France in 1527, and to Rome in 1528 and 1529. One other of Henry's chief agents and ambassadors was Richard Sampson, who like John Bell served as a proctor for the king in the 1529 legatine trial, and in the same year was sent with the former "minion" Sir Nicholas Carew on an embassy first to Rome, to plead the king's case with the pope, and then to Charles V. Others traveling between Henry's and Clement's courts were William Benet, William Knight, Sir Gregory Casale, Peter Vannes, and Edward Lee (see Parmiter's account of these negotiations in *The King's Great Matter*, pp. 11–95).

[18] Croke pursued his task doggedly, sending back to England not only the sealed judgments of respected doctors of the Church, but – to the amusement of the foreign ambassadors at Henry's court – the opinions of Jewish rabbis, and the determination of a theological school that did not exist. Croke's many letters are calendared in *LP*, vol. 4, pt. 3. No. 6514 records the discovery that he had acquired the opinion of Padua's theological college, complete with official seal and signatures of learned

From the perspective of those who opposed the king's divorce, then, Henry's court contained quite a number of men – some formerly expelled minions, no less – who were helping the king to bring himself and his realm to ruin, and who could thus be taken as objects of *Magnificence*'s satire in 1530. We can point to several of the play's features that would have increased its aptness for such contemporary application. First, the ridicule of French manners and influences remained topical, because not only were several of the minions again serving in the capacity of ambassadors to France, but at Henry's court French ways were in rising favor due to the presence of Anne Boleyn. She had spent the years from 1515 to 1521 at the court of Francis I, where she was accepted into the household of Queen Claude. Besides serving as a companion for the queen (they were about the same age), Anne was valuable as an interpreter, since she picked up the French language as quickly as she did its fashions, dances, and that "continental polish" that later would so much offend (just as it had offended the enemies of the minions) her enemies at home.[19] Back in England, Anne's ascent at court was accompanied by the elevation in status of others in the Boleyn family. Anne's father and, as we have noted, her brother George served as ambassadors to France. With this in mind, we see that in 1530 Skelton's ridicule of foolish French fashions strikes not only at several of Henry's courtiers, but at his mistress and her family.

Aping the French is but one of the vices' milder sins. More serious is their encouragement of Magnificence toward debauchery, as Courtly Abusion does in the following passage:

> *Courtly Abusion:*
>
> So as ye be a prince of great might,
> It is seeming your pleasure ye delight,
> And to acquaint you with carnal delectation;
> And to fall in acquaintance with every new fashion,
> And quickly your appetites to sharp and address;
> To fasten your fancy upon a fair mistress
> That quickly is envied with ruddies of the rose,
> Inpurtured with features after your purpose,
> The strains of her veins as azure Indie blue,
> Enbudded with beauty and color fresh of hue,
> As lily white to look upon her leer,
> Her eyen reluctant as carbuncle so clear,
> Her mouth embalmed, delectable and merry,

divines, despite there being no Paduan theological college at the time (Kelly discusses this embarrassment in *Matrimonial Trials of Henry VIII*, p. 177).

[19] See E. W. Ives, *Anne Boleyn* (Oxford: Basil Blackwell, 1986), pp. 35–43, 57.

Her lusty lips ruddy as the cherry –
How like you? Ye lack, sir, such a lusty lass.

Magnificence:

Ah, that were a baby to brace and to bass [i.e., kiss]!
I would I had, by him that hell did harrow,
With me in keeping such a Philip Sparrow.
I would hawk whilst my head did work,
So I might hobby for such a lusty lark.
These words in mine ear, they be so lustily spoken,
That on such a female my flesh would be wroken.
They touch me so thoroughly and tickle my conceit,
That wearied I would be on such a bait.
Ah, Cock's arms! Where might such one be found?

Courtly Abusion:

Will ye spend any money?

Magnificence:

Yea, a thousand pound.   (lines 1545–70)

Walker makes no attempt to argue that this or similar passages refer to any particular royal infidelity encouraged by the minions before their expulsion.[20] He rightly takes these passages as standard morality-play matter, representing a typical corrupting influence to be expected from vice-characters.[21] But in 1530, any suggestion that the king was lustful was tantamount to opposition to the divorce. We saw in the previous chapter that William Barlow, in *A Dialogue on the Lutheran Factions*, similarly condemns so-called "learned persons" who would "approve the lusts" of their rulers. But in the case of Skelton's *Magnificence* it is far clearer that Henry VIII is *the* referent, so it is worth reminding ourselves how much Henry resented the accusation that he wanted to divorce Catherine because he lusted for Anne. As Hall recounts, when the reason for Campeggio's coming in 1528 became known the talk of the people (especially those "being ignorant of the truth") was "that the king would for his own pleasure have another wife" (p. 754), so when the legatine trial opened Henry stood before the assembly himself to swear that it was his only desire "to have a speedy end, according to right, for the quietness of [his] mind and conscience only, and for no other cause as God knoweth" (p. 757). Three years later, as we saw in chapter 2, Henry sent More into both houses of Parliament to repeat this message,

---

[20] It is true that in that time Henry was having an affair with Elizabeth Blount (she bore him Henry Fitzroy in 1519), but this relationship was several years old. The minions could have had nothing to do with it.

[21] Also on this point see Harris, *Skelton's* Magnyfycence, pp. 90–5.

instructing the members to return into their counties and tell their neighbors that "the king hath not attempted this matter of will or pleasure, as some strangers report, but only for the discharge of his conscience and surety of the succession of the realm" (Hall, p. 780). One would have to believe that in 1530 Rastell knew how overdetermined and risky an act it was to print a play portraying a king eager to "hobby" for a "lusty lark."

But the privilege of deniability is just another of the advantages in printing Skelton's *Magnificence.* It is, after all, just an old play; and if Walker is correct about the satirical and propagandistic function of its original performance, those who remember it will recall that *Magnificence* was devised to congratulate the king, not to rebuke him. Even if readers do not remember those circumstances, they would understand that it was written by the "king's own orator," as Skelton often styled himself, or, as Rastell's title page advertises, that it was "devised and made by master Skelton, poet laureate late deceased." In other words, this is a play from a former time, composed under the patronage of the king.

The fact that it is now printed by John Rastell, and with the royal privilege, only strengthens the impression that the play has the king's official blessing. But as we have seen, most of the works that had "official blessing" in this period were not supposed to be taken as mere mouthpieces for the king. The court also encouraged tracts like Elyot's *The Governor*, a *speculum principis* that through its inquiry into the general question "What makes an ideal ruler?" publicly counsels the king toward virtue, and through its publication by the royal printer publicly attests to the king's intention to follow good counsel. As a morality play *Magnificence*, too, is concerned with the question of what makes a good ruler. Despite its being a record of decade-old events, however, Skelton's *speculum principis* now offers Henry advice specific to 1530: to avoid his ruin, he should give up this idea of a divorce and expel those who support him in it, because those particular courtiers and scholars are not "wise men" but deceivers.

Indeed, *Magnificence* contains many lines that can be taken as warnings that Henry has surrounded himself with phony scholars, exegetes, and philosophers. Liberty compliments Felicity, for instance, on a piece of illiterate Bible-glossing (line 1427), and not only is pretentious French banter satirized, so too is the vices' pretended Latin learning.

> *Fancy:*
>
> I am yet as full of game
> As ever I was, and as full of trifles –
> *Nil, nichelum, nihil – anglice* nifils.[22]

---

[22] That is, "Nothing, nothing, nothing – in English, worthless nothings."

Folly:

What! Canst thou all this Latin yet,
And hath so massed a wandering wit?

Fancy:

Tush, man! I keep some Latin in store.   (lines 1140–5)

Similarly, other passages in the play seem to mock the image of Henry's court as a place of humanist discourse. Crafty Conveyance says that "the guise nowadays" is to "crake great words" (lines 812–13); Cloaked Collusion boasts "I sow seditious seeds of discord and debates" (line 737); and on one of the occasions when the vices congratulate themselves for successfully duping Magnificence, Crafty Conveyance praises Folly for his ability to argue *in utramque partem*:

Folly:

So how, I say, the hare is squat!
For, frantic Fancy, thou makest men mad;
And I Folly bringeth them to *qui fuit* gad;
With *qui fuit* brain seek I have them brought;
From *qui fuit aliquid* to sheer shaking nought.

Crafty Conveyance:

Well argued and surely on both sides.   (lines 1299–1304)

Such boasts are typical of dissembling vice-characters in morality plays, but at this time of Henry's self-representation as a philosopher-king gravely weighing the opposing viewpoints in debates among wise men, these scenes appear to challenge the integrity of that image. The passage in which Magnificence expresses his admiration for his new courtiers' bogus eloquence would have the same result:

As I be saved, with pleasure I am surprised
Of your language, it is so well devised;
Polished and fresh is your ornacy.   (lines 1529–31)

Finally, one other damning allusion seems to appear in the way that Magnificence's moral plummet begins when he is taken in by a fraudulent written recommendation – a letter ("closed under seal" [line 312]) introducing Fancy as Largess, who "stinteth great debates" (line 371). *Magnificence* appeared at the very moment that Henry's project of gathering letters in support of his cause was underway. These were letters of a different sort than Fancy's, it is true, but Henry was acquiring them primarily by means of "largess," distributed through Croke and Stokesley, and they were meant precisely to "stint debate" rather than encourage it.

The printing of *Magnificence* in 1530 thus allowed John Rastell to do indirectly what Bishop Fisher was the last to get away with openly, in his speech at the legatine trial.[23] That is, Rastell questions Henry's claim to be relying on good counsel. For all the talk of philosopher-kings, this play implies, Henry defines eloquence and reason according to the opinion he wants to hear in favor of his divorce, and hears only counsel that articulates his wayward will. That is what Courtly Abusion recommends to Magnificence:

> *Courtly Abusion:*
>
> Wisely let these words in your mind be weighed:
> By wayward willfulness let each thing be conveyed;
> What so ever ye do, follow your own will,
> Be it reason or none, it shall not greatly skill;
> Be it right or wrong, by the advice of me,
> Take your pleasure and use free liberty;
> And if you see any thing against your mind,
> Then some occasion or quarrel ye must find,
> And frown it and face it, as though ye would fight;
> Fret yourself for anger and for despite;
> Hear no man what so ever they say
> But do as ye list and take your own way.[24]
>
> *Magnificence:*
>
> Thy words and my mind oddly well accord.
>
> *Courtly Abusion:*
>
> What should ye do else? Are not you a lord?
> Let your lust and liking stand for a law.   (lines 1593–1607)

In 1519, Walker maintains, *Magnificence* was praising Henry for rejecting just this advice. But the shift in context between the play's performance and its printing also shifts the stance of the play in its relation to Henry. Now it is a call for *future* action, because now the play looks forward to a time when the king will be undeceived, when he will reject the dangerous advice of false philosophers. Another way to put it is that in 1530 *Magnificence* was posing as general, deliberative discourse on the conduct of kings, but really it was delivering a specific and imperative message to Henry VIII: "You are in the middle section of the drama, duped and headed toward ruin, rather than in the final state of salvation – as the play had once, in 1519, represented you." And by implication,

---

[23] Discussed in the introduction, pp. 9–12.
[24] Cf. Plato's description of the tyrant Dionysius in Thomas Elyot's *Of the Knowledge which Maketh a Wise Man* (pp. 18–21), quoted above, p. 79.

Rastell is making the more general claim that truly wise counsel, such that will save the king from dissembling tempters, is coming from his press. If Henry wants to live up to his philosopher-king image – if he wants, as well, the happy ending that Skelton's play has scripted for him – he should, it seems clear, listen to that wisdom.

III

If Walker is correct about the original date of *The Play of the Weather* (1529), then William Rastell sent a similar message to the king in his 1533 edition of this play. John Heywood, like Skelton, was employed by the court during the 1520s, and like Skelton and William Rastell, Heywood remained a Catholic all his life. Around 1529 Heywood married the daughter of John Rastell, Eliza, but even before this connection to the Rastell family he belonged to the More circle.[25] Heywood's Catholicism and connections did not reduce his activity at court, however, at least not until 1544 when he was indicted (though he escaped conviction) for his supposed involvement in a plot against Archbishop Cranmer.[26] Up to the time of that affair he remained steadily employed by Henry as a court entertainer, and in fact within eight years after his indictment for treason Heywood was back at work, putting on plays and other entertainments for Edward, Mary, and the princess Elizabeth, until Elizabeth's coronation prompted him to leave England for good.[27]

Heywood's plays are essentially moralistic farces, and many poke fun at the abuses of the clergy in the tradition of Chaucer's *The Parson's Tale* and Skelton's *Colin Clout*. This sort of satire, Walker emphasizes, is not at all "anti-clerical" in the way that contemporary Protestant tracts were anti-clerical. Heywood, he says, exhibits a conservative, "Erasmian" conception of reform (p. 166). Or as James Sutherland puts it, "John Heywood's satire is that of a good Catholic who wishes that his Church were better."[28] William Rastell's 1533–1534 editions of Heywood's plays, for this reason, are among the last books of the decade to affirm religious loyalty to Rome. This loyalty is indicated in such passages as the concluding speech of *The Play Called the Four Ps:*

[25] See Hogrefe, *The Sir Thomas More Circle*, pp. 289–98; Robert Bolwell, *The Life and Works of John Heywood* (New York: Columbia University Press, 1921), pp. 19–29.

[26] Bolwell, *John Heywood*, pp. 35–41.

[27] Bolwell lists all of Heywood's "pageants, masks, and other revels" mentioned in *LP* (*John Heywood*, pp. xi–xiii; and chronological table, pp. 169–74).

[28] In *English Satire* (Cambridge: Cambridge University Press, 1962), p. 134.

Then to our reason God give us his grace,
That we may follow with faith so firmly
His commandments, that we may purchase
His love, and so consequently
To believe his church fast and faithfully;
So that we may, according to his promise,
Be kept out of error in any wise . . .
Beseeching Our Lord to prosper you all
In the faith of his church universal.[29]

The Play of the Weather is different from *The Four Ps* and Heywood's other works in that it contains no obvious references to the Church or to corrupt priests, and it is drawn from classical sources.[30] It begins with Jupiter's report that he has taken upon himself the task of resolving a dispute between Phoebus, Saturn, Phoebe, and Aeolus, who have accused each other of overusing their respective elements – the sun, frost, rain, and wind – to the disadvantage of the others. In order to secure counsel to help him make his decision, Jupiter appoints Merry Report as an usher to invite and receive mortals who want to make their wishes known on the matter. But the mortals turn out to be in as much disagreement as the gods: the Merchant asks for steady winds for the sails of his ships; the Ranger requests gales because he profits by windfalls; the Water Miller wants constant rain and the Wind Miller only wind; the Gentlewoman demands endless fair weather for her fair complexion, while the Laundress needs a strong sun for her drying; and last of all, a boy asks for year-round snow to play in. After Jupiter hears each of these suitors he gives his judgment. All will get the weather they desire, but only for short spans of time. He will allow the continued balance between the elements.

Walker begins his analysis of *The Play of the Weather* by stressing the similarity between the image of Jupiter in the play and the king for whom the play was most likely performed. He points out that "Jupiter is not encountered in some Olympian or neutral *mise en scène*, but in the great hall of a Tudor palace, where in the style of the monarch on progress he establishes a temporary presence chamber clearly based upon the Tudor model." By this means, says Walker, "Heywood ensured that analogies would be drawn between Henry VIII and Jupiter. Indeed Henry had already been compared to Jupiter in encomiastic literature prior to this performance," so "the association was a natural as well as an obvious

---

[29] *The Plays of John Heywood*, ed. Axton and Happé, lines 1221–34. The following references to *The Play of the Weather* are also to this edition.

[30] These sources are Lucian's *Icaromenippus* and *The Double Indictment* (see *The Plays of John Heywood*, pp. 47–8; Walker, *Plays of Persuasion*, p. 136; Altman, *The Tudor Play of Mind*, pp. 121–2).

one" (p. 148).[31] Walker then observes about Heywood's play what I have been saying of other works that came from the Rastells' presses (especially the polemics of Thomas More): that Heywood takes advantage of Henry's professedly neutral stance at the time, a stance which necessarily leaves space for dissenting voices. In Walker's words, Henry was "posing as the concerned but impartial judge" in the disputes between reformers and conservative ecclesiastics, and *The Play of the Weather* is evidence that once Henry had "employed the rhetoric of free debate" – even though everyone knew he did so with "predetermined answers" in mind – there would "necessarily be scope for individuals who were either consciously or unconsciously out of step with current royal thinking to raise issues and opinions far removed from those which the crown was seeking to encourage" (pp. 167–8).

In Walker's view *The Play of the Weather* responds to the attacks on Church privileges that had occurred in the first session of Parliament, which, even if it did not quite live up to its name of the "anti-clerical Parliament" in the number of anti-clerical bills passed, nonetheless was vocal enough about Church enormities to alarm conservative Catholics like More and Heywood (pp. 158–63).[32] Perhaps what alarmed them even more, Walker continues, was the knowledge that "Protestant literature was openly circulating at court" (p. 159).[33] Meanwhile Henry was promoting his image as defender of the faith, the champion of orthodoxy and the Church, by such means as his proclamations against heretical books in 1530 (p. 158). Walker suggests that Heywood and others in the More circle wanted to encourage Henry's resolve in defending the Church's position within England because they felt that despite his quarrel with the pope he was not at that time likely to defy Rome. "Certainly," he says, "Thomas More did not at this stage see anti-clericalism and heresy as connived at by the crown, for he accepted the

---

[31] The prior comparison between Henry and Jupiter that Walker refers to is in Skelton's *Speak, Parrot*, lines 405–10. Walker also explains that the role of Merry Report "offers a parody of the office of yeoman usher of the chamber," whose duties included "keeping the doors of the king's chamber, and ensuring that only those individuals of gentle status and above, or those with legitimate business within, were permitted to pass into the chamber beyond." In 1528, Walker then notes, Heywood became a "sewer of the chamber," which is "a kind of Tudor head-waiter to the crown," and "thus Heywood would have witnessed at first hand the activities of the chamber staff, and the protocol which governed access to the presence or audience chamber" (p. 138).

[32] Walker cites Christopher Haigh's article on this subject, "Anti-clericalism and the English Reformation," in *The English Reformation Revised*, ed. Christopher Haigh (Cambridge: Cambridge University Press, 1987), pp. 56–74.

[33] Walker cites here the report to this effect calendared in *SP, Spanish*, vol. 4, pt. 1, no. 160.

chancellorship from Henry and retained it until 1532, evidently believing that [More's own] harsh repression of heresy met with royal approval" (p. 158).[34] Heywood's play therefore encourages Henry's assertion of royal independence. In Henry, Walker claims, Heywood saw the salvation of the Church from its detractors and maligners in Parliament:

> What Heywood seems to have done in *Weather*, then, is take up and extrapolate to its absolutist extreme this rhetoric of royal independence fostered by Henry himself. By stressing the absolutist possibilities, even the absolutist obligations, inherent in such an active, personal, sovereignty, Heywood reminded the king of his own resolution, and suggested that he pursue it to its logical conclusion. If he intended to rule personally, then he did not need to countenance either a fractious Parliament or anti-clerical advisers . . . Evidently the author's hope was that the king would dissolve Parliament and pursue the sort of Erasmian reforms in the Church that Heywood approved of and thought the king desired. (p. 166)

In my view Walker underestimates the More circle's awareness of Henry's strategy during this time. I agree that More and Heywood did not believe Henry was "conniving at" anti-clericalism or heresy, but certainly he was conniving at the exploitation of popular anti-clericalism, heresy, and the Protestant threat to the Church for the purpose of pressuring Rome and obtaining his divorce from Catherine. Neither Heywood nor More could have had any misconceptions about Henry proving the salvation of the Church during this period of the divorce crisis, for I assume they both recognized that Henry had called Parliament because he knew he might have to achieve through it what he hesitated to do alone: defy the pope. If the play indeed praises Jupiter for acting alone rather than with his Parliament because Heywood wanted to encourage Henry to do the same thing, it does not have to be the case that Heywood offered this counsel because he feared Parliament itself. I suspect, if Heywood did write the play in 1529, that he rather hoped Parliament would be dissolved because he knew that Henry, without its cover and assistance, would be in a weaker position to oppose Rome, or to effect the kinds of domestic jurisdictional reforms that would be required in order for him to obtain his divorce legally within England.

In any case William Rastell could not have printed *The Play of the Weather* in 1533 with a 1529 design. If the original aim of the play was to nip Henry's plans for Parliament in the bud, by the time it appeared in print Parliament was already convening or finished with its fourth

---

[34] On this point Walker is in agreement with and cites Guy, *The Public Career of Thomas More*, pp. 50–64; and Marius, *Thomas More*, pp. 325–70.

meeting,[35] and unless Rastell printed the play before the 25th of January, 1533, it appeared after Henry's marriage to Anne was already accomplished. Just as the contemporary political situation had changed, therefore, so would have *The Play of the Weather*'s relevance. In the context of 1533, it could only be condemning, not praising, a king who was increasingly augmenting the extent of his royal powers – as were Jupiter on stage and Henry VIII actually. This apparent condemnation of Henry leads Richard Axton and Peter Happé to suggest, in their preface to Heywood's works, that *The Play of the Weather* was not written until late 1533 (pp. 51–2), when the looming supremacy legislation seems to make the play more relevant than it would have been to the late 1520s. It may be, therefore, that my analysis of the play will support Axton's and Happé's proposal. For I will argue that *The Play of the Weather*, like Skelton's *Magnificence* in the context of the 1530s, is aimed at satirizing Henry's philosopher-king image, starting with the uncanny resemblance between Jupiter's repeated professions of neutrality and Henry's rhetoric of reticent delicacy.

"For, in faith, I care not who win or lose," Jupiter characteristically boasts (line 215), and he promises to listen to "each man indifferently," only interested as he is in what "best may stand to our honor infinite, / For wealth in common and each man's singular profit" (lines 281–4). But earlier in the play Jupiter reveals his deeper conviction that his judgment alone is sufficient for wielding the supreme power that is in his hands. After recounting the dispute between Phoebus, Saturn, Phoebe, and Aeolus, Jupiter declares:

> Thus can these four in no manner agree.
> Which seen in themselves, and further considering,
> The same to redress was cause of their assembly.
> And also that we, evermore being,
> Beside our puissant power of deity,
> Of wisdom and nature so noble and so free –
> From all extremities the mean dividing,
> To appease and plenty each thing attempering –
> They have in conclusion wholly surrendered
> Into our hands (as much as concerning
> All manner weathers by them engendered)
> The full of their powers for term everlasting,
> To set such order as standeth with our pleasing;
> Which thing, as of our part, no part required
> But of all their parts right humbly desired

---

[35] There were sessions in 1529, 1531, and 1532, and the 1533 meeting was held in the first part of the year, from January 26 to April 7.

To take upon us;[36] whereto we did assent.
And so in all things, with one voice agreeable
We have clearly finished our aforesaid Parliament,
To your great wealth which shall be firm and stable,
And to our honor far inestimable.
For since their powers as ours added to our own,
Who can, we say, know us as we should be known?

(lines 63–84)

Jupiter's version of events makes for ironic allegory in 1533. Because the Parliament of gods could "in no wise agree," he says, they requested him to take over – *they* appealed to *him* to assert his supremacy. *The Play of the Weather* represents Jupiter doing exactly what Henry was striving to accomplish at the time, to appropriate the voices and thus the power of Parliament but to all appearances to do so by Parliament's own invitation. By 1533, for instance, Cromwell had started to write those bills that directly address the king, as if they represented appeals from Parliament as a whole and single body urging Henry to take the actions it concluded he should take.[37]

More notoriously, there had recently occurred a very public grab for power on Henry's part, and this supplied a particular occasion for the play's criticism of a king who professes neutrality but strips others of their authority. That incident was the Submission of the Clergy (in May, 1532), in which Convocation, the assembly of bishops that coincided with parliamentary sessions, agreed upon Henry's demand to submit a document conceding its independent law-making powers to the king.[38] As discussed in chapter 2, it was this "ignominious and complete"

---

[36] I follow Joseph Quincy Adams, in *Chief Pre-Shakespearean Dramas* (New York: Houghton Mifflin, 1924), in ending the sentence here rather than at the end of the preceding line.

[37] These bills are discussed in chapter 1, pp. 44–5.

[38] The "bishops' answer" to the king's request opens in a manner that seems to betray their and Henry's anticipation that their surrender of power would be viewed by the realm as less than freely volunteered:

We your most humble subjects, daily orators, and bedemen of your clergy of England, having our special trust and confidence in your most excellent wisdom, your princely goodness, and fervent zeal to the promotion of God's honor and Christian religion; and also in your learning far exceeding, in our judgment, the learning of all other kings and princes that we have read of; and doubting nothing but that the same shall still continue and daily increase in your majesty; First do offer and promise *in verbo sacerdotii* here unto your highness, submitting ourselves most humbly to the same, that we will never from henceforth presume to attempt, allege, claim or yet put in ure, or to enact, promulge or execute any canons, constitution or ordinance provincial, or by any other name whatsoever they may be called in our convocation in time coming; Which convocation is always, hath been and must be assembled only capitulation, as Parmiter calls it,[39] that so clearly spelled the end for the Catholic Church in England and prompted Thomas More immediately to resign the chancellorship. After this capitulation, Jupiter's boast at the "addition" of Parliament's powers to his own would seem all the more naturally to invoke the steps Henry appeared to be taking toward royal supremacy.

It also represents the attendant drawbacks. Debate and wise counsel, as the play demonstrates, have no place under a supreme monarch. What there is exists only for show. The amusingly foolish and fractious opinions that Jupiter hears in *The Play of the Weather* only reconfirm for him his own "wisdom and nature so noble," and in his opinion they warrant his supremacy as the best means to a "firm and stable" realm. The petitions of the suitors, each asking for an eternity of one kind of weather, can hardly represent an "encomium of the method of arguing *in utramque partem*," as Joel Altman claims,[40] for it contributes nothing to the obvious solution to the problem, which is the one Jupiter finally offers: to leave things as they were.

If one needs the hint that this "judgment" is not as impressive as Jupiter seems to think, Merry Report provides it:

> God thank your lordship. Lo, how this is brought to pass!
> Sirs, now shall ye have the weather even as it was.
>
> (lines 1239–40)

Jupiter does not pick up on the irony of Merry Report's expression of gratitude, but readers must. And that makes the self-congratulation of Jupiter's concluding lines appear all the more ominous:

> We need no wit our self any farther to boast,
> For our deeds declare us apparently.
> Not only here on earth in every coast,
> But also above in the heavenly company,

by your high commandment of writ; Unless your highness by your royal assent shall license us to make, promulge and execute the same, and thereto give your most royal assent and authority. (Pocock, *Records of the Reformation*, vol. 2, pp. 257–8)
Several slightly different MS drafts of the Submission exist (other versions are in *Documents*, no. 6, and *Documents Illustrative of English Church History*, ed. Henry Gee and William John Hardy [London: MacMillan, 1910], pp. 176–8), such differences "probably indicating," according to Pocock, "the great difficulty there was in satisfying the king." It was officially subscribed on May 16 (see Lehmberg, *The Reformation Parliament*, pp. 149–53), and passed by Parliament during the 1534 session as 25 Henry VIII, c. 19, in *Statutes*.

[39] *The King's Great Matter*, p. 192.
[40] *The Tudor Play of Mind*, p. 123.

Our prudence hath made peace universally.
Which thing, we say, recordeth us as principal
God and governor of heaven, earth, and all.

Now unto that heaven we will make return,
Where we be glorified most triumphantly.
Also we will all ye that on earth sojourn –
Since cause giveth cause – to know us your lord only,
And now here to sing most joyfully,
Rejoicing in us; and in mean time we shall
Ascend into our throne celestial.   (lines 1241–54)

Jupiter gloats over his supposed wisdom and the people's "rejoicing in us," in language that mimics the rhetoric of royal supremacy – the "know us your lord only" mode of discourse such as that which Cromwell was drafting for the next sessions of Parliament. *The Play of the Weather* represents Henry as he seemed in 1533 on the verge of becoming, a supreme ruler. But the supreme ruler in this play is a windbag, easily deflated by Merry Report's jests. It was not too late for Henry VIII to refuse this role. The Submission of the Clergy had occurred, foreshadowing the supremacy legislation to come, but it had not yet been introduced to Parliament. Henry could still take the wiser course by conforming his actions more closely to the philosopher-king image that he was, even yet, promulgating through the royal press. According to the testimony of this propaganda, wise counsel and fruitful debate are available at Henry's court and in his Parliament, and Henry prizes that counsel and debate, listening to "each man indifferently" in order to obtain the wisest guidance. In its satirical depiction of Jupiter, *The Play of the Weather* pressures Henry to keep the pledge of this public image, for in truth, as the supreme god admits with unknowing irony, "our deeds declare us apparently."

Conclusion
The Rhetoric of Supremacy

In the context of a discussion of seventeenth-century religious polemics and apologetics, Richard Helgerson looks back on the earliest years of the Tudor struggle over the powers of church and state and says that, "when in 1534 Parliament declared that England was and always had been an empire and that its king was supreme head of church and state, it invented Leviathan." That is, it invented "the body of the beast, a body that includes us all," a metaphor for the state that mandates the realm speak with one voice.[1] During the period of the divorce crisis Henry was of course ever moving closer to this mandate. Even while he was encouraging open dialogue, Berthelet's ostensible examples increasingly hemmed dialogue in, and as early as *A Glass of the Truth* (in late 1531) it was very clear that Henry viewed his conscience as appropriately the conscience of England, and his subjects were only his *good* subjects if their speech accorded with his will. But not until 1534 was this consensus explicitly required by law. The supremacy legislation, for this reason, abruptly brings my story to a close, because it marks a total reformation of the discursive practices that had attended Henry VIII's philosopher-king image.

There were five statutes passed during the fifth and sixth sessions of Parliament in 1534, and subsequently printed by Berthelet, that effected this absolute and unambiguous censorship: the Restraint of Annates and the First Succession Act came first,[2] followed by the Act of Supremacy, the Act Ratifying the Oath for the Observation of the Act of Succession (also known as the Second Act of Succession), and the Treasons Act.[3] The implicit threats of *A Glass of the Truth* were now published in plain speech. The First Act of Succession, for instance, states that subjects who "by writing, print, deed or act" say or do "any thing or things to the prejudice, slander, disturbance or derogation" of the king's matrimony, "shall be adjudged high traitors . . . and suffer

---

[1] *Forms of Nationhood*, p. 292.

[2] 25 Henry VIII, c. 20 and c. 22, in *Statutes*.

[3] 26 Henry VIII, c. 1, c. 2, and c. 13, in *Statutes*. Except for the Act Ratifying the Oath (reprinted in Gee, *Documents*, no. 56), the supremacy legislation is in Elton, *The Tudor Constitution*, nos. 4, 30, 178, and 180. *Documents* contains the Act in Restraint of Annates (no. 8) and the Act of Supremacy (no. 13).

pains of death."[4] The final section of this act calls for a loyalty oath, the base text of which soon afterwards appeared as part of the Second Act of Succession. The ultimate "form, or example of the profession and oath exhibited to Henry VIII" was provided in Latin and English, and stated on behalf of the king's subjects, "We, not constrained by force or fear, not hereunto induced or seduced by any deceit or other sinister machination, but out of our own certain knowledge, deliberate minds and mere and spontaneous wills, do, purely of our own accord, and absolutely in the word of our priesthood, profess, promise, and swear, unto your most illustrious majesty, our singular and most high lord and patron, Henry the eighth, by the grace of God, king of England and France, defender of the faith, lord of Ireland, and on earth of the English Church, immediately under Christ, supreme head."[5] The same act also required the execution of anyone who refused to take this oath, while the Supremacy Act further established that Henry "shall have full power and authority" to "repress, redress, reform, order, correct, restrain and amend" all "errors" and "heresies," as well as other "abuses, offenses, contempts and enormities" that need to be "reformed, repressed, redressed, corrected, restrained or amended."[6] Henry's right to determine the meaning of scripture, and to call dissent heresy, was now in the statute books.

II

Not surprisingly, 1534 was William Rastell's last year in the printing trade, and it appears that he was winding down his business quickly. We know of only six books that he published in that year: an abridged edition of the statutes passed in 1532–1533, two editions of the *Natura Brevium*, Heywood's *Play of Love*, and finally, the Rastells' last expression of Catholic dissent posing as support for government policy, German Gardiner's *Letter of a Young Gentleman wherein Men May See the Demeanor and Heresy of John Frith late Burned* (*STC* 11594).

This *Letter of a Young Gentleman* purports to record two dialogues, the first between John Frith and Bishop Stephen Gardiner, the second between Frith and the author of the tract, German Gardiner (probably the bishop's nephew), while Frith was imprisoned in the Tower.[7] The

---

[4] Elton, *The Tudor Constitution*, no. 4.

[5] Sir Walter Scott, ed. *The Somers Collection of Tracts: A Collection of Scarce and Valuable Tracts . . . of the Late Lord Somers*, 2nd ed., 13 vols. (London: T. Cadell and W. Davies, etc., 1809–15), vol. 1, p. 37 (both the Latin and English versions are printed in this volume [pp. 35–8]).

[6] Elton, *The Tudor Constitution*, no. 180.

[7] It was Stephen Gardiner who drafted Henry's response to Bishop Fisher in the

tract was written and printed in order to confirm in the public's mind that the government was right in having Frith burned, by corroborating Thomas More's assertion in *The Apology* that Frith was a "proud unlearned fool" who could never be persuaded to revoke his "pestilent heresy against the sacrament."[8] Because *A Letter of a Young Gentleman* was printed "cum privilegio," the impression is made that German Gardiner speaks from a position that has the king's favor. The impression is strengthened when Gardiner observes how shamefully Frith's opinions contradict those of "the king's highness in his most excellent and erudite assertion of the sacraments" (sig. 23ᵛ), meaning Henry's *Assertio ad Lutherum.*

Despite this surface show of government support, German Gardiner's motive for writing *A Letter of a Young Gentleman*, and William Rastell's for printing it, was clearly subversive. As Richard Marius explains, the very topic of John Frith was a potentially embarrassing one for Henry, since Frith had been "a pawn in Henry VIII's elaborate game against the Catholic church" since early 1531. After the court's overtures to Tyndale had been rebuffed, says Marius, "the king – or at least his agents – believed that [Frith] could be won over, made to forsake his radical beliefs, and persuaded to take up the king's side in the divorce."[9] Henry therefore offered Frith his favor for a time. There is even an extent letter, from Chapuys to Charles V, which Marius plausibly suggests describes not only Henry's kindly treatment given Frith (referred to as a "young priest"), but his bargaining for Frith's services as a propagandist in return.[10] According to Chapuys,

> the priest, fearing lest the archbishop of Canterbury should proceed against him, appealed to the king, as chief and sovereign of the said archbishop, and was conducted to the royal presence before several bishops, who disputed with him and asked him to retract [his erroneous doctrines]. Upon which the king taking in his hand a parchment role, where the priest's errors were stated, his eyes fell on the very first article wherein it was expressly stated that the Pope was not the sovereign chief of the Christian Church. I have been told that the king said immediately: "This proposition cannot be counted as

legatine trial of 1529 (see above, p. 9). Though Gardiner was a staunch defender of Church doctrine he did support the divorce and Henry's supremacy. A recent study of Gardiner's career is Glyn Redworth, *In Defence of the Church Catholic: The Life of Stephen Gardiner* (Oxford: Basil Blackwell, 1990), but on Gardiner's efforts to persuade Frith to recant his heresies see James Arthur Muller, *Stephen Gardiner and the Tudor Reaction* (New York: MacMillan, 1926), pp. 52–3.

[8] *CW*, vol. 9, pp. 124–5.

[9] *CW*, vol. 7, pp. cxxiii, cxxix (Introduction to More's *Letter Against Frith*).

[10] Ibid., pp. cxxx–ii. The letter, excerpted below, is calendared in *SP, Spanish*, vol. 4, pt. 1, no. 664.

heretical, for it is both true and certain." Therefore, after the king had heard what the priest had to say in his own defence, he was set free and sent back to his own dwelling on condition of preaching one of these days a sermon, and retracting some of his doctrines which the king does not consider as thoroughly orthodox.

For Thomas More at the time, Henry's "deal" with John Frith followed by his release could only have been "a crushing humiliation," says Marius. But once it became "Henry's policy" in 1533 "to prove that he was as Catholic as anyone else in Christendom," that deal would have been "embarrassing or even dangerous" to the king if it became public. Hence, when "the government turned from wooing Frith to making an example of him" (he was burned on July 4, 1533), "to gloat over Frith's death" could be interpreted as trying to "call attention to the government's flirtation with the young man."[11] In many places in *A Letter of a Young Gentleman*, in fact, "gloating" seems to best characterize German Gardiner's tone. At one point, for example, Gardiner says that Frith "hath brought his filthy carcass to the temporal fire, and his silly wretched soul to the fire everlasting." This is as it should be, Gardiner goes on, for "neither good man nor almost evil, could without abhoring and detesting his wickedness hear him named" (sig. 4ʳ⁻ᵛ). Those who were aware of Henry's attempts to recruit Frith would understand readily enough where on the spectrum of good to evil this sentence places Henry. With Gardiner's treatise, William Rastell's press moved from publishing counsel to condemnation.

This shift is more obvious when we come to Gardiner's explicit statements of loyalty to the Roman Catholic Church. "There is but one truth, and one Church which professeth that truth," he says, and that is "the holy Catholic Church of Christ." And make no mistake, Gardiner emphasizes, he does not mean any "universal church of the elect" as Frith would define it, but "the known Church" and "the governors of the same" – whom, says Gardiner, "if you disobeyed, ought we not then answer and were we not bound by the word of God, to take you as an heathen?" (sig. 37ʳ⁻ᵛ). Bold words in 1534, given that Henry had defied the pope to marry Anne the year before, and that this was the year Parliament would declare him head of church and state in England.

More interesting, to my mind, is the way that *A Letter of a Young Gentleman* professes to record dialogues, but presents instead mockeries of dialogue. When the Gardiners attempt to persuade Frith from his heresies, they do not so much debate Frith as knock their heads against a wall, continually frustrated as they are by Frith's nonsensical answers

[11] *CW*, vol. 7, pp. cxxxi, cxliii, clv, clviii.

and stalling tricks. Stephen Gardiner, for example, thinks he has won a crucial point when Frith agrees at the outset "to follow the authority of the Catholic doctors" in their dispute. The concession made those who were present in the room "rejoice," we are told, because they assumed Frith "had meant good faith" in his "promise," and had "yielded himself to reason" (sig. 9^r). But when confronted with passages from Augustine and Chrysostom that contradict his opinions, Frith refuses to accept them as decisive answers to the questions under dispute, based on what German Gardiner dismisses as Frith's random interpretations of the passages. The young heretic "would rather say anything whatsoever" to avoid retracting his errors, we are told. In the end, Frith responds to the arguments against him with "answers so inconstant and variable" that Bishop Gardiner abandons the cause, declaring that it is "most meet to proceed with [Frith] judicially, and either cure the infected sheep, or if it were desperate, cast it out of the fold" (sig. 8^{r-v}).

With the optimism of youth, German Gardiner decides to keep up the battle. But as before, Frith will only "trifle" and "babble" and "play with every thing," offering "nothing else but inventions of his own brain" as evidence for his opinions (sigs. 16^{r-v}, 39^v). When Gardiner points to relevant passages in scripture or the Church fathers, Frith responds by "shaking off [the] matter with a certain grinning laughter after his fashion, as though it had been nothing to the purpose" (sig. 19^r), or by ignoring the challenge to his position, sitting "still a while, without either speaking or making any semblance to speak" (sig. 23^r).

Worse yet, Frith toys with his examiner. When he is told that Irenaeus and Hilary had verified the real presence in the Eucharist, "then," says Gardiner, "began he as it had been in a tragedy, to ruffle and cry why had not the bishop [Stephen Gardiner] told him this, complaining sore, that they had showed him no such place, so that a man would have thought him very sorry, that he knew it not before, and desirous to know it then." But Frith's show of desire to know the truth "proved afterward clean contrary." When "the next day after" the books were "brought unto him" and "the places showed," Gardiner reports, then Frith only "blamed therein my hasty judgment," declaring the passages "were somewhat to the purpose, but not so much as I said they were" (sig. 27^{r-v}). After all this, says Gardiner, Frith had the audacity to complain that he was being used harshly, since he had "offered himself to be reformed" (sig. 28^r).

Obviously we should not assume Gardiner's treatise to be a fair and accurate record of his debate with Frith, but as a publication of 1534 that reflects on its times and on its own literary form it *is* accurate, because this is a dialogue that announces the end of dialogue. Readers see the spectacle of debate in which "all reason and craft [have] failed" (sig. 35^v). Unguided by the authority of Church doctrine, each man may use a "new logic" (sig. 24^r) to concoct perverse, idiosyncratic interpretations of God's word. Unless, that is, the reigning temporal power succeeds in asserting its own "logic" on the realm. Frith has been "late burnt" as a heretic, Gardiner may gloat, but what shall result from the supremacy legislation that casts all England "out of the fold" and into one man's church?

We know that in 1534 William Rastell was called before Cromwell to justify his publication of Thomas More's *Answer to a Poisoned Book*. We can only wonder if *A Letter of a Young Gentleman* came up in that or in another conversation between Cromwell and Rastell on the topic of Rastell's loyalty to the king. In any case, in 1534 William Rastell left the printing business and devoted himself to the full-time study of the law.[12] The next time he had anything to do with his former trade was in 1557, under Mary's reign, when he edited the first collection of More's English works for Richard Tottel.

III

John Rastell, in contrast, underwent a religious conversion, reportedly after meeting John Frith in 1531 while Frith was a prisoner in the Tower, and as a consequence he threw in his lot with Thomas Cromwell and the political reformers in Parliament.[13] He also let out half his printing house to John Gough, a Protestant who had been briefly imprisoned in 1528 for publishing heretical books,[14] and in extant letters to Cromwell we find Rastell offering to print a primer he had undertaken to write, "to bring people from the naughty doctrine of the pope."[15] But Rastell's career was

[12] William Rastell entered Lincoln's Inn, where More had studied and where he was joined by Richard Heywood, the younger brother of Thomas. Early in Elizabeth's reign the families of William Rastell and John Heywood fled to Louvain to live in exile (Reed, *Early Tudor Drama*, pp. 78–83, 90).

As for German Gardiner, in 1544 he was executed, together with five Franciscan priests, for denying the royal supremacy; see Muller, *Stephen Gardiner*, p. 113, based on an entry in *Monumenta Franciscana*, Rerum Britannicarum Medii Aevi Scriptores (Rolls Series), no. 4, vol. 2, edited by Richard Howlett (London: HMSO, 1882), p. 206.

[13] See Clebsch, *England's Earliest Protestants*, pp. 109–10; Devereux, "John Rastell's Press," pp. 39–40; Elton, *Reform and Renewal*, pp. 144–6; Geritz and Laine, *John Rastell*, p. 21; and the entry for John Rastell in Bindoff, *The Commons, 1509–1558*, vol. 3, pp. 176–9.

[14] Reed, *Early Tudor Drama*, p. 23; Devereux, "John Rastell's Press," pp. 44–5; Geritz and Laine, *John Rastell*, pp. 24–5.

[15] Calendared in *LP*, vol. 7, nos. 1071–3. One book from John Rastell's press that argues for reform does survive, though it lacks Rastell's identifying device: *A Dialogue between Clement and Bernard* (1532; *STC* 6800.3). On the question of its authorship see my "*A dyaloge betwene Clemente and Bernarde*, c. 1532: A Neglected

coming to an end. Cromwell did not finance or, it seems, even take an interest in Rastell's project. His printing services were not needed, for there were plenty of other printers in London already busy bringing people from "the naughty doctrine of the pope." The court was no doubt content just to have the two Rastells out of the way, their opposition silenced. In 1535 John Rastell was apparently tried for refusing to pay his tithes, and his biographers have surmised that on these grounds Rastell was sent to prison. He died there, estranged from his family and penniless.[16]

Thomas Berthelet, on the other hand, began in 1534 to print the kind of heavy-handed tracts that we normally think of as government propaganda. No one had to read between the lines any longer. The *Articles Devised by the Whole Consent of the King's Council* (first edition, 1533) was printed again in 1534,[17] in addition to *A Treatise against the Muttering of Some Papists in Corners*, and *A Treatise wherein Christ and his Teachings are Compared with the Pope and His Doings.*[18] The king's counselors now began to speak in specific terms on particular issues and with no pretense of a variety in opinions, as we see in Edward Fox's *Opus eximium, de vera differentia regiae potestatis et ecclesiasticae* (1534; *STC* 11218), Stephen Gardiner's *Episcopi de vera obedientia oratio* (1535; *STC* 11584), and Richard Sampson's *Regii sacelli decani oratio, qua docet anglos, regiae dignitati ut obediant* (1535; *STC* 21681). With "the Pilgrimage of Grace" uprising of 1536, Berthelet's press was even more active publishing the king's demands for national consensus. He printed five editions of *The Ten Articles of 1536, Devised by the King's Highness to establish Christian Unity, approved by the Whole Clergy of this Realm*, followed by the *Injunctions Given by the Authority of the King's Highness to the Clergy.*[19] Berthelet also printed Thomas Starkey's *Exhortation to the People, Instructing them to Unity and Obedience* (*STC* 23236), and two books by Sir Richard Morrison: *A Lamentation in Which is Showed What Ruin and Destruction Cometh of Seditious Rebellion*, and *A Remedy for Sedition Wherein are Contained Many Things concerning the True and Loyal Obeisance that Commons Owe unto Their Prince and Sovereign Lord the King.*[20] In 1535–36 Henry also issued a proclamation against

---

Tract Belonging to the Last Period of John Rastell's Career," *Sixteenth Century Journal* 29 (1998): 55–65.

[16] The accounts of Rastell's final years are based on letters calendared in *LP*, vol. 7, nos. 10713, and vol. 10, no. 248. See Reed, *Early Tudor Drama*, pp. 26–7; Devereux, "John Rastell's Press," p. 45; Geritz and Laine, *John Rastell*, pp. 24–5.

[17] Reprinted in Pocock, *Records of the Reformation*, vol. 2, pp. 523–31.

[18] *STC* 23551.5 and 14575. The first is reprinted in Pocock, *Records of the Reformation*, vol. 2, pp. 539–52.

[19] *Documents*, nos. 16 and 17.

[20] *STC* 18113.3 and 18113.5–7; reprinted with contemporary documents and an

seditious rumors and unlawful assemblies,[21] and another ordering the confiscation of Bishop Fisher's books.[22] The free speech that supposedly had been encouraged before was now unmistakably proscribed, by law and by example, and that left just one route for London's other printers: to publish books like Berthelet's or not publish political or religious works at all.

This does not mean Henry ceased to cultivate a public image. Several studies show that he styled himself a modern-day David in portraits and in the illustrations that appeared on the title pages of the Coverdale and Great Bibles of the period.[23] Nor does it mean that other printers had not already found ways to follow and go beyond the king's rules for discourse, both old and new. From the beginning of the decade printers with Protestant sympathies welcomed the anti-Rome themes of the king's books, and, sometimes through the roundabout sponsorship of Thomas Cromwell, published reformist pamphlets that complemented Henry's propaganda but also advanced Protestant doctrine further than Henry was ultimately comfortable with. In 1534 they were even more free to do so.[24] Their strategy, of course, was to speed the ship of state in its course toward a Protestant reformation, so that its momentum would be too great – even for the king – to bring it easily to a halt. Robert Wyer, for instance, printed a translation of Martin Luther's *A Book Made by a Certain Great Clerk, against the New Idol, and Old Devil* (1534, but without its author's name, to be sure; *STC* 16962), as well as *The Image of a Very Christian Bishop and of a Counterfeit Bishop* (1536; *STC* 16983.5). John Byddell published *A*

---

analysis of the government's polemical response to the Pilgrimage of Grace uprising in David Sandler Berkowitz, *Humanist Scholarship and Public Order: Two Tracts against the Pilgrimage of Grace by Sir Richard Morrison* (Washington: Folger, 1984).

[21] This survives only in MS; printed in *TRP*, vol. 1, no. 168.

[22] Reprinted in *TRP*, vol. 1, no. 161.

[23] See John N. King, "Henry VIII as David: The King's Image and Reformation Politics," in *Rethinking the Henrician Era: Essays on Early Tudor Texts and Contexts*, ed. Peter C. Herman (Urbana: University of Illinois Press, 1994), pp. 78–92; King, *Tudor Royal Iconography: Literature and Art in an Age of Religious Crisis* (Princeton: Princeton University Press, 1989), chapter two (especially pp. 54–6 and 76–80); and Pamela Tudor-Craig, "Henry VIII and King David," in *Early Tudor England: Proceedings of the 1987 Harlaxton Symposium*, ed. Daniel Williams (Woodbridge, Suffolk: Boydell Press, 1987), pp. 183–205. A collection of studies on the representation of Henry VIII that ranges from the coronation panegyrics to modern film is in Uwe Baumann, *Henry VIII in History, Historiography and Literature* (Frankfurt: Peter Lang, 1992).

[24] This is the subject of Riegler, "Printing, Protestantism, and Politics: Thomas Cromwell and Religious Reform," which documents that many of the works mentioned below, and others of a similar nature, were sponsored by William Marshall, who in turn received his money from Thomas Cromwell; also see Clebsch, *England's Earliest Protestants*, pp. 253–6.

Muster of Schismatic Bishops of Rome (1534; *STC* 23552) and *A Mandate to the Clergy against the Pope, Recognizing the Supremacy of the King as head of the Church* (1534; *STC* 16794.5 A3) by John Longland. Thomas Godfray, who in 1532 printed the first collected works of Chaucer, brought out in the same year the Chaucerian *Prayer and Complaint of the Ploughman unto Christ*, which rather daringly contained a preface initialed "W.T."[25] Other works by banned authors were also printed by Godfray: a primer of prayers taken from George Joye's *Ortulus anime* (*STC* 15988), and a *Treatise Declaring and Showing that Images are not to be Suffered in Churches* (*STC* 24238) translated from Martin Bucer's *Das einigerlei Bild* (both 1535). Godfray was also, it seems, the first to print Tyndale's New Testament and *Pathway into the Holy Scripture* in England (1536; *STC* 2831 and 24462–3). At the same time, Godfray was careful to place his printing activity within the context of the king's own program. He printed in 1536 "a panegyric of Henry VIII as the abolisher of papist abuses,"[26] and the first edition of Christopher St. German's *Answer to a Letter*, a pamphlet defending the royal supremacy (*STC* 21558.5).

These printers also published translations of Erasmus, but they chose the early polemical and satirical works that were popular among Lutheran printers on the Continent, rather than the more philosophical and pedagogical treatises favored by the royal press. In 1534, for instance, Robert Wyer twice printed William Roy's translation of *Paraclesis* (*STC* 10493.5 and 10494). It is in this famous essay that we find Erasmus wishing the farmer at his plow might someday be able to sing the Gospel to himself in his native tongue, a favorite image in the reformers' arguments for vernacular Bible translations.[27] Similarly, in 1534 John Byddell printed *The Paraphrase of Erasmus Roterdame upon the Epistle of Paul unto Titus* (1534; *STC* 10503), and the same year he commissioned Robert Copland to publish for him translations of two dialogues by Erasmus: *Funus*, famous for its attack on the greed of

[25] *STC* 20036.5. The preface is thought to be Tyndale's or by George Joye (see the entry in *STC* for the first edition [Antwerp; 20036]). Thomas Godfray also printed Skelton's *Colin Clout* (1531). On the subject of sixteenth-century Protestant pastoral satire see John N. King, *English Reformation Literature*; and King, "Spenser's *Shepheardes Calendar* and Protestant Pastoral Satire," in *Renaissance Genres: Essays on Theory, History, and Interpretation*, ed. Barbara K. Lewalski (Cambridge, Mass.: Harvard University Press, 1986), pp. 369–98, which is reworked in chapter 1 of King's *Spenser's Poetry and the Reformation Tradition* (Princeton: Princeton University Press, 1990).

[26] Only a fragment survives, and this is how it is described in *STC* (13089a).

[27] See the translation of *Paraclesis* in *Christian Humanism and the Reformation: Selected Writings of Erasmus with the Life of Erasmus by Beatus Rhenanus*, ed. John C. Olin (New York: Fordham University Press, 1975), p. 97.

clergymen (*STC* 10453.5), and *Julius exclusus e coelis*, in which Saint Peter denies Pope Julius II entrance into heaven (*STC* 14841.5 and 14842).

These would be the primary materials, then, for a history of a different discursive formation in England, one that was generated in the latter years of the divorce crisis but that characterized the second half of the 1530s. There were, of course, other concurrent formations. Sharon Jansen has shown, for example, that religious prophecies, not printed but spoken and circulated in manuscript, provided an important means for voicing political protest during this period.[28] The traces of another formation survive in the introspective writings from this decade that today we most value: Thomas More's "Tower works,"[29] and the poetry of Thomas Wyatt.

It is with a poem attributed to Wyatt that I will bring my story to a close, for it seems an especially poignant reflection of Henry's clamping down, once and for all, on dialogue and counsel. Wyatt probably composed it in 1536 while he was imprisoned in the Tower, and perhaps after he had witnessed the execution of Anne Boleyn. The poem is short and can be quoted in full:

> *V. Innocentia*
> *Veritas Viat Fides*
> *Circumdederunt me inimici mei*
>
> Who list his wealth and ease retain,
> Himself let him unknown contain.
> Press not too fast in at that gate
> Where the return stands by disdain,
> For sure, *circa regna tonat.*
>
> These bloody days have broken my heart.
> My lust, my youth did them depart,
> And blind desire of estate.
> Who hastes to climb seeks to revert.
> Of truth, *circa regna tonat.*

[28] In "'And he shall be called Edward': Sixteenth-Century Political Protest and Folger MS Loseley b. 546," *English Literary Renaissance* 23 (1993): pp. 227–43; and *Political Protest and Prophecy under Henry VIII* (Woodbridge, Suffolk: Boydell Press, 1991).

[29] These are *A Dialogue of Comfort, Instructions and Prayers, A Treatise Upon the Passion*, and *De Tristitia Christi*, in vols. 12–14 of *CW*. We would also include in this genre John Fisher's "Spiritual Consolation," a letter to his sister Elizabeth written in the Tower and reprinted in *The English Works of John Fisher, Bishop of Rochester*, ed. John E. B. Mayor, Early English Text Society, Extra Series, no. 27, pt. 1 (London: EETS, 1876), pp. 349–63.

> The bell tower showed me such a sight
> That in my head sticks day and night.
> There did I learn out of a grate,
> For all favor, glory, or might,
> That yet *circa regna tonat.*
>
> By proof, I say, there did I learn;
> Wit helpeth not defense to yearn,
> Of innocency to plead or prate.
> Bear low, therefore, give God the stern,
> For sure, *circa regna tonat.*[30]

Wyatt, we see, is repeating in verse Hythlodaeus's contention that the courts of kings are dangerous places, though he does so from the perspective of one already burned by glory's luster. The theme is underscored by the refrain, "around thrones it thunders" (*circa regna tonat*), a line taken from Seneca's *Phaedra* which concludes an analogy between Jupiter and tyrants:

> *Chorus:* Seldom does the moist valley suffer the lightning's blast; but Caucasus the huge, and the Phrygian grove of mother Cybele, quake beneath the bolt of high-thundering Jove. For in jealous fear Jove aims at that which neighbors on high heaven; but the low-roofed, common home never feels his mighty blasts. Around thrones he thunders (*Circa regna tonat*).[31]

The wisest course in such circumstances, Wyatt says, is to "bear low."[32] Yet, consider further the refrain *circa regna tonat*. In *Phaedra* the line is satisfactorily translated as above, because the previous sentences make clear that Jupiter ("he") is doing the thundering. Since the subject is not explicitly identified, however (it is in the verb *tonat*), the line could just as well be translated in a way that plainly states the allegorical meaning of the passage: "Around authority (or, in the vicinity of kings) it thunders."[33]

---

[30] *Sir Thomas Wyatt: The Complete Poems*, ed. R. A. Rebholz (Harmondsworth: Penguin, 1978), p. 155.

[31] Seneca, *Hippolytus, or Phaedra*, lines 1132–40.

[32] Cf. Annabel Patterson's statement, in *Censorship and Interpretation*, that "the poetry of Sir Thomas Wyatt . . . deserve[s] reinvestigation in the light of the intimidating circumstances of the 1530s and 1540s, the onset of the Reformation in England, the divorce of Catherine of Aragon, and the execution of Queen Anne Boleyn. The secret refrain of much of the poetry of this period is made explicit in one of Wyatt's 'unpublished' poems: *Circa Regna tonat*" (p. 17). One study that answers this call is Michael Holahan, "Wyatt, the Heart's Forest, and the Ancient Savings," *English Literary Renaissance* 23 (1993): pp. 46–80.

[33] Some translators would also have it, "He [Jupiter] thunders through (or around) the realm," because *regna* may mean (a) the power of a ruler, meaning authority, kingship, or (as often in Cicero) tyranny; as well as (b) a realm or kingdom.

In Wyatt's poem, where *circa regna tonat* occurs without any prior reference to Jupiter or the heavens, but only within the context of mortal and specifically Wyatt's cares, we would likely incline toward the second rendering. But in the last stanza of the poem it is fitting to read the line in still another way, because there it seems more relevant than it does in Seneca's *Phaedra* that the verb *tonare*, like *thunder* in English, often denotes in Latin literature a loud, thunderous voice. When Wyatt follows the statement that "Wit helpeth not defense to yearn, / Of innocency to plead or prate" shortly after with the words "For sure, *circa regna tonat*," he provides an apt characterization of how, for Wyatt and (as we have seen in this study) for More and his circle, the rules of public discourse were changed and the space for public dissent was constricted. We are left with the impression by this last stanza that that pleading or prattling voice, really any voice but the royal one, is drowned out.

Bibliography

I. Primary Works

Adams, Joseph Quincy. *Chief Pre-Shakespearean Dramas.* New York: Houghton Mifflin, 1924.

Arber, Edward, ed. *English Reprints.* Westminster: A. Constable, 1895.

——, ed. *An English Garner: Ingatherings from our History and Literature.* 8 vols. Westminster: A. Constable, 1893–97.

Barlowe, Jerome and William Roye. *Rede Me and Be Nott Wrothe.* Edited by Douglas Parker. Toronto: University of Toronto Press, 1992.

Barlow, William. *The Work of William Barlowe, including Bishop Barlowe's Dialogue on the Lutheran Factions.* Edited by Andrew M. McLean. The Courtenay Library of Reformation Classics, edited by G. E. Duffield, no. 15. Appleford, Berkshire: Sutton Courtenay Press, 1981.

Bray, Gerald, ed. *Documents of the English Reformation.* Cambridge: James Clarke, 1994.

Brewer, J. S., James Gairdner, et al., eds. *Letters and Papers, Foreign and Domestic, of the Reign of Henry VIII.* 21 vols. and *Addenda.* London: Longmans and HMSO, 1862–1932.

Brown, Rawdon, ed. *Calendar of State Papers, and Manuscripts, relating to English Affairs, existing in the Archives and Collections of Venice, and in Other Libraries of Northern Italy.* 38 vols. London: Longmans and HMSO, 1864–1947.

Cicero. *Brutus, Orator.* Translated by G. L. Hendrickson and H. M. Hubbell. Loeb Classical Library. London: W. Heinemann, 1939. Revised, 1962.

——. *De Officiis.* Translated by Walter Miller. Loeb Classical Library. London: W. Heinemann, 1913.

——. *De Oratore.* Translated by E. W. Sutton and H. Rackham. Loeb Classical Library. 2 vols. London: W. Heinemann, 1942.

——. *De Senectute, De Amicitia, De Divinatione.* Translated by W. A. Falconer. Loeb Classical Library. London: W. Heinemann, 1923.

——. *Letters to His Friends.* Translated by W. Glynn Williams. Loeb Classical Library. 3 vols. London: W. Heinemann, 1927.

A Dialogue between a Knight and a Clerk concerning the Power Spiritual and Temporal. London: T. Berthelet, 1533. Printed as a parallel text in Trevisa, *Trevisa's Dialogus inter Militem et Clericum.*

Disputatio inter clericum et militem. London: T. Berthelet, 1531.

Elyot, Thomas. *A Critical Edition of Sir Thomas Elyot's* The Boke named the Governour. Edited by Donald W. Rude. New York: Garland, 1992.

——. *The Boke Named The Governour devised by Sir Thomas Elyot, Knight.* Edited by Henry H. S. Croft. 2 vols. London: Kegan Paul, 1880.

———. *Four Political Treatises.* Facsimile reproductions with introduction by Lillian Gottesman. Gainesville, Florida: Scholars' Facsimiles and Reprints, 1967.

———. *The Letters of Sir Thomas Elyot.* Edited by K. J. Wilson. *Studies in Philology* 73 (1976).

———. *Of the Knowledge which Maketh a Wise Man.* Edited by Edwin Johnston Howard. Oxford, Ohio: Anchor Press, 1946.

Erasmus. *Christian Humanism and the Reformation: Selected Writings of Erasmus with the Life of Erasmus by Beatus Rhenanus.* Edited by John C. Olin. New York: Fordham University Press, 1975.

———. *The Collected Works of Erasmus.* Edited by R. J. Schoeck, B. M. Corrigan, et al. Toronto: Toronto University Press, 1974– .

———. *The Colloquies of Erasmus.* Translated by Craig R. Thompson. Chicago: Chicago University Press, 1965.

———. *Erasmi Opuscula.* Edited by Wallace K. Ferguson. The Hague: Martinus Nijhoff, 1933.

———. *Opera omnia Desiderii Erasmi Roterodami.* Amsterdam: North Holland Pub. Co., 1972– .

———. *Opus epistolarum Des. Erasmi Roterodami.* Edited by P. S. Allen, M. H. Allen, and H. W. Garrod. 12 vols. Oxford: Oxford University Press, 1906–58.

Fish, Simon. *A Supplication of Beggars.* In *The Complete Works of St. Thomas More,* vol. 7, pp. 407–22.

Fisher, John. *The English Works of John Fisher, Bishop of Rochester.* Edited by John E. B. Mayor. The Early English Text Society, Extra Series, no. 27, pt. 1. London: EETS, 1876.

Foxe, John. *The Acts and Monuments of John Foxe.* Edited by Rev. Stephen Reed Cattley. 8 vols. London: R. B. Seeley and W. Burnside, 1837–41.

Frith, John. *The Work of John Frith.* Edited by N. T. Wright. The Courtenay Library of Reformation Classics, no. 7. Oxford: Sutton Courtenay Press, 1978.

Furnivall, Frederick, ed. *Ballads from Manuscripts.* 2 vols. London and Hertford: Ballad Society, 1868–73.

Gardiner, German. *A Letter of a Young Gentleman named Master German Gardiner, written to a friend of his, wherein men may see the demeanor and heresy of John Frith, late burned.* London: W. Rastell, 1534.

Gardiner, Stephen. *Obedience in Church and State: Three Political Tracts by Stephen Gardiner.* Edited by Pierre Janelle. Cambridge: Cambridge University Press, 1930.

de Gayangos, Pascual, ed. *Calendar of Letters, Despatches, and State Papers, relating to the Negotiations between England and Spain.* 13 vols. London: Longmans and HMSO, 1862–1954.

Gee, Henry and William John Hardy, eds. *Documents Illustrative of English Church History.* London: MacMillan, 1910.

Hall, Edward. *Hall's Chronicle containing the History of England . . . to the end of the reign of Henry Eight.* Edited by Sir Henry Ellis. London: J. Johnson, 1809.

Henry VIII. *A Glass of the Truth.* In *Records of the Reformation,* edited by Pocock, vol. 2, pp. 385–421.

Heywood, John. *The Pardoner and the Friar, 1533; The Four Ps, ?1544.* Ed. G. R. Proudfoot. Malone Society Reprints. Oxford: Oxford University Press, 1984.

——. *The Plays of John Heywood.* Edited by Richard Axton and Peter Happé. Tudor Interludes, no. 6. Cambridge: D. S. Brewer, 1991.

Horace. *Satires, Epistles, Ars poetica.* Translated by H. R. Fairclough. Loeb Classical Library. London: W. Heinemann, 1929.

Hughes, Paul and James F. Larkin, eds. *Tudor Royal Proclamations.* 2 vols. New Haven: Yale University Press, 1964.

Luther, Martin. *D. Martin Luthers Werke.* 64 vols. Weimar: Kritische Gesammtausgabe, 1883– .

——. *Luther's Works.* Edited by Jaroslav Pelikan and Helmut T. Lehmann. 55 vols. Philadelphia: Muhlenberg and Fortress Press, 1955–86.

Machiavelli, Niccolò. *The Prince.* Translated by George Bull. Harmondsworth: Penguin, 1961.

Monumenta Franciscana, Rerum Britannicarum Medii Aevi Scriptores (Rolls Series), no. 4. vol. 1 edited by J. S. Brewer; vol. 2 edited by Richard Howlett. London: HMSO, 1858 and 1882.

More, Thomas. *The Complete Works of St. Thomas More.* Edited by Louis L. Martz, Richard S. Sylvester, Clarence H. Miller, et al. 15 vols. New Haven: Yale University Press, 1963–97.

Volumes cited:

Vol. 4: *Utopia.* Edited by Edward Surtz and J. H. Hexter, 1965.

Vol. 6, in 2 pts.: *A Dialogue concerning Heresies.* Edited by Thomas Lawler, Germain Marc'hadour, and Richard Marius, 1981.

Vol. 7: *Letter to Bugenhagen, Supplication of Souls, Letter Against Frith.* Edited by Frank Manley, Germain Marc'hadour, Richard Marius, and Clarence H. Miller, 1990.

Vol. 8, in 3 pts.: *The Confutation of Tyndale's Answer.* Edited by Louis A. Schuster, Richard Marius, James P. Lusardi, and Richard Schoeck, 1973.

Vol. 9: *The Apology.* Edited by J. B. Trapp, 1979.

Vol. 10: *The Debellation of Salem and Bizance.* Edited by John Guy, Ralph Keen, Clarence H. Miller, and Ruth McGugan, 1987.

Vol. 11: *The Answer to a Poisoned Book.* Edited by Stephen Merriam Foley and Clarence H. Miller, 1985.

Vol. 12: *A Dialogue of Comfort against Tribulation.* Edited by Louis L. Martz and Frank Manley, 1976.

Vol. 13: *Treatise on the Passion, Treatise on the Blessed Body, Instructions and Prayers.* Edited by Garry E. Haupt, 1976.

Vol. 14, in 2 pts.: *De Tristitia Christi.* Edited by Clarence H. Miller, 1976.

——. *The Correspondence of Sir Thomas More.* Edited by E. F. Rogers. Princeton: Princeton University Press, 1947.

The Noble Triumphant Coronation of Queen Anne, Wife unto the Most Noble

Bibliography

King Henry VIII. In *An English Garner,* edited by Arber, vol. 2, pp. 41–51; and *Tudor Tracts,* edited by Pollard, pp. 1–19.

Plato. *Plato: The Collected Dialogues.* Edited by Edith Hamilton and Huntingdon Cairns. Bollingen Series, vol. 71. Princeton: Princeton University Press, 1961.

Pocock, Nicholas, ed. *Records of the Reformation: The Divorce, 1527–1533.* 2 vols. Oxford: Carendon Press, 1870.

Rastell, John. The Pastyme of the People *and* A New Boke of Purgatory *by J. Rastell with a facsimile of* The Pastyme: *A Critical Edition.* The Renaissance Imagination, vol. 14. New York: Garland, 1985.

———. *Three Rastell Plays: Four Elements, Calisto and Melebea, Gentleness and Nobility.* Edited by Richard Axton. Tudor Interludes. Cambridge: D. S. Brewer, 1979.

Rhetorica ad Herennium. Translated by H. Caplan. Loeb Classical Library. London: W. Heinemann, 1954.

Roper, William. *The Life of Sir Thomas More.* In *Two Early Tudor Lives,* edited by Richard S. Sylvester and Davis P. Harding, pp. 196–254. New Haven: Yale University Press, 1962.

Sallust. *Sallust.* Translated by J. C. Rolfe. Loeb Classical Library. London: W. Heinemann, 1931.

St. German, Christopher. *St. German's Doctor and Student.* Edited by T. F. T. Plucknett and J. L. Barton. Selden Society, vol. 91. London: Selden Society, 1974.

Scott, Sir Walter, ed. *The Somers Collection of Tracts: A Collection of Scarce and Valuable Tracts, on the Most Interesting and Entertaining Subjects, but chiefly such as relate to the History and Constitution of these Kingdoms, selected from an Infinite Number in Print and in Manuscript, in the Royal, Cotton, Sion, and other Public, as well as Private, Libraries, particularly that of the Late Lord Somers.* 2nd edition, 13 vols. London: T. Cadell and W. Davies, etc., 1809–15.

Scriptores Historiae Augustae. Translated by David Magie. Loeb Classical Library. 3 vols. London: W. Heinemann, 1921–32.

Seneca. *Tragedies.* Translated by Frank Justus Miller. Loeb Classical Library. 2 vols. London: W. Heinemann, 1917. Revised, 1929 and 1987.

Skelton, John. *John Skelton: The Complete English Poems.* Edited by John Scattergood. New Haven: Yale University Press, 1983.

———. *The Poetical Works of John Skelton.* Edited by Rev. Alexander Dyce. 2 vols. London: Thomas Rodd, 1843.

Starkey, Thomas. *A Dialogue between Cardinal Pole and Thomas Lupset, Lecturer in Rhetoric at Oxford.* In *England in the Reign of Henry the Eighth, Pt. 2,* edited by J. M. Cowper, Early English Text Society, Extra Series, no. 32. London: EETS, 1871.

———. *Starkey's Life and Letters.* In *England in the Reign of King Henry the Eighth, Pt. 1,* edited by Sidney J. Herrtage, Early English Text Society, Extra Series, no. 32. London: EETS, 1878.

———. *Thomas Starkey: A Dialogue between Pole and Lupset.* Edited by T. F.

Mayer. Camden Fourth Series, vol. 37. London: Royal Historical Society, 1989.

State Papers, Published under the Authority of His Majesty's Commission, of King Henry VIII. 11 vols. G. Eyre and A. Strahan, 1830–52.

The Statutes of the Realm (1225–1713) Printed by Command of His Majesty King George the Third. 9 vols. London: G. Eyre and A. Strahan, 1810–22.

Strype, John. *Ecclesiastical Memorials, relating chiefly to Religion, and the Reformation of it, and the Emergencies of the Church of England, under King Henry VIII, King Edward VI, and Queen Mary I.* 3 vols. Oxford: Clarendon Press, 1822.

Surtz, Edward, S. J. and Virginia Murphy, eds. *The Divorce Tracts of Henry VIII.* Angers: *Moreana*, 1988.

Tacitus. *The Histories and the Annals.* Translated by Clifford Moore and John Jackson. Loeb Classical Library. 3 vols. London: W. Heinemann, 1931.

Tanner, J. R. *Tudor Constitutional Documents, A.D. 1485–1603, with an Historical Commentary.* Cambridge: Cambridge University Press, 1922.

Trevisa, John. *Trevisa's* Dialogus inter Militem et Clericum. Edited by Aaron Jenkins Perry. Early English Text Society, Original Series, no. 167. London: EETS, 1925 for 1924.

Tyndale, William. *An Answer to Sir Thomas More's Dialogue, The Supper of the Lord after the True Meaning of John VI. and 1 Cor. XI. and Wm. Tracy's Testament Expounded, by William Tyndale, Martyr, 1536.* Edited for the Parker Society by Rev. Henry Walter. Cambridge: Cambridge University Press, 1850.

———. *Doctrinal Treatises and Introductions to Different Portions of the Holy Scriptures, by William Tyndale, Martyr, 1536.* Edited for the Parker Society by Rev. Henry Walter. Cambridge: Cambridge University Press, 1848.

———. *Expositions and Notes on Sundry Portions of the Holy Scriptures, together with the Practice of Prelates, by William Tyndale, Martyr, 1536.* Edited for the Parker Society by Rev. Henry Walter. Cambridge: Cambridge University Press, 1849.

Wakefield, Robert. *Kotser Codicis R. Wakfeldi.* London: T. Berthelet, 1533.

Wyatt, Thomas. *Sir Thomas Wyatt: The Complete Poems.* Edited by R. A. Rebholz. Harmondsworth: Penguin, 1978.

II. Secondary Works

Adams, Robert. *The Better Part of Valor: More, Erasmus, Colet, and Vives, On Humanism, War, and Peace, 1496–1535.* Seattle: University of Washington Press, 1962.

Altman, Joel B. *The Tudor Play of Mind: Rhetorical Inquiry and the Development of Elizabethan Drama.* Berkeley: University of California Press, 1978.

Ames, Joseph. *Typographical Antiquities, being a Historical Account of Printing in England.* London: W. Faden, 1749.

Anglo, Sydney. *Spectacle, Pageantry, and Early Tudor Policy.* Oxford: Clarendon Press, 1969.

——. "William Cornish in a Play, Pageants, Prison and Politics." *Review of English Studies,* New Series, 10 (1959): pp. 357–60.

Armstrong, J. R. "The Dialectical Road to Truth." In *French Renaissance Studies, 1540–70: Humanism and the Encyclopedia,* edited by Peter Sharratt, pp. 36–51. Edinburgh: Edinburgh University Press, 1976.

Bagchi, David V. N. *Luther's Earliest Opponents: Catholic Controversialists, 1518–1525.* Minneapolis: Fortress Press, 1991.

Bainton, Roland H. *Here I Stand: A Life of Martin Luther.* New York: Abingdon-Cokesbury Press, 1950.

Baumann, Uwe. *Henry VIII: In History, Historiography and Literature.* Frankfurt: Peter Lang, 1992.

Baumer, Franklin le van. "The Church of England and the Common Corps of Christendom." *The Journal of Modern History* 16 (1944): pp. 1–21.

——. "The Conception of Christendom in Renaissance England." *Journal of the History of Ideas* 6 (1945): pp. 131–56.

——. *The Early Tudor Theory of Kingship.* New Haven: Yale University Press, 1940.

——. "England, the Turk, and the Common Corps of Christendom." *The American Historical Review* 50 (1944): pp. 26–48.

Bedouelle, Guy. "The Consultations of the Universities and Scholars Concerning the 'Great Matter' of King Henry VIII." Trans. by John L. Farthing in *The Bible in the Sixteenth Century,* edited by David C. Steinmetz, pp. 21–36. Durham: Duke University Press, 1990.

—— and Patrick Le Gal, eds. *Le "Divorce" du Roi Henry VIII: Etudes et documents.* Travaux d'Humanisme et Renaissance, no. 221. Geneva: Librairie Droz S.A., 1987.

Berkowitz, David Sandler. *Humanist Scholarship and Public Order: Two Tracts Against the Pilgrimage of Grace by Sir Richard Morrison.* Washington: Folger, 1984.

Bernard, G. W. "The Fall of Wolsey Reconsidered." *Journal of British Studies* 35 (1996): 277–310.

Bevington, David. *Tudor Drama and Politics: A Critical Approach to Topical Meaning.* Cambridge, Mass.: Harvard University Press, 1968.

Bindoff, S. T. *The House of Commons: 1509–1558.* The History of Parliament. 3 vols. London: Secker and Warburg, 1982.

Birch, David. *Early Reformation English Polemics.* Salzburg Studies in English Literature. Salzburg: Institut für Anglistik und Amerikanistik, 1983.

Block, Joseph S. *Factional Politics and the English Reformation, 1520–1540.* London: Royal Historical Society, 1993.

Bolwell, Robert W. *The Life and Works of John Heywood.* New York: Columbia University Press, 1921.

Caspari, F. *Humanism and the Social Order in Tudor England.* Chicago: University of Chicago Press, 1954.

Chambers, R. W. *Thomas More.* New York: Harcourt Brace, 1935.

Chastel, André. *The Sack of Rome, 1527.* Translated by Beth Archer. The A. W. Mellon Lecures in the Fine Arts, Bollingen Series, vol. 35, no. 26. Princeton: Princeton University Press, 1983.

Clebsch, William A. *England's Earliest Protestants, 1520–1535.* Yale Publications in Religion, edited by David Horne, vol. 11. New Haven: Yale University Press, 1964.

Conrad, F. W. "The Problem of Counsel Reconsidered: The Case of Sir Thomas Elyot." In *Political Thought and the Tudor Commonwealth: Deep Structure, Discourse, and Disguise,* edited by Paul A. Fideler and T. F. Mayer, pp. 75–107. London: Routledge, 1992.

Cooper, J. P. "The Supplication against the Ordinaries Reconsidered." *English Historical Review* 72 (1957): pp. 616–41.

Crosset, John. "More and Seneca." *Philological Quarterly* 40 (1961): pp. 577–80.

Daniell, David. *William Tyndale: A Biography.* New Haven: Yale University Press, 1994.

Davenport, Cyril. *Thomas Berthelet: Royal Printer and Bookbinder to Henry VIII, King of England.* Chicago: The Caxton Club, 1901.

Davis, J. C. "More, Morton, and the Politics of Accomodation." *Journal of British Studies* 9 (1970): pp. 27–49.

Deakins, Roger Lee. "The Tudor Prose Dialogue: Genre and Anti-Genre." *Studies in English Literature, 1500–1800* 20 (1980): pp. 5–23.

Devereux, E. J. "John Rastell's Press in the English Reformation." *Moreana* 49 (1976): pp. 29–47.

Dickens, A. G. *The English Reformation.* 2nd edition. University Park, Pennsylvania: Pennsylvania University Press, 1989.

——. *Thomas Cromwell and the English Reformation.* London: English Universities Press, 1959.

Dowling, Maria. *Humanism in the Age of Henry VIII.* London: Croom Helm, 1986.

——. "Humanist Support for Katherine of Aragon." *Bulletin of the Institute of Historical Research* 57 (1984): pp. 46–55.

——. "Scholarship, Politics and the Court of Henry VIII." Ph.D. dissertation, University of London, 1981.

Duff, E. Gordon. *A Century of the English Book Trade: Short Notices of all Printers, Stationers, Book-Binders, and Others Connected with it from the Issue of the First Dated Book in 1457 to the Incorporation of the Company of Stationers in 1557.* London: Bibliographical Society, 1905.

——. *The Printers, Stationers and Bookbinders of Westminster and London from 1476 to 1535.* Cambridge: Cambridge University Press, 1906.

Edwards, H. L. R. *Skelton: The Life and Times of an Early Tudor Poet.* London: Jonathan Cape, 1949.

Elton, G. R. *"The Body of the Whole Realm": Parliament and Representation in Medieval and Tudor England.* Charlottesville: University of Virginia Press, 1969.

———. "The Commons' Supplication of 1532: Parliamentary Manoevres in the Reign of Henry VIII." *English Historical Review* 66 (1951): pp. 507–34.

———. *England Under the Tudors.* 3rd edition. London: Routledge, 1991.

———. *Policy and Police: The Enforcement of the Reformation in the Age of Thomas Cromwell.* Cambridge: Cambridge University Press, 1972.

———. "The Political Creed of Thomas Cromwell." *Transactions of the Royal Historical Society*, Fifth Series, 6 (1956): pp. 69–92.

———. *Reform and Reformation: England, 1509–1558.* The New History of England, vol. 2. London: Edward Arnold, 1977.

———. *Reform and Renewal: Thomas Cromwell and the Common Weal.* Cambridge: Cambridge University Press, 1973.

———. "Reform by Statute: Thomas Starkey's *Dialogue* and Thomas Cromwell's Policy." *Proceedings of the British Academy* 54 (1968): pp. 165–88.

———. "Sir Thomas More and the Opposition to Henry VIII." *Bulletin of the Institute of Historical Research* 41 (1968): pp. 19–34.

———. "Sir Thomas More, Councillor." In *St. Thomas More: Action and Contemplation*, edited by Richard S. Sylvester, pp. 86–122. New Haven: Yale University Press, 1972.

———. *Studies in Tudor and Stuart Politics and Government.* 3 vols. Cambridge: Cambridge University Press, 1974–83.

———. *The Tudor Constitution: Documents and Commentary.* 2nd edition. Cambridge: Cambridge University Press, 1982.

Erickson, Norma Nadine. "A Dispute between a Priest and a Knight." Ph.D. dissertation, University of Washington, 1966.

Ferguson, Arthur B. *The Articulate Citizen and the English Renaissance.* Durham, North Carolina: Duke University Press, 1965.

Fischer-Galati, Stephen A. *Ottoman Imperialism and German Protestantism, 1521–1555.* Harvard Historical Monographs, vol. 43. Cambridge, Mass.: Harvard University Press, 1959.

Foucault, Michel. *The Archaeology of Knowledge.* Translated by A. M. Sheridan Smith. New York: Pantheon, 1972.

Fox, Alistair. *Politics and Literature in the Reigns of Henry VII and Henry VIII.* Oxford: Basil Blackwell, 1989.

———. *Thomas More: History and Providence.* Oxford: Blackwell, 1982.

—— and John Guy. *Reassessing the Henrician Age: Humanism, Politics and Reform, 1500–1550.* Oxford: Blackwell, 1986.

Gaisser, Julia Haig. *Catullus and his Renaissance Readers.* Oxford: Clarendon Press, 1993.

Geritz, Albert and Amos Lee Laine. *John Rastell.* Twayne's English Authors Series. Boston: Twayne Publishers, 1983.

Gogan, Brian. *The Common Corps of Christendom: Ecclesiological Themes in the Writings of Sir Thomas More.* Studies in the History of Christian Thought, edited by Heiko A. Oberman, vol. 26. Leiden: E. J. Brill, 1982.

Gordon, Ian A. *John Skelton: Poet Laureate.* Melbourne: Melbourne University Press, 1943.

Graham, Howard Jay. "'Our Tong Maternall Maruellously Amendyd and Augmentyd': The First Englishing and Printing of the Medieval Statutes at Large, 1530–1533." *UCLA Law Review* 13 (1965–66): pp. 59–98.

——. "The Rastells and the Printed English Law Book of the Renaissance." *Law Library Journal* 47 (1954): pp. 6–25.

Graham, Howard Jay and J. W. Heckel. "The Book that 'Made' the Common Law: The First Printing of Fitzherbert's *La graunde abridgement*, 1514–1516." *Law Library Journal* 51 (1958): pp. 100–16.

Greenblatt, Stephen. *Renaissance Self-Fashioning: From More to Shakespeare.* Chicago: University of Chicago Press, 1980.

Guy, John. *Christopher St. German on Chancery and Statute.* Selden Society Supplementary Series, vol. 6. London: Selden Society, 1985.

——. *The Public Career of Sir Thomas More.* Brighton, Sussex: Harvester Press, and New Haven: Yale University Press, 1980.

——. "The Rhetoric of Counsel in Early Modern England." In *Tudor Political Culture*, edited by Dale Hoak, pp. 292–310. Cambridge: Cambridge University Press, 1995.

——. *Tudor England.* Oxford: Oxford University Press, 1988.

Gwyn, Peter. *The King's Cardinal: The Rise and Fall of Thomas Wolsey.* London: Barrie and Jenkins, 1990.

Haas, Steven. "The *Disputatio inter clericum et militem:* Was Berthelet's 1531 Edition the First Henrician Polemic of Thomas Cromwell?" *Moreana* 14 (1977): pp. 65–72.

——. "Henry VIII's *Glasse of Truthe.*" *History* 64 (1979): pp. 353–62.

Haigh, Christopher, ed. *The English Reformation Revised.* Cambridge: Cambridge University Press, 1987.

Happé, Peter. "Fansy and Foly: The Drama of Fools in *Magnyfycence.*" *Comparative Drama* 27 (1993–94): pp. 426–52.

Harris, William O. *Skelton's Magnyfycence and the Cardinal Virtue Tradition.* Chapel Hill: University of North Carolina Press, 1965.

Heinze, R. W. *The Proclamations of the Tudor Kings.* Cambridge: Cambridge University Press, 1976.

Heiserman, A. R. *Skelton and Satire.* Chicago: University of Chicago Press, 1961.

Helgerson, Richard. *Forms of Nationhood: The Elizabethan Writing of England.* Chicago: Chicago University Press, 1992.

Hexter, J. H. "Thomas More and the Problem of Counsel." In *Quincentennial Essays on St. Thomas More: Selected Papers from the Thomas More College Conference*, edited by Michael J. Moore, pp. 55–66. Boone, North Carolina: Albion, 1978.

Hobson, Geoffrey D. *Bindings in Cambridge Libraries.* Cambridge: Cambridge University Press, 1929.

Hogrefe, Pearl. *The Life and Times of Sir Thomas Elyot, Englishman.* Ames: Iowa State University Press, 1967.

——. "The Life of Christopher St. German." *Review of English Studies* 13 (1937): pp. 398–404.

——. "Sir Thomas Elyot's Intention in the Opening Chapters of *The Governour*." *Studies in Philology* 60 (1963): pp. 133–40.

——. *The Sir Thomas More Circle: A Program of Ideas and their Impact on Secular Drama.* Urbana: University of Illinois Press, 1969.

Holahan, Michael. "Wyatt, the Heart's Forest, and the Ancient Savings." *English Literary Renaissance* 23 (1993): pp. 46–80.

Hughes, Philip. *The Reformation in England.* 3 vols. London: Hollis and Carter, 1950–54.

Hume, Anthea. "A Study of the Writings of the English Protestant Exiles, 1525–35." Ph.D. dissertation, University of London, 1961.

Hunter, James McVey. "Christopher St. German's 'Doctor and Student': The Scholastic Heritage of a Tudor Dialogue." Ph.D. dissertation, University of Colorado at Boulder, 1984.

Ives, E. W. *Anne Boleyn.* Oxford: Basil Blackwell, 1986.

——. "The Fall of Wolsey." In *Cardinal Wolsey: Church, State and Art*, edited by S. J. Gunn and P. G. Lindley, pp. 286–315. Cambridge: Cambridge University Press, 1991.

Jansen, Sharon. "'And he shall be called Edward': Sixteenth-Century Political Protest and Folger MS Loseley b. 546." *English Literary Renaissance* 23 (1993): pp. 227–43.

——. *Political Protest and Prophecy under Henry VIII.* Woodbridge, Suffolk: Boydell Press, 1991.

Johnston, Stanley Howard, Jr. "A Study of the Career and Literary Publications of Richard Pynson." Ph.D. dissertation, University of Western Ontario, 1977.

Jones, G. Lloyd. *The Discovery of Hebrew in Tudor England: A Third Language.* Manchester: Manchester University Press, 1983.

Kelly, Henry Ansgar. *The Matrimonial Trials of Henry VIII.* Stanford: Stanford University Press, 1976.

King, John N. *English Reformation Literature: The Tudor Origins of the Protestant Tradition.* Princeton: Princeton University Press, 1982.

——. "Henry VIII as David: The King's Image and Reformation Politics." In *Rethinking the Henrician Era: Essays on Early Tudor Texts and Contexts*, edited by Peter C. Herman, pp. 78–92. Urbana: University of Illinois Press, 1994.

——. *Spenser's Poetry and the Reformation Tradition.* Princeton: Princeton University Press, 1990.

——. "Spenser's *Shepheardes Calender* and Protestant Pastoral Satire." In *Renaissance Genres: Essays on Theory, History, and Interpretation*, edited by Barbara K. Lewalski, Harvard English Studies, vol. 14, pp. 369–98. Cambridge, Mass.: Harvard University Press, 1986.

——. *Tudor Royal Iconography: Literature and Art in an Age of Religious Crisis.* Princeton: Princeton University Press, 1989.

Kinney, Arthur F. *Humanist Poetics: Thought, Rhetoric, and Fiction in*

Sixteenth-Century England. Amherst: University of Massachusetts Press, 1986.

——. *John Skelton: Priest as Poet.* Chapel Hill: University of North Carolina Press, 1987.

Kipling, Gordon. *The Triumph of Honour: Burgundian Origins of the Elizabethan Renaissance.* Leiden: Leiden University Press, 1977.

Koszul, A. "Was Bishop Barlow Friar Jerome Barlow?" *Review of English Studies* 4 (1928): pp. 25–34.

Lancashire, I. *Dramatic Texts and Records of Britain: A Chronological Topography to 1558.* Cambridge: Cambridge University Press, 1984.

Lehmberg, Stanford E. *The Reformation Parliament, 1529–1536.* Cambridge: Cambridge University Press, 1970.

——. *Sir Thomas Elyot: Tudor Humanist.* Austin: University of Texas Press, 1960.

Loach, Jennifer. "The Function of Ceremonial in the Reign of Henry VIII." *Past and Present* 143 (1994): pp. 43–68.

Logan, George M. *The Meaning of More's "Utopia."* Princeton: Princeton University Press, 1983.

Major, John M. *Sir Thomas Elyot and Renaissance Humanism.* Lincoln: University of Nebraska Press, 1964.

Marius, Richard. *Thomas More.* New York: Knopf, 1984.

Mayer, Thomas F. "Faction and Ideology: Thomas Starkey's *Dialogue.*" *Historical Journal* 28 (1985): pp. 1–25.

——. "A Mission Worse than Death: Reginald Pole and the Parisian Theologians." *English Historical Review* 103 (1988): pp. 870–91.

——. *Thomas Starkey and the Commonweal: Humanist Politics and Religion in the Reign of Henry VIII.* Cambridge: Cambridge University Press, 1989.

——. "Thomas Starkey's Aristocratic Reform Programme." *History of Political Thought* 7 (1986): pp. 439–61.

McConica, James Kelsey. *English Humanists and Reformation Politics under Henry VIII and Edward VI.* Oxford: Oxford University Press, 1965.

McKerrow, R. B. and F. S. Ferguson. *Title Page Borders used in England and Scotland, 1485–1640.* London: Bibliographical Society, 1932.

McLean, Andrew Miller. "A Note on Thomas More and Thomas Starkey." *Moreana* 41 (1974): pp. 31–35.

Mozley, J. F. *William Tyndale.* New York: MacMillan, 1937.

Muller, James Arthur. *Stephen Gardiner and the Tudor Reaction.* New York: MacMillan, 1926.

Murphy, Virginia Marie. "The Debate over Henry VIII's First Divorce." Ph.D. dissertation, Cambridge University, 1984.

——. "The Literature and Propaganda of Henry VIII's First Divorce." In *The Reign of Henry VIII: Politics, Policy, and Piety*, edited by Diarmaid MacCulloch, pp. 135–58. London: MacMillan, 1995.

Neville, Pamela Ayers. "Richard Pynson, King's Printer (1506–1529): Printing and Propaganda in Early Tudor England." Ph.D. dissertation, University of London, Warburg Institute, 1990.

Nicholson, Graham. "The Act of Appeals and the English Reformation." In

Law and Government Under the Tudors, edited by Claire Cross, David Loades and J. J. Scarisbrick, pp. 19–30. Cambridge: Cambridge University Press, 1988.

Nixon, Howard M. "Early English Gold-Tooled Bookbindings." In *Studi di Bibliografia e di Storia in onore de Tammaro De Marinis*, 4 vols., edited by Romeo De Maio, vol. 3, pp. 283–308. Verona: G. Mardersteig, 1964.

Nixon, Howard M. and Mirjam M. Foot, *The History of Decorated Bookbinding in England.* Oxford: Clarendon Press, 1992.

O'Donovan, Joan Lockwood. *Theology of Law and Authority in the English Reformation.* Emory University Studies in Law and Religion, no. 1. Atlanta: Scholars Press, 1991.

Parmiter, Geoffrey de C. *The King's Great Matter: A Study of Anglo-Papal Relations, 1527–1534.* New York: Barnes and Noble, 1967.

Patrides, C. A. " 'The Bloody and Cruell Turke': the Background of a Renaissance Commonplace." *Studies in the Renaissance* 10 (1963): pp. 126–35.

Patterson, Annabel. *The Conditions of Writing and Reading in Early Modern England.* Madison: University of Wisconsin Press, 1984.

Pineas, Rainer. *Thomas More and Tudor Polemics.* Bloomington: Indiana University Press, 1968.

Pollard, A. W. and G. R. Redgrave. *A Short-Title Catalogue of Books Printed in England, Scotland, and Ireland and of English Books Printed Abroad, 1475–1640.* 2nd edition. Revised and enlarged by W. A. Jackson, F. S. Ferguson, and Katherine F. Pantzer. 3 vols. London: The Bibliographical Society, 1986–91.

Pollet, Maurice. *John Skelton: Poet of Tudor England.* Translated by John Warrington. London: Dent and Sons, 1971.

Redworth, Glyn. *In Defence of the Church Catholic: The Life of Stephen Gardiner.* Oxford: Basil Blackwell, 1990.

Reed, A. W. *Early Tudor Drama: Medwall, the Rastells, Heywood, and the More Circle.* London: Methuen, 1926.

Riegler, Edward R. "Printing, Protestantism, and Politics: Thomas Cromwell and Religious Reform." Ph.D. dissertation, UCLA, 1978.

Rupp, E. Gordon. *Studies in the Making of the English Protestant Tradition, Mainly in the Reign of Henry VIII.* Cambridge: Cambridge University Press, 1947.

Scarisbrick, J. J. *Henry VIII.* Berkeley: University of California Press, 1968.

Scattergood, John. "Skelton's *Magnyfycence* and the Tudor Royal Household." *Medieval English Theatre* 15 (1993): pp. 21–48.

Schenk, Wilhelm. *Reginald Pole, Cardinal of England.* London: Longmans, 1950.

Schmitt, Charles B. and Quentin Skinner, eds. *The Cambridge History of Renaissance Philosophy.* Cambridge: Cambridge University Press, 1988.

Schwoebel, Robert. *The Shadow of the Crescent: The Renaissance Image of the Turk (1453–1517).* New York: St. Martin's Press, 1967.

Setton, Kenneth. "Lutheranism and the Turkish Peril." *Balkan Studies* 3 (1962): pp. 133–68.

Shaw, Stanford. *History of the Ottoman Empire and Modern Turkey, Volume I: Empire of the Gazis: The Rise and Decline of the Ottoman Empire, 1280–1808*. Cambridge: Cambridge University Press, 1976.

Skinner, Quentin. *The Foundations of Modern Political Thought*. 2 vols. Cambridge: Cambridge University Press, 1978.

——. "Sir Thomas More's *Utopia* and the Language of Renaissance Humanism." In *The Languages of Political Theory in Early Modern Europe*, edited by Anthony Pagden, pp. 123–57. Cambridge: Cambridge University Press, 1987.

Solt, Leo F. *Church and State in Early Modern England, 1509–1640*. Oxford: Oxford University Press, 1990.

Starkey, David, et al. *The English Court: from the Wars of the Roses to the Civil War*. London: Longman, 1987.

——. *The Reign of Henry VIII: Personalities and Politics*. London: G. Philip, 1985. 2nd edition, London: Collins and Brown, 1991.

Starnes, Colin. *The New Republic: A Commentary on Book I of More's Utopia, Showing its Relation to Plato's Republic*. Waterloo, Ontario: Wilfrid Laurier University Press, 1990.

Surtz, Edward, S. J. *The Works and Days of John Fisher: An Introduction to the Position of St. John Fisher (1469–1535), Bishop of Rochester, in the English Renaissance and the Reformation*. Cambridge, Mass.: Harvard University Press, 1967.

Sutherland, James. *English Satire*. Cambridge: Cambridge University Press, 1962.

Thorne, S. E. "St. German's 'Doctor and Student.'" *The Library*, Fourth Series, 10 (1930): pp. 421–6.

Tinkler, J. F. "Humanism and Dialogue." *Parergon*, New Series, 6 (1988): pp. 197–214.

Tudor-Craig, Pamela. "Henry VIII and King David." In *Early Tudor England: Proceedings of the 1987 Harlaxton Symposium*, edited by Daniel Williams, pp. 183–205. Woodbridge, Suffolk: Boydell Press, 1989.

Vaughan, Dorothy M. *Europe and the Turk: A Pattern of Alliances, 1350–1700*. Liverpool: Liverpool University Press, 1954.

Walker, Greg. "The Expulsion of the Minions Reconsidered." *The Historical Journal* 32 (1989): pp. 1–16.

——. *John Skelton and the Politics of the 1520s*. Cambridge Studies in Early Modern British History. Cambridge: Cambridge University Press, 1988.

——. *Persuasive Fictions: Faction, Faith and Political Culture in the Reign of Henry VIII*. Aldershot: Scholar Press, 1996.

——. *Plays of Persuasion: Drama and Politics at the Court of Henry VIII*. Cambridge: Cambridge University Press, 1991.

Winser, Leigh. "*Magnyfycence* and the Characters of Sottie." *Sixteenth Century Journal* 12 (1981): pp. 85–94.

Zeeveld, Gordon. *Foundations of Tudor Policy*. Cambridge, Mass.: Harvard University Press, 1948.

Index

Footnotes are indexed when references include material other than bibliographical citations, and when such material does not occur in the text.